Cae Cordell

THE HAT MAN - FATHERS' TRANSGRESSIONS

THE STATE OF IDAHO vs. NOEL SNOW

CASE NO. CR-91-08467C

D1556960

JUMPING GOAT
PUBLISHING, PLLC
Dover, Arkansas

Rebekah Garza Graphic Design

rgarza.design@gmail.com

479-264-6935

Custom designs included but not limited to:

- Book covers
- Custom Logos
- Illustrations
- Websites

Consultations available

ISBN – 978-1514256268

THE HAT MAN – FATHERS' TRANSGRESSIONS

This is an autobiography. This book is based on facts, court documents, living testimony, and surviving the events and the memories of the author. This is her story of marital sexual abuse and violence.

This book is published in the USA by various forms of electronic and print forums. To contact author, please write the author at cae234@msn.com

Books by Cae Cordell

Red Bird Phoenix May 2015
The Hat Man – Fathers' Transgressions July 2015

Coming Soon:

Romance Novel:
Charity Rose – The Rising Moon

Murder Mystery:
Deadly Connection

Counseling book:
The ABC's of Understanding Sexual Abuse

Redemption's Song

Spirit runners - dancing ghosts that disturb,
Wrongs claim our mourning,
Lingering in our sleeping hours,
Causing despair in our whispered awakening,
Those empty memories,
From the past that we have tried to outrun,
Until the past overtakes.
Memories that demand an accounting,
Rasping answers, sometimes come,
Unwillingly so far from within,
From the things, we oft already know.
But things let lie hidden in the awesome fear of
waiting,
Raining ghosts embraced,
Wrenched tears advance toward redemption,
Unlikely surprises, like white wisp clouds -
At the windows of the soul.
Those sad refrains - melodies - that the soul had
forgotten how to sing,
Those buried songs, soul resurrections harmony,
Twofold whispers in the night.
Warped like a wing-back rocker in the mind,
Summits climbed, high crags surpassed,
Gained a foothold of the soul,
Chained gently from our past unfolding,
Pages written, redemption song begun.

A note to the reader:

Thank you for sharing in my story. I am hopeful this book will open your heart to the harm so many children are suffering. Possibly, you have had to live with such abuse. Lifelong abuse is an insidious crime that lingers on; I pray you have found a place of peace and a quiet heart, knowing you are guiltless. You are an important person. You have a right to hope, for fulfillment, and a life of joy. May this book be a part of your journey beyond the pain into the light of life. I have found my peace in my Heavenly Father and in His service. God be with you wherever you are.

Cae Cordell
Author

Incest, the ugly word,
The hidden shadows,
Devouring the soul,
Rendering helplessness,
Loss of innocence,
The taker that never gives back,
Generational blight,
The capstone of hate,
Incest!

As long as there is life, there is hope for healing, restoration, and forgiveness of one's self. It is a journey of anger, pain, and often times of hopelessness, but when one takes control of self, there is power in that control!

Prologue

Matriarchal rape is rare and has seldom been written about, but sexual abuse in all forms knows no social, economic, gender or religious preference. The generational damage to children or spouses is permanent, but our choices for reform must be based in logic rather than the continuing destructive behavior of generational predators. In sharing the pattern of violence and abuse as it has played out in my life, the damage, the horror, and the lack of choices, the reader can get a glimpse beyond the curtain of ignorance into the reality of daily abuse. A child of incest or sexual abuse craves a "normal" live in spite of the trauma, compensating in horrific ways to be like other children – how a child craves normalcy! Mental and body memories drive children to murder parts of their emotional being to survive. Some turn to cutting themselves, develop lifetime anger issues, or addictions to alcohol, sex and drugs. Many may act out in an eroticized sexual way as they have been taught with other children or adults. Others become sexual predators carrying forward the generational curse of dark secrets. Children are desperate for acceptance and finding a façade of 'love' from those responsible for them – wanting *their lives to be normal. Children of abuse crave acceptance.* Children find justification for the actions and treatment of a parent and or other incestuous relationships. Too many live in fear of sexual predators and further exploitation. Often the exploitation and rape rage lives with them until death.

We must realize no child chooses to be raped and abused or lures a predatory adult to assault them. This predatory action is an adult decision, thus their sole crime and sin. Many times the child abuse builds in the lives of the abused until they are driven to become predatory, thinking this will stop their pain. There aren't any healthy boundaries in incestuous sexual abuse or any other such linked relationships. Children are forced to carry a load of self-blame and useless guilt living with abuse. So many children never accept and understand they are without sin. My two books are a hard look at sexual abuse, but there is no denial that incest, violence and sexual molestation exists; the fight must continue to eradicate any and all sexual abuse in the world.

The Hat Man – Fathers Transgressions is about my ex-husband, Noel Snow, his court conviction, my life decisions and the heinous part he played in our marital story. I pray the affirmation of this book will give courage to the hurting, freedom for the victimized and bolster changes in the law to protect the vulnerable - our children. Mending the lives of my children's devastation has forever changed me and made me stronger. My losses have been horrific.

Where It All Began

Incest is a dirty, nasty little word,
It is like mud,
it sticks like hummus,
Growing mold over everything,
Mind chains that exist without seeing them,
Gripping, destroying, holding down the mind,
Psyche death, twisted ties of family,
Wretched secrets vile, gag reflex!
Damaged goods,
Sold to the devil,
Scolded by the living,
Twisted, stunted,
Blamed, shamed, put in the closet,
Fighting for one's life,
I survived the aftermath.

Going back to Madison County, Arkansas wasn't easy!
After all, I had fled fifty years ago, running away from the
horror of incest and violence. Hurt on top of hurt mired my
growing up years with the painful violation of my body by
Betty, my mother, my brother, Samson, my father, Aaron
and others.

Incest is painful. The betrayal of a child's trust is
abhorrent! How does a child's faith reconcile with the evil
done to the body, soul and mind?

I decided I would not honor my parents with the softer
mother and father names as an adult – my survival
depended on it. The choices of violence and abuse by my
parents forfeited their right to be called those names, so I
began to call them Betty and Aaron as they had abandoned
all parental rights.

Nothing was the same as I drove along the twisty roads

into the Loy community. The old dirt roads were wider and many were paved. The changes were in contrast to the simplicity of my walking away and the fear that lay on the road ahead. Nothing I saw fit into my memories of consternation, nightmares and distorted thinking. Things seemed smaller.

I remember the heart-wrenching day in August 1965 when I had fled the only home I had known carrying three small suitcases. The road had been dusty, long, and unforgiving as the leaving terror lodged in my soul. I caught a ride with Burl Weathers as I had pre-arranged. He wasn't afraid of Aaron and encouraged my leaving, "Girl, ya' are doin' the right thing, gettin' away like this. Don't ya' be scared of leavin'. Ya' are a tough girl and if anybody can make it out of this holler, ya' can. Don't look back as I drive away, either. Once I get ya' away, don't ever come back here, if ya' wanna' amount to anythin'."

I hugged my sister and brother to my heart. I knew they didn't understand my going, but I did. I whispered words of love in their ears, but I knew the anguish in their hearts. Would they ever be able to forgive my leaving them behind? My heart was ripped out of my chest as I left my beloved sister, Ruth, and baby brother, Ezra Joel, in the situation of horrific abuse by our parents. I despaired of their surviving the separation and loss – leaving was a grief digging deep in my guts – cutting into my mind like a raw meat saw.

Scalding tears poured down my face as the two-toned Chevy traveled the miles to Fayetteville allowing me to catch the Greyhound bus to Little Rock. I swallowed hard and managed to gather my courage, guts, gumption, and clung to the hot car seat with all my might. The slow burn of worry niggled harshly. I zipped it in my brain – I couldn't carry that sack with me. My breath came in a short burst of need in letting go, fear was a tarantula burrowing deep into my brain.

I knew this was my beginning, but Ruth and Ezra Joel's would be years in the earning.

The sights and smells of the valley stirred deep-seated memories in my mind like rolling bumblebees, stumbling, stinging, and tossing me into the frothing mouth of the past. It was as if my whole body gave painful protest in my returning. My heart twisted with many 'might haves' and 'what ifs'. I was facing the failure of my past, gathering the dusty web-like vines of memories, twining them to build a bridge for my future.

I pulled to a stop by the old cement low-water bridge where I had sat on just such a day, so long ago, to plan my future, and to think about escaping my parents and my older brother who took such joy in abusing me. The kaleidoscope of recollections came rushing back, paced by the sound of the water dredging up the old insecurities and fears of a lifetime.

I faced my future, accepting that my damage is forever.

Prayer provides answers. Psalms 83:1   "O God, don't sit idly by, silent and inactive when we pray. Answer us! Deliver us!

Chapter 1

Those insidious questions of the "what ifs",
The powerless child that could have held so much promise,
Abused, used, and abandoned without a place of solace.
How does one answer the "what ifs" of life?

Whispers in the dark,
sucking down into the mire of the bad,
Shadows dancing in the flickering edges of the mind,
Satiation is not to be found.
Why is the good outweighed by the evil?

Overcoming good with damages beyond compare,
Shadow dances, do not accept this dance,
Unseen fire that burns forever,
Without any answers of the "whys"!

Mid-1930s

To understand the Shadow Man, one must grasp he is like a glimpse out of the corner of one's eye caught over a shoulder. When turning to find him, he slips into the shadows and is gone into the dusty mist as if he never existed – just a figment of the imagination. Such was the figure slipping along in the dragging evening gloominess searching with determined tentacles to latch onto any substance in human form to punish. The shifty shadow crept into the old barn, seeking a place to rest. It was a malevolent presence - maybe an invention of the imagination or was it demonic? The fighting, the building pressure, the feeling of being trapped by a woman, the inadequacy and the craving to find a human vessel to incapacitate and wound was just too much - so the shadow took on substance waiting to garner a victim. This devilish being was observed through the passing clouds in the night sky by the critters inside. It was hard to distinguish the caped silhouette from the rest of the darkness in the barn. The brimmed black hat obscured its identity, if the shadow even existed outside of Hell.

The quiet *whoo-whoo* of a lone screech owl reverberated in the night air, but the echo halted when the bird sensed the wicked presence below. The old tomcat looked through the cracks of the shabby barn. The sight of the Shadow Man caused the hair on his back to rise and hissing, he scurried to a safe place beneath the hay manger at the back of the barn.

Was it man or demon entering the dilapidated old barn with vengeance in mind? Whatever the evil, the silent manner in which it moved facilitated the smell of fear. The quiet itself should have been a warning for the wary. A step could be heard outside the barn, walking forward steadily with a purpose toward the sagging door.

Carefully, the young boy opened the door. His hands trembled with nervousness. His mother had ordered him to go find his father. He hated it when she fought with his father. His mother was a religious zealot and jealousy ruled her life. His father, Houston Columbus Snow, was a Communist, a bigot, a gamester, and carried a hatred of all women, especially his wife, like a virtuous brand. Before marrying Bertie Lambdin, Columbus had been dating and was in love with a woman who was his obsession. She'd refused sex with him. He wanted to marry her, but he caught her being forced to have sex with her uncle. He dropped her like a hot potato, blaming her for the incestuous relationship, never admitting she was victimized. A fierce hatred colored his thinking process as he watched her betrayal through a window. He had not analyzed if she might have been forced into the relationship at her young age by her uncle. He married Bertie on the rebound, but never loved her as she deserved, blaming her for his former love's deception. The woman's lingering influence controlled his life – so much so – Bertie in a jealous rage punched the woman's eyes out in all the photos Columbus had carefully secreted.

Columbus ranted how all men were fools to be taken in by any woman. His continuous diatribe left the boy with a distrustful, warped and poisonous view of women. He spouted his communist theories to the other men he gambled with, and especially to his son, and withdrew into a world of blame. He even espoused the Bible promoted the communist platform of having all things in common. All the men that associated with him were wrongdoers, drunks and men who liked to whore around. Men who were faithful to their wives did not come near him or his family. He made moonshine and sold it to anyone who had money to buy it. It was his main source of income and he imbibed his share of his profits.

The boy understood his mother had reasons to be jealous of his father because he was a gambler and rambling kind of man - often seeking out loose women and then boasting of his conquest in front of Bertie. He was not a faithful man to anyone but himself - and to his partner - Satan. Bertie held grudges, embedded from years of hate, and taught her children this requiem. She fought for family hierarchy control and worked the children against their father. Columbus withdrew into a quilt of anger and wrapped his loathing around himself like a tattered blanket living in a dredged world of misunderstandings, working little, and living a riotous life – a prodigal son he was not. He kept a six-foot black snake whip handy to dominate the children and to keep Bertie in line.

Noel knew where his father kept a stash of moonshine so when he had stormed out of the house more than three hours earlier, he knew 'the old man' would be liquored up and full of anger. When his father got drunk, he would do vicious things. He had taken a horse whip to one of his sisters, wounding her badly. The rest of them all tried to placate him as much as possible. He bragged how he could snap the flesh off their backs with just a flick of the horsewhip.

"Father, are you in here?" Noel asked timidly, pushing on the creaking barn door. Nothing moved. He could hear the cow munching hay, and then heard her as she suddenly moved farther into the darkness. Something had spooked her. He slid inside the door expecting to confront his father. He sensed a movement to his left. He felt in front of him, trying to find the wall without stumbling over something. Again, he called, "Dad, where are you?" No answer was forthcoming!

"Dad, it's me, Noel. Where are you?" Silence answered him. He figured by now the 'old man' was passed out from drinking or ready to burst into a knot of anger, possibly taking that anger out on him. He stood in wary uneasiness, hoping he could flee before a beating occurred.

"Dad, answer me. I just want to help you." The silence was stifling in the night.

Out of the corner of his eye, he caught a glimpse of a shadow on the old barn wall in the light of the pale moon - was it beast, demon or man?

He spoke again, "Dad where are you? Please, it's me, Noel. Are you okay? Mother sent me; she is worried sick about you. She's sorry she made you mad and wants you to come back to the house and eat supper – it's being kept in the warming oven."

The shadow moved as Noel turned to the left inside the stable. He was trying to see if his father was there in the hay – maybe he was passed out before. His mother claimed his father was demon-possessed and sometimes he wondered if she knew the truth. She claimed to be a Holy Ghost-filled woman of God, but her anger and jealousy often put their family in turmoil.

Noel was forced to be the "man of the house" and as

such, expected to hunt and fish to help feed the large family of eight children. The squirrels were plentiful and he got a deer as often as possible, but his efforts were never enough. Suddenly, Noel felt a hand clamp on his shoulder, shoving him down into the hay, and a body tumbling on top of him. There was no escaping the grip around his throat or the weight pressing the air from his lungs. He fought with all his ten-year-old might, but was overcome by the strength of the Shadow Man. His clothing was ripped from his body as he convulsed from the choking.

The owl shivered as an eerie scream ripped through the old barn, muffled as the hand clamped over the boy's mouth. The hay rustled as the demonic force began its act of violation. The shadow was all-encompassing. Its grip was relentless. Obscenities poured out of the faceless shadow, describing to the boy what he must do or die.

"I am tired of being dragged down. You all are a weight around my neck, drowning me with your yammering and your constant demand for food. I don't have any freedom without one of you clinging to my back. You are nothing. I am going to train you how to handle women. You will know when the future is yours to hold. Women ain't nothin' but putrid pussies. You've gotta' know how to control them and make them believe your control is their idea."

"Do you understand what I am telling you to do, boy?" asked the disembodied voice.

"Yes," answered the terror-filled youth even as he resisted, still trying to fight for his life.
"Father, is that you? Why are you talking so funny?" asked the trembling boy.

"Shut up, you little coward. You ain't nothin' like your old man. Your mother has made a pussy out of you. If you're a pussy, then I'm gonna' treat you like you wear a skirt, and show you what real men do to pussies."
The pain was unbearable as sobs shook his body; he

pleaded with the voice to stop the pain. "Please, stop hurting me, pleaaaase!" The screams echoed in the throat of the child.

"Roll over, and show me what you learned," commanded the shadow.

Trembling, the boy complied, tears running down his narrow dirty face. He was broken and compliant. Thus began his education. The training was relentless and violent. His "lessons" would follow him for the rest of his life, affecting all of his choices and treatment of others.

He was sent from the barn back to his mother to do for her what she ordered - and thus the yoyo effect pulled at his mind. He was a spindly boy with blonde hair and gray eyes, and emaciated from the hard work of the farm. The boy was ordered to keep the secret and forced often to replay the hilltop horror; often with a look or a touch on the shoulder and a nod in the direction of the barn. The horrible secret was like a maggot in his brain. He dared not refuse. Noel learned to conform to the deviant demands even if his body rebelled.

The Shadow Man beat his sisters into submission so Noel learned hitting, kicking, and beating females as appropriate behavior. He yearned to copy the ecstatic look the Shadow Man got when he was beating the girls; control was the key of power.

The supremacy wielded by the Shadow Man aroused him and gave him sexual pleasure. He readily got a "hard-on" as the beatings become more eroticized. The 'chastisement' became exciting. His hand stroking his penis seemed to excite the Shadow Man. Noel never grew used to the penis penetrating his rectum and its accompanying pain, but the urge for dominance grew. He became twisted, deriving pleasure as his abuser had, using the rectum for molestation and rape. He postulated that he was going to have a "tight ass" to use and nothing would deny him that gratification.

The Shadow Man was teaching him all he needed to know. He got to help Father drink his whiskey, listen to his ramblings, watch him gamble and it gave him the feeling of belonging. The Shadow Man became easier to endure. Sharing brought approval.

His mother detested the drinking and lack of respect by his father, but she was powerless to stop his behavior. Noel had three older sisters. There were three younger than he and then a baby brother. As the first-born son, his mother expected him to be the "man of the house". She was a wonderful housekeeper and an excellent cook, but lacking in wifely warmth due her extreme low self-esteem. She helped work in the garden, canning and preserving, or they wouldn't have any food to fill their bellies. His older sisters worked alongside her faithfully. They were forced to work long hard hours being diligent not to stir up their father's wrath.

Noel was torn between her religious world and his father's world of depravity. His mental conflict turned to an internal raging fire burning anything he touched. He was expected to join his mother and sisters in church, sing praises to God, share their shouting and talking in tongues in the Holy Ghost. He kept an eye half-open to see how people were reacting to his spiritual side-show. If he perceived even a smidgen of disrespect, he *knew* they were plotting against him and were out to destroy him.

He became adept at soulful praying, bending his knees as others watched, and putting on a show of spirituality. According to his father, church goers were all hypocrites, liars, whores, and the preacher was having sex with all of the women.

He could not excuse his mother's controlling nature and demand for obedience as it belittled his manhood. In church he began to feel roiling anger and a pulsating desire to murder. He often fantasized how to cut up, stab, maim and demolish people he assumed were "crossing him." He took his rage out on the farm animals. Bestiality was against nature, but that didn't stop his thirst for this extreme sexual deviancy.

Noel's rage built with intensifying regularity. He would explode, screaming at people, threatening them verbally, and often running into the house grabbing a shotgun to shoot at them. Brandishing guns was his infantile way of showing personal supremacy to the world as if the guns were the extension of his *pecker* power. Many people ran in fear believing they would be killed if they didn't escape.

> *Which hat are you wearing today, Hat Man?*
> *Your jumpity-jiggity-jack silhouette is glowing.*
> *Which hat is ruling?*
> *Pain, Anger, Hatred, Jealousy, Control, Power,*
> *Manipulation*
> *Seven-in-one personalities!*
> *Voices of horror speaking,*
> *Who wears the hat?*
> *Shadow Man drifting - just out of gazing range,*
> *Only glimpsed with a glance over the shoulder.*
> *Frosted like a glass of nether reality.*
> *The Piper must be paid his due,*
> *Jiggity-jack; jack-in-the-box, pop-goes-the-weasel.*
> *The sandbox is ready - say it quickly!*
> *Who will rule the man - at this moment?*

Noel's formative years were influenced by his father's actions and he spent energy emulating him. Columbus openly manipulated, derided and used Bertie for sexual gratification. Noel noticed his father's actions provided him with unequaled power in his parent's marriage relationship. This power was more and more attractive as he reached manhood - he began to be ruled by what he saw and reacted with rage and furious outbursts. He idolized his father for being a "man".

Noel absorbed Columbus' message into the pores of his being that women were to be used, hated, manipulated, and controlled by a show of force. Father was wont to say, "Son, if you want a woman to know you are the boss, keep her pregnant and barefoot, and then slap her around plenty so she will show respect. You are a man and a woman can't refuse you sex. You are the boss. A woman must learn to do as you say."

Noel's life and marriage to his first wife, Clara Galantine, reflected his father's philosophy.
Noel was careful to hide his bitter rage in public, but the neighbors were learning, bit-by-bit, what was inside of him. Many were terrified of him and avoided being around him. He held in his rage around outsiders, but his family suffered consequently. If he drank, he was mellow and easier to get along with, and those around him had rather he stayed drunk than sober.

Noel rode horses everywhere. When he was riding, he was a man in control of his universe, cocky, boastful and demanding. He took perverse pleasure in riding a mean horse, showing people his manly prowess. His oldest son was nearly dragged to death because Noel was showing him who was boss. He recklessly raced his horses for miles, proving he was "the man" by his horsemanship.

Noel plagued the countryside spying on the neighbors from his youth to old age. He was a Peeping Tom extraordinaire! Women were afraid of him, but kept quiet about his clandestine overtures in the surrounding countryside, too afraid to let their husbands intervene. He would develop a crush on a woman and stalk her for months. He would suddenly give up his "reign of terror" decreeing the woman wasn't worth his attention, fixate on another hapless woman and repeat the cycle. He convinced some women to engage in short-lived affairs whether by force or persistence. He would imagine some evil being done to him, threaten and rage against that woman in his pursuit of her.

In secret, he began to fantasize about sex with others, both men and women; after all, he was "The Man". Seeing fear in the faces of the people he was watching when they noticed him was a sexual high - he loved the adrenalin rush. He could be someone he wasn't with a horse between his legs. He held the ultimate power over their minds and bodies with a heavy hand on the reins.

He began to confront neighbors with "Why are you staring at me? What do you think you are doing with my girl?" He would go into a rage and act peculiarly. People began to avoid him. The voices in his head were tormenting and driving him to even wilder episodes of behavior. He was wretched and friendless; yet, he would claim he had many friends, and blame others for them not visiting, claiming *his friends* weren't welcome by this or that one.

Noel never accepted accountability for any of his wrongdoing, rages, his feelings, nor did any of his sisters or mother. They always had a scapegoat to blame misdeeds on rather than themselves. Noel's carnality began to accelerate. He disrespected women, ranting they used sex for control, power and manipulation.

At home, he was a conniving, macho Neanderthal man controlling his family with a flattening fist - in his cave he was 'The Man' – the ruler of his domain. He exhibited very low self-esteem, angry because people recognized his cowardice, but pumped himself up to be a "big man." After all, he was a male and had a right to be domineering and mean-spirited. He was the man of the house; he could spend hours bragging about his manhood.

When did the Shadow Man pass along this heritage and his personality blend as one with his son? Did the son separate into 'The Hat Man' with several personalities to

survive or to participate? Eventually Noel became 'The
Man' later in his life, often referring to himself in the third
person. Noel became a shadow within a shadow where
only darkness existed. In the shadows of his life he was
even more dangerous. On the other hand this sin was
generational, handed down from father to son.

Noel's years of abuse and internal scars by the Shadow
Man never healed. His soul oozed putrid pus. He rebelled
and resented being a mama's boy. He fumed his entire life
that his mama wanted to control him as she had his father.

His mother ordered him to plow the fields so the
family could eat. His overalls clung to his bony body like
the ripe fruit of the tomatoes. His father hired all them out
to cotton farmers in the *bottoms* each summer. They
dragged the cotton sacks up and down the rows in burning
resentment because, at the end of the harvest, Father took
their money and gambled it away. Food was scarce except
for Bertie's preserving.

Columbus continued to prefer gambling, drinking and
whoring - it didn't matter in what order – to his family. He
ran a moonshine still down under the Hollow near Silex, a
few miles out of Dover, at the "Boar's Den" as he called
his "hideout". Truth be told, it was an escape from Bertie
and the family - a place where he lived out his private
fantasies. Silex, at one time, had been a small town with its
own post office, but the town had burned to the ground and
never recovered, though the old foundations linger on in the
vine and brush of the hillsides.

Columbus was the son of a Baptist preacher, Houston
Snow, who'd believed in living a strict, but godly life
preaching the gospel of Jesus Christ. Columbus was the
son of rebellion, a hellion, never buying into the gospel
according to his father - living opposite of the Hell and
damnation sermons. Noel cloaked his evil in righteous

clothing.

Psalm 23

The Lord is my shepherd, I shall not want.
He makes me lie down in green pastures;
He leads me beside still waters;
He restores my soul.
He leads me in right paths!
For His name's sake.

Even though I walk through the darkest valley,
I fear no evil;
For you are with me;
Your rod and your staff -
They comfort me.

You prepare a table before me
In the presence of my enemies;
You anoint my head with oil;
My cup overflows.
Surely goodness and mercy shall follow me
All the days of my life,
And I shall dwell in the house of the Lord
My whole life long.
(1)(New revised Standard Version Bible, 1989)

Life is exciting, tiring, and though sometimes it is unexplained, it can be hurtful. It is our choice to complete the journey in denial or walking in freedom.

Chapter 2

The Man, the Man, come and see,
From my fingers, take the candy,
Dandy, dandy, dancing mind.
Come closer; see there is no face,
Empty eyes, figuring wild -
Come; come to me, my little love.
Hurly, girly, it doesn't matter
I am but a dancing silhouette.

Noel volunteered for the Navy in the early 1940s choosing to enlist rather than be drafted. He did not finish high school. He was already drifting on the edges of the Lee's Chapel Community radar, becoming known for his rages and slyness. Joining the military was one of his first free will choices outside the domination of his mother and father. He was an effeminate boy to the point of prettiness. Due to his father's savaging, he experienced thoughts of homosexuality. He was resentful and angry at his mother for sending him to report for service in overalls and a white shirt as it made him look less than a man. Many of the other enlistees made fun of him. He carried a lifelong festering resentment against her.

He entered the US Navy and was shipped to the Solomon Islands from boot camp training in San Diego. As Noel's ship took him across the equator, the Shadow Man was lying in wait. Several Navy sailors and officers aboard the ship gang raped Noel as his ship crossed the equator. He was informed it was an "initiation" custom of military manhood.

A high-pressure fire hose was then used to blow him around the ship deck, nearly drowning him, to get him 'used to the waves'. He believed they meant to murder him. He was too ignorant and ashamed to report the attacks to the ship commander. These military sexual attacks added to a series of events that drove him into an abyss of mind-hell. He was filled with rage by his weakness because he couldn't or didn't fight back. He thought the men must have known of his abuse by his father. He found the Shadow Man came out to play even in the Navy, just like at home.

Weeks after arriving in the Solomon Islands, an officer attacked and raped him in his tent at the edge of the ocean threatening to drown him if he didn't cooperate. He spoke of the officer as one of the "Shadow Men." It was a slow recovery from the trauma of the officer's rape. His mother had written she'd had a spiritual premonition of his death, begging him to cut off his hand, punch out his eye, shoot himself in the foot, or slash his wrist, anything to get a medical discharge. He was being pummeled from all directions and dealing with intrusive thoughts and flashbacks of his sexual abuse. His mother's psychological battering brought the appearance of "The Man" persona. "The Man" ruled Noel for the rest of his life. His fragile hold on reality snapped and he ran screaming through the base totally broken.

He was put on a medical ship and sent to a California VA hospital psych unit. After a few months there, he was sent to a psych unit in Texas, and eventually back to an Arkansas unit. He was discharged with a 100% VA disability.

His family informed the community Noel was lost at sea for weeks, but this was not the truth. He lived a lie for more than forty years, refusing to disclose to the community that he suffered a fugue break from reality due to the war and rapes.

Noel developed sociopathic behavior with several other personalities manifesting themselves plus hypochondria. The multiple personalities slowly developed as he aged. None of the separate entities remembered the other personalities or their actions. Late in life he was diagnosed as being bi-polar and paranoid schizophrenic.

His social development was hindered from these episodes of rape causing self-effacing behavior and erratic anger issues. He never developed mentally beyond his psych test of the early 1950s.

> *War drums beat,*
> *Hearts pounding,*
> *Water surrounding,*
> *Mama's boy, Mama's boy,*
> *Crying in the rain,*
> *Rage boiling,*
> *Pulses beating,*
> *Mama's boy, Mama's boy,*
> *Find a way to run home.*

Noel was subjected to much abusive behavior from his mother after his return from the war. She wanted him to shape up, be a man – just get a hold of himself, deny his mental instability and hop to her every demand. She wielded a great deal of psychological power over his actions, as did his sisters. He grew to hate her, as she wanted him to replace his father after their divorce. Columbus escaped to California where he found work and then got an old age pension and eventually welfare supplementation. Noel's mother had never worked. Her daughters found out the California Welfare System would provide her a way to survive so she followed them to California in the mid-50s. She lived with one of her daughters for a while and then in a subsidized housing unit until her death. She constantly demanded Noel's loyalty through letters, openly criticizing all he did or didn't do.

What is life? A train ride or a wreck waiting to
happen? Standing tall requires backbone, a fighting spirit
and a will to survive. Difficulties break us or make us
stronger! Demand all you can of yourself, be strong, live
with joy, hope and peace. Leave the world a better place
than you found it. Find peace among the flowers, the trees,
and the beauty of each sunset. Run into the future knowing
you have place your stones well!

Chapter 3

Marriage on the mind,
Fitting in, finding a place,
A place to hide, to prey!
A young man must take a bride,
Family values to uphold,
The name must be carried on,
Take a wife, take a wife,
Lullabies singing,
Manhood proving,
With a wife, with a wife,
No one will know your secret,
You have fooled them all!

1947-1968
Silex, Arkansas

Noel Snow married his first wife, Clara Galantine, in 1947. He bought a forty-acre farm next to the Snow family farm in the Lee's Chapel Community in Johnson County.

Their twenty year marriage produced eight children, six girls and two boys. Noel returned from WWII with full-blown paranoid schizophrenia. The VA doctors later explained his development of schizophrenia was environmentally produced by the personal trauma of his young life and his abusive parents. Usually environmental schizophrenia manifests around seventeen, but Noel claimed to have only 'nervous problems', never admitting deep psychological issues. His months in the service exacerbated the condition. His family was ashamed of him. They demanded he give up his 100% Federal Veterans Compensation in the early 1950s and just be a *normal man* and get a job. No thought was given to hardship and the near starvation of his wife and children.

He claimed to have *'sinking spells'* and was too ill to work. He took to his bed for weeks being dictatorial and abusive to the children. The bottom dropped out of his marriage relationship with him accusing his wife, Clara, of poisoning their baby son, Timothy, who died from supposed Drain-o poisoning in 1968. There wasn't enough known about sexual abuse in the sixties to suspect sexual trauma and the filing of abuse charges. Criminal charges were never filed in little Timothy's death. Later, when the autopsy report was read by Idaho law enforcement in 1991, they felt the little boy and been sexually molested by Noel, thus causing his death. Idaho law enforcement officers believed Noel got away with molesting and causing the death of his son.

I do know each time Noel walked into the little boy's hospital, he died and had to be resuscitated. I believe it was the trauma of hearing his abuser's voice. He and Clara divorced in the late '60s after a twenty-year rocky marriage.

Noel's callousness drew strength and substance from the ugly shadow things in his life. He was not a poster 'boy' for fatherhood. He and Clara's martial discord did not offer a stable home life for the children's developmental well-being.

In the VA records, comments indicated he and his wife didn't have the economic or emotional wherewithal to offer a stable home life to their children. The VA hospital records gave a picture of a slatternly wife and housekeeping that was loathsome. Noel and Clara developed an open triangulating hostility toward each other in front of the children, the community and became spiritually bankrupt.

Noel was often brutal to his children, beating them savagely at the least offense. He broke his second oldest daughter's tailbone by kicking her with his booted foot. He forced them to work in the hot fields, often berating them for their 'laziness'. The children unfortunately bore the brunt of his brutality and were left with messed-up lives. Noel heard voices, living with auditory hallucinations, and the presence of evil gnawed at his inward man. His mind's tricks drove him down a road desiring evil rather than righteousness, conspiring with his mother and sisters against the world.

Though filled with evil and hate, Noel kept up desultory church attendance because it made him look good in the community to be a church goer. He continued to shout, speak in tongues and flaunt his spirituality, but holiness never lodged in his heart. He took his family to various churches over the years, changing churches as he did his hats. Noel was easily offended by some perceived wrong in each church; soon he was moving on to another church after finding fault with whatever church the family was attending.

The malevolence of his actions was directly related to his maternal family. His wife and children didn't have a chance of a social or safe environment. Two of his younger sisters appeared to be *'in love'* with him according to one of their husbands. They fawned over him like jealous lovers when he was around and hated any woman they deemed a threat to their control, such as his first wife.

The shallowness of his soul and wickedness filtered into every moment of his waking and treatment of his innocent children. The children bore no fault. When Noel was in a full rage, he would shake, puff up like a toad, clench his fist and grit his teeth until his jaw jerked like it was on a rubber band. He had a livid, sadistic face and his anger was a living, fire-breathing dragon on the prowl. No one or anything was safe when he was in a rage, especially women, children and animals.

He was a certified by his VA doctors in the late

forties/early fifties as being a hypochondriac. He wallowed
in his hypochondria, using his *illnesses* to keep from
supporting his family. He only worked eleven quarters in
his life according to Social Security records. He was
always going to get a job "next week" when he could pull
his *nerves* together. He claimed amnesia when confronted
with his delusions of illnesses, but was vocal in his
perceived mistreatment by neighbors and family.

The ignorance of his wife, Clara, offered little solace
or protection to the children, but to her credit, she did the
best she could with the knowledge she possessed. Clara
was uneducated and isolated in her marriage. She was
morally weak offering little defense in the mistreatment of
their children, but fed into his mental illness, the paranoia,
and the evil that ruled Noel's life with deep resentment.
She never held Noel accountable even after she caught him
molesting her fourteen year old niece.

Noel often laughed that Clara had caught him in the act
of molesting her niece, but she was so dumb he was able to
explain his way out of it. He told her the girl had tempted
him and he was unable to resist the sex she offered. He
molested one of his cousins near his own age and then
molested one of her sister's daughters, as a young child, in
a swimming hole on Piney River near Hagarville,
Arkansas. Clara was on the riverbank - and did nothing to
stop his molestation of the young girl. He just turned his
back and molested the girl while his other children were
swimming near by. He was a risk-taking molester, liking
the adrenaline rush of the nearness of being caught. His
ego was fed by his cleverness and getting away with the
crime. He bragged he'd had sex with all of his children.

His wife, Clara, had too many children to keep a nice
home. She had no self-management skills to make a
difference in those efforts so living in squalor was her only
recourse. She had to wash on a wringer washing machine
and often was without water to do so. Noel did install

water to the house from a well near a pond. It was
unhealthy for drinking and minnows often came through
into the bathtub or wash water. It was too much for her to
make a garden, help in the fields and do what she could
with Noel laying in the bed pretending to be ill. He would
badger her in rages until she would angrily do things. Clara
bore eight children in twenty years. She piled dirty
clothing up in the attic, and it took several pickup loads to
clean them out when I married him. Noel did nothing to
make things easier for her. The old 1867 farmhouse was
isolated, cold, and not fit for children. He did not provide
them with bedding to keep them warm at night. They slept
in a screened-in porch mostly in the open air even during
the wintertime. There was an old wood stove for heating in
the living area and wood cooking stove in the cabinet-less
kitchen. The cracks in the walls were so big a cat could
have been thrown easily through them! Noel's mind-set
was if the boards held up the walls of the old house; his
family shouldn't be complaining as his mother stated it was
good enough.

Tears are the window washers of the soul.

Chapter 4

War Drums beat,
Heart pounding,
Water surrounding,
Mama's boy! Mama's boy!
Crying in the rain,
Rage boiling,
Heart beating,
Helplessness,
Mama's boy, mama's boy!
Find a way to run home.

Noel's mother, Bertie, hated his wife, Clara, and undermined the marriage at every crossroad. Because Bertie deemed Clara to be a whore, Noel accepted her word as righteousness in his life. Bertie and his sisters, Gladys, Flora and Katherine bragged how they had 'fixed' Noel's relationship with her, convincing him he wasn't the father of any of their children.

His mother told him he wasn't much of a man producing only girls, and he just didn't have what it took to produce a boy. He began telling people he was letting his beard grow as a 'Nazareth vow to God' until he got a son from his wife. He grew it for some time and finally got the son that his mother told him he wasn't man enough to sire. He certainly kept Clara pregnant and barefoot!

Even though Clara was victimized by Noel's family, she made unwise extra-curricular sexual choices during her marriage and after her divorce from Noel. VA records listed letters and phone calls from Noel's sisters and mother accusing Clara of being a lazy whore who wouldn't cook for the family, was an unfit mother and a wife who sought to have Noel put away in a mental institution.

They preyed on Noel's insecurities and fears accusing her of having affairs with many of the sleaziest farming community men and named which child belonged to whom. Their choices of *fathers* would have gagged a dog off a 'gut wagon', but this was how they chose to demean Clara - and Noel let them. Clara's lifestyle later confirmed many of Noel's fears after their divorce, which he pointed to as his redemptive claims of non-fatherhood. Was she driven to seek sexual affirmation as confirmation of her of worth by her choices?

Noel's children all share a strong physical resemblance to him. His children didn't deserve his malice or the degradation of his family's claims. Clara was from plain country stock. She did not know how to deal with such spitefulness. Noel was often spoon-fed a litany of vile diatribe by his mother and three sisters reacting as they guided him in his belligerence and mean-spiritedness toward his precious children.

Chapter 5

Hat Man, shake and bake,
I've got the sugar if you a cake will make.
Sift the flour, pour and stir, blight on the mind!
Bring a cup of love; add to the mix, you are in a fix.
My apple love dumpling!
Come, come, be my honey dove, fly to me quickly.
I am looking for love only my way.
Come, come, says the Hat Man!

1965

I walked seven miles twice a day mowing yards at the Kingston High School to earn money to leave at summer's end. I helped the young'uns milk the cows after I trudged home from work. It felt like my feet would crumble from the tiredness of the many miles I walked behind the mower, plus the trek there and back. Sometimes someone would give me a ride, but this seldom happened. Jim Fancher gave me permission to walk across his fields which cut down the miles considerably and was a blessing.

My fear was a live breathing dragon feeding the fire of determination and gumption to leave the Hollow in August 1965. My name had become synonymous with NOTHING. I thought perhaps that my real name was 'Nothing'. I had lost all value to Aaron and Betty by refusing to be sold, bartered or used for any more sexual exploitation. Not a person in my family stepped forward to acknowledge I existed outside of Aaron's demands. I had outgrown my corncob dollies and discarded them. My beautiful wedding dollies rotted on the walls, crumbling like many of my dreams.

It was the hardest choice I'd ever made leaving Ruth and Ezra behind, but I gathered my courage to follow my dreams or sink into the soil of the Hollow without escaping. Apprehension was a snake in my bosom just waiting to strike at my fragile existence.

I took my meager belongings, God in my pocket and climbed in Mr. Weathers' car, thus making my escape from the Hollow. Pieces of God were torn from my flesh as I watched my young'uns beloved tear-stained faces while I rode away in Burl Weathers' car.

In spite of all the beatings, the violence and abuse, I loved my parents. I was their prisoner while growing up and even into early adulthood - a prisoner of circumstances kept behind a barbed wire fence of fear and hate.

How could I find the words to express the horror of my life, the dirtiness of my inner self, the guilt of abandoning Ruth and Ezra Joel? I felt filthy from the constant sexual abuse, but knew I had been cleansed in my heart by Jesus' forgiving love. My nerves were near the breaking point from the many years of abuse by Pap and Mam, but I was determined to leave and learn in the outside world.

Fear ate at my gut facing the unknown. I was scared spitless to go and too afraid to stay. I was taught the outside world was a place where the Devil waited to entrap me.

I had been taught in church I was supposed to honor my father and my mother. The small tree of parental forgiveness had not taken root in me. It was spiritual torment because I couldn't do what the scriptures stated. I knew parents weren't to cause sorrow for their children, but raise them in kindness and loving care – mine hadn't. How could I honor my parents? I prayed for God to show me the secret of obedience. What had I missed in my psyche causing

me to be the way I was? Where was my
blamelessness? How could I ever find the sunshine I
saw in innocent faces of others? I envied the other
children their carefree lives.

I survived by enduring the violent experience of
my parents; finding survival gave me strength. When
the burden of their physical and mental debasement
gave me more than I could stand, I knelt! My hands
and knees turned black with hard work and
supplication before God. I grew hope like a vine in my
secret place alone with God. My hope in Jesus fueled
my determination to become more than *Nothing*. My
childhood was forever lost, but I was determined not to
stay lost. I was emotionally damaged by the abuses of
my childhood, but I vowed to become a living,
breathing successful survivor.

The psychological violence cycle formed a mind
dependency. I was repelled by my parent's violence,
yet I sought their approval and longed to hear the
magic words, "I love you". Being vulnerable and
needy pushed me to work tirelessly hoping I could
'earn' those coveted words. As violent as the family
dynamics were, they were the only safety net I
understood. How could I find existence outside of
their "normal"? My parents were the only "normal"
I'd ever known.

The cycle of violence had brainwashed me into
believing I couldn't exist outside of the family unit,
much like the Stockholm syndrome.

*The Stockholm syndrome is a psychiatric term,
which describes an emotional attachment to a captor
formed by a hostage because of continuous stress. The
hostage creates identification with one's abuser or
captors. Dependence is created when there is total
reliance on those who hold the power. The victim's
thinking becomes distorted.*

Facing outsiders caused a fearful, painful
breathing entity of dread in my very soul. Dealing
with alien faces was terrifying, causing me much
emotional distress. I wanted to scurry home after each
encounter. Crazy as it was, I wanted the reassurance
of my "safety net" with Aaron and Betty. Even though
being with them brought near death, I understood their
parameters. No matter how horrifying they were - they
were a part of my life like an ingrown toenail.
Obeying was a habit. Fear was a leash. Even though I
was resistant, they warned me about the 'outside
world' and its dangers. They were so 'knowing' in
their assurances, I was going to find out and regret
defying them by leaving. If I were to trust any
outsider, I would be tricked. Those strangers would
take me to the Devil.

Leaving the Hollow farm filled me with 'snot
provoking terror', but my feet kept walking. Every
unknown person might want to harm me, to destroy me
and thus, were unsafe, but I had faith in God in my
pocket. Little Rock was a dreadful place in my dazed
mind – sights, sounds, evil, hope, fear, doubts, and
most of all freedom. I wasn't trustful of anyone's
motives outside of God's. I saw everything through
Aaron's controlling paranoia with nothing substantial
to explain my fears, but the fears were real dragons just
waiting. At night I sweated fear knowing someone
was going to break in due to my parent's prediction of
doom!

Aaron beat me all summer of 1965 trying to
prevent my attending Draughon's Business School
where I'd received free tuition and a work scholarship.
As difficult as it was to leave the young'uns, I meant to
attend Draughon's Business School and even though
facing strangers was terrifying – I went!

After arriving at school, I hid at lunchtime, sitting

on top of one of the commodes in the bathroom so no
one could see me eat. I looked at myself through
Betty's eyes - how ugly I was chewing my food.
Aaron deemed me unworthy to eat at the table,
throwing my food in the corner. I felt undeserving to
eat with decent people and thought my habits offended
people even after all the training by Mrs. McCollough.
I faced the torturous guillotine of self-doubt trying to
fight my way through an existence outside of Aaron's
and Betty's world. I was like a lost puppy without a
saucer to lick from for sustenance. Prayer and
supplication to God were my strength.

I lived and worked at a daycare owned by Harold
and Hazel Goodfellow for my room and board for
several months. When I arrived at the Goodfellow
home, there had been a break-in while Mrs.
Goodfellow was at work at her daycare center. My
first introduction to her home was to deal with
questioning from the police: who was I, how had I
gotten to Little Rock, and why was I in her home. She
got scared for a bit wondering if I was a trustworthy
person – maybe I had known about her beforehand.
Here I was hours from home, no one to turn to for help
and her with a break-in! I was terrified, what if she
kicked me out? How was I going to survive, no
money, and nowhere to go?

They turned out to be wonderful people and were
good to me. I lived in the daycare center and my
bedroom was at the back of the center. The other
workers were older than I and to them I was an
ignorant "hillbilly". They treated me badly from the
start. I didn't know or have life skills to deal with
them. I was folding the center's wash and heard them
talking when they thought I was back in my bedroom.
The shame of their contempt pushed me inside of
myself even more. I didn't know how to be a normal

human being so Aaron and Betty must have been right
- I was nothing. I was too ignorant to know I should
have spoken with Mrs. Goodfellow about her
employee's treatment of me and ask her to help me
work through their tactics. I didn't trust anyone, so in
my pain and shame at their comments, after a few
months of their bullying, I left.

I started attending a church while at the daycare
just down the street a few blocks. I became involved
in the familiar Assembly of God Church worship
services. As I was a member, I was asked to be their
janitor. I took the job. I needed to earn extra money. I
also took ironing jobs on the side for a nickel an
article. It was a meager existence, but free of Aaron
and Betty.

One day the Assembly of God pastor, Darrell
Teeter, asked me to come down to the parsonage
which was being used as Sunday School classrooms,
stating he wanted to show me how to clean better. As I
entered the parsonage, he turned and locked the door
behind me. I instinctively knew I was in trouble. He
immediately attacked me, trying to rape me. He
rubbed my breasts, squeezing painfully. He tried to
kiss me and began rubbing his engorged penis against
my crotch. He was panting and sexually aroused. He
told me I might as well not fight him because he was
too turned on to stop from having me. He kept trying
to push me back onto the couch, panting and thrusting
against me. I was terrified! I fought like a wildcat out
of sheer animal terror, but he almost accomplished the
job before I got away. I ran away into the
neighborhood, cowering in fear like a cornered animal.
What was wrong with me that a 'man of God' would
attack me? I thought I had a target on my back which
stated, "I am nobody, attack me!" I hid like a wounded
creature, going to school in a fog, not daring to tell

anyone, just knowing that every noise I heard outside at night was the preacher at my door trying to get in to hurt me. I licked my wounds in silence and horror. I learned to separate myself into two people as I had at home. I was a professional at school and a cowardly nobody in my personal life.

The pastor, Darrell Teeter, came to Draughon's Business School, pulled me from class and told me no one would believe me if I dared to tell what he had tried to do. He was the pastor and I was supposed to 'relieve the saints' - and he was a Saint. He informed me since his wife was not sexually satisfying him, he had chosen me. I saw the same look in his eyes I had seen in Aaron's, Betty's, Samson's and Uncle Paul's. I was frightened into the next week of Sundays. I was too afraid to tell any of the school administration fearing dismissal from the school. I had no understanding the school would have helped me report him to the police and defend me – ignorance was my worst enemy. There was no safety anywhere for me where a sexual predator couldn't find me! How I needed to see the young'uns! My parents were useless in the help department. I told them what happened and they bragged to the Kingston church that they were right and I was paying the Devil for leaving home. According to them, I was receiving recompense for my disobedience against the "will of God" for my life because I had left home. I never ever told them another thing.

I quit going to that church. Finally, the Sunday School Superintendent of the Little Rock Church and his wife came to my house late one night. They wanted to know why I hadn't been in church. I refused to answer them. The couple demanded to know why I wasn't coming to church. I was a member there and they informed me I was under an obligation to continue being a part of the church. I had taken the job as janitor and the church needed to be cleaned. I broke down sobbing, "Pastor Teeter tried to rape me!" I told them how he had locked the parsonage door and how I managed to fight him off. There was a shocked silence and disbelief on their faces.

"Surely not!" exclaimed the Sunday School Superintendent. He kept questioning me in disbelief. I couldn't stop crying like a whipped dog. I knew I was dirty and evil from Betty's and Aaron's beatings and abuse, but I didn't want anyone else to know my shame. Maybe I did deserve what the preacher had tried to do me.

After a bit, the Sunday School Superintendent's wife started crying and stated, "The preacher tried to rape me also." Hearing that, his face turned white as a sheet. He stumbled in his doubtful questioning, looking from her to me. "Why didn't you tell me?" She said she was afraid it would shut the church down and make God look bad. She said he tried to overpower her and rape her. After a long talk and some praying, he told me he would report the preacher to the Assembly of God headquarters in Hot Springs. I trusted him to do so, but years later found out it had all been covered up and still being hidden today.

Darrell Teeter attempted to assault several women in the church besides me. I was assured he would be taken care of and never preach again. I was lied to by the Assembly of God Church. He is still an ordained minister to this day. I was young and a nobody so the church allowed him to hold credentials and continues the ongoing cover-up of his crimes to this day. I was heartbroken and spiritually abandoned. What a "holy man' he was! This pastor's spiritual betrayal added tremendous stress to my life. This left a hole in my God-life with more added distrust of those who rape and abuse. I had no one to turn to for hope, healing and an explanation of why a preacher would try to rape me.

I was able to find an apartment, after leaving the daycare, but I did stay in touch with the Goodfellow's over the years. During the following weeks at Draughon's Business School, one of my fellow students, an older man, tried to break into my apartment one evening after midnight. I believe he was intent on molesting me. I shook with terror. I peed in one of my cooking pots during the night rather than use the bathroom just outside of my room in the hallway. I was afraid he would be waiting for me. I could see his black and white shoes backlit underneath the front door of my apartment and could identify him. He wore the same shoes to school. I had no phone. He followed me for weeks at school until one day I got brave enough to tell some of the other students within his hearing, "Girls, I have figured out who is trying to break into my apartment. I know I am right and I am going to tell his wife," I told my new friends. They all agreed and talked about creeps in school. The man was listening to us as we talked. He was only a seat or so away from us in the school.

His actions stopped immediately and he moved to another section of the school and soon left the apartment complex. Going to the police was out of the question for me because of my distrust. Police weren't my friends. I had been trained to be afraid of anyone in law enforcement.

They agreed I should let my landlady know who he was and which apartment he lived in. I told my landlady of my suspicions and she arranged a signal for me to use. I was to use my broom handle to knock on her ceiling, which was just beneath my apartment

floor. If I knocked a certain amount of times, she
would call the police.

Thank God for Beverly Carter and Linda
Thompson for being my friends and rescuing me from
the fear of my existence at Draughon's Business
School.

After living in my apartment for a few weeks, I
found a city library and started frequenting it as
reading always had given me a place to hide. One day,
a man attacked me in an upper floor of the library,
muttering, "I want your cherry, I am going to have
your cherry." Fear slithered through my being as he
tried to drag me into an empty reading room still
insisting I was going to give him my 'cherry.' I fought
out of blind fear. Blackness almost overcame my
mind. I managed to shove him down a set of stairs.
As I fled in panic, he hit the bottom floor yelling at me
that he was going to catch me. I never went back to
the library again, and I never reported his attack to the
librarian or to the police. I lost a place of safety where
I could heal from the loneliness eating at my soul.
Fear almost drove me mad.

Several weeks later, I was waiting to catch the city bus
to school. A man in a station wagon pulled up and
demanded I get into his vehicle. I told him, "What are you
trying to do? I am not getting into your car, I don't know
you."

He touched a pistol on the seat of his car,
motioning for me to come closer, insisting I get in the
car with him. I took a step backwards and then
another; I was not going to get in that car. I was
terrified and cried out to God to help me. I was
inspired, I believe, by Him at that moment.

"Can't you see my Father is standing right here
with me and He is bigger than you? No, I won't get in
the car. You had better move along as He is going to

take care of you for me. Now you leave me alone. Here comes the bus and I am getting on it." What he saw, I don't know, but he turned sickly pale, cussed me loudly, and sped off into the morning. That night, a girl was raped in a city park. The description matched the man who tried to force me into his car. They had an APB out for him. I was too afraid of the police to report the incident. I was glad I knew God. I felt His strength and presence with me that morning.

The pastor's attempted rape, the break-in attempt, the man at the library, and now this incident created extreme anxiety and fear in my heart- almost breaking me to the point of no return. My heart cried, "Oh God, what is wrong with me?" I wanted to tuck my tail between my legs and run like a dog for the Hollow farm. I didn't know that once I was a rape victim, there could be multiple attempts by various individuals with whom I came in contact. There is something in our victimized psyche that alerts a predator to our pre-conditioning.

Where is wisdom for the young and a medal of bravery for
their souls? Who will equip them to be bold as a lion in
telling of their abuse? Who will defend them when they
are brave? Where is the law, the safety and the public
outcry against the lifetime harm of the children?

Chapter 6

Trials severe,
Clinging to hope
Fingernail hanging,
Toes digging in,
Treasures none,
Hope of default,
No reasoning available,
Insanity teeming,
Hate is supreme.

1965-66

My heart bled with anxiety and fear for Ruth and Ezra Joel's safety. When I left the Hollow, Aaron and Betty, with revenge in mind, forbade me to have any contact with them. I contacted Ruth secretly by writing her at the Kingston High School. I would send her a letter and a stamped self-addressed envelope. My parents found one of my letters she had forgotten to destroy and beat her badly. I got so worried; I caught the bus home during the Christmas break. I was beaten every day I was there. Ruth would cower in the corner afraid Aaron and Betty were going to kill me and turn on her. She pretended to hate me to keep from being beaten. The fright on the faces of my precious sister and brother was difficult to bear. What were they enduring while I was away? I knew I wasn't any good for them, so I stayed away from them as long as I could stand it. I had no one in the family to turn to for help, nor did the young'uns.

I ran out of money to finish school in the late spring of 1966. I knew then I was a nothing, and felt any man could look at me and see I was damaged goods. I was devastated to the core of my being. I quit school and returned to the Hollow farm. At least the beatings there were familiar.

Finally, I was able to move out to Huntsville to live with my beloved Grandpa and Grandma. I helped them around their place for rent so I could save my money to further my education. I was not going to give up now. Grandma urged me not to give up, but to get my education. With the help of Judge Clarence Watson, I found a job in Huntsville working for the Arkansas State Revenue Office. He hadn't forgotten how I was a hard worker. He encouraged me to stay in school. Aaron was sure mad I got a good job of my choosing and was staying with my grandparents. I didn't get to see the young'uns but a time or two that summer because going home meant a beating.

Grandpa walked me the mile and a half every morning to work and then met me at quitting time. It was a wonderful time of being with my grandparents, helping them garden, repair fences or cut brush, singing in the evenings after work and praying with them. How they loved one another! Grandma made a wonderful supper and had it ready to eat when I got home. I had never gotten such loving care as I received that summer.

Grandpa would sit on the front porch and play his violin or banjo and we would sing hymns. I wanted to stay there forever and never leave! They shared a lot of their faith - adult to adult - and why they felt as they did about God. Sometimes, Grandpa would play an old dance song from his pre-preacher days and talk of what a sinner he had been – not a good man, but saved by grace. He would often say, "These aren't nice songs, but your grandma sure used to like to dance to these tunes before we found Jesus." He could make that violin sing! Grandma would smile and give him that secret look only lovers can recognize in their mate's face.

Grandma shared with me her simple country woman philosophy: love God, raise a family, and do what you can to make life easier on those around you. I learned so much from her through my childhood. She wanted me to understand a good marriage was nothing like Aaron and Betty's. She shared a good marital loving relationship that was satisfying and wonderful. We often spoke of the beatings. She and Grandpa told me they believed Aaron hated me because God had placed a call on my life to preach. Did the Devil urge him in trying to destroy me because of my God-Calling? They believed Aaron had abandoned God's calling on his life, thus turning more evil as the years passed.

Grandma cried and told me of her lifelong love of God. She and Grandpa prayed daily for my survival. She and Grandpa never knew how to stop Aaron from being so mean. It was wonderful to have her and Grandpa give me hugs and tell me at least twice a day they loved me. At night, they would come to my bedroom, have prayer with me, and give me a goodnight kiss on the forehead. It was a time I treasured. We shared a like faith and often walked to a little country church down the highway every time there was a service. Grandma raised her voice in song and how I wished I could sing like her!

Grandpa John Riley Russell died in 1969. I got to attend his funeral. Grandma Lillie Carter Russell died in 1985. Aaron sent word he would kill me if I came to her funeral because of the doctor's finding out Betty was a sociopath. Out of respect for Grandma, I didn't go because of the dangerous anger of Aaron and Betty. I had visited Grandma, weeks earlier at Aunt Jewel's and said my goodbyes then. It hurt to see my Grandma not in her right mind. She asked if she could crawl on my lap and rest her head against my shoulder as I used to do as a child in her lap. I held her in my arms and then laid her gently on the bed as she slept. It was enough of a wonderful goodbye because I know I will see her in heaven.

The pattern of brainwashing and broken dynamics of my dysfunctional family was familiar to me, though stunting in my emotional maturity, it was my life. I sought to get 'things just right' to escape the low-self esteem, the socially inept feelings and burden of terror. As long as I had the young'uns, I could deal with the pain, the self-loathing and keep hope, but without them, I was a shattered rock. There were no normal social boundaries of give and take in my family or a child's rights to live without fear. When gentleness and caring were distributed, my family was absent that day and received a failing grade.

Did Aaron and Betty's triangulation give them satisfaction in the thirst for power in the family unit to build up their low self-esteem? Did each of them believe if they fought hard enough, one would have power over the other one? They both were losers. In the Hollow, no one cared what happened to us young'uns; we were society's blight, an embarrassment and the butt of jokes in the Kingston community. Personal filth, along with Aaron, was not an easy bedfellow for people to snuggle up to, especially steeped in ignorance.

In the fall of 1966, I was accepted at Arkansas Polytechnic College in Russellville. My Uncle John asked me to go to college with my sixteen year old cousin. He felt she was too immature and flighty to be away from home.

I laugh often to keep the tears at bay because there

are those in my family who are very angry at me for writing this book, but incest lives in our family, damaging not only me but many others. I urgently want to eradicate it as my last gift for Grandma and my children. I want my children to understand how much I love them and to know, in the end, I did everything I could to set them free of the madness that has been in my family for generations.

When I was in my early twenties, I went to my Uncle John's house for the night. To my shock and horror after I was in bed, I heard someone scuttling down the hallway toward the bed where I was sleeping with my cousin. Suddenly a hand crept up under the covers, shoving my clothing up above my waist. I started screaming, "Rape! Rape!" and discovered it was my Uncle John!

Shh, Shh!" He kept trying to put his fingers inside me and put his other hand over my mouth. I began screaming, kicking and fighting. My cousin lay there offering not a word in my defense or helped me fight so I assume Uncle John had been sexually abusing her too. My Aunt Jewel ran into the room with her cornbread skillet and began beating Uncle John over the head. She was very angry. "What do you think you're doing?"

The pervert protested, "I was only trying to see if Catherine is still a good girl!" I was in shock. She whipped him good and told him "You are a bastard. Get out of this room right now." My Aunt Jewel was a godly woman, who did care, but she never learned to drive and was dependent upon my Uncle John's bounty, so she had no choices open to her. She neither held a job nor had an education to have helped her do things differently.

It was awkward to visit with my Aunt Jewell after this incident. Uncle John destroyed, in a few minutes,

a lifetime of trust I'd had in him. Sexual abuse digs
deep and its tentacles cling to the soul.

During my second year of college, Betty began
threatening to commit suicide. She would call me in
the dormitory, demanding I come home or she was
going to do '*the deed*' and murder Ezra Joel and Ruth.
She would describe how she had a gun pointed at Ruth
or Ezra Joel's head and if I didn't promise to come
home, she was going to kill them. I lived in terror she
would actually kill my sister and brother. I had no way
of knowing if she was telling me the truth or not I
went home reluctantly; I did not want to see her or
Aaron. I got a beating, but it seemed to satisfy her
sexually to help Pap beat me.
She hadn't tried to touch me since I had almost
killed her. Other than leering, lewd remarks and
sexually explicit jokes, she'd left me alone. The
beatings were her only weapon. She was obsessed
with me and humiliated me often. Her insane pressure
made it difficult to try to go to school and the stress
affected my grades. Her threats got so bad that my
college house mother or one of the nurses at the school
would take her calls rather than me. I trembled in fear
knowing any call could be a death sentence for the
young'uns.
I know it was hard for Ruth and Ezra Joel to
survive after I left home. I lived with a boatload of
guilt for abandoning them. Being ignorant of the law,
I could see no other alternative. If only I had known to
ask Aunt Mary Russell for help. There wasn't much in
place in Arkansas during the late '60s to help children.
A father or mother was the law. I was a
disenfranchised female and worthless because of the
abuse I suffered as Aaron Russell's child. In fact, at
that time the law offered little protection for children

from any kind of abuse, especially as most everyone was afraid of Aaron. He could lie smoother than Southern Comfort Whiskey going down slow and easy, or so he claimed.

Bragging was all Aaron seemed much good at, and laying the lash to our backs. He did live up to his brags with the beatings!

If I had known what Ruth and Ezra Joel were enduring, I think I would have died. My precious sister, Ruth, has been able to share about some of the torment she encountered after I left. She had to take over the farm chores and milk the dairy herd. She made up her mind she was not going to be the 'slave' I had been. She began her own campaign for freedom.

She told me every day, Aaron and Betty claimed I was the 'perfect daughter' and why couldn't she be like me. She became very angry and grew to hate me because she didn't know what else to do to survive after I left home without her. Brainwashing by my parents took many forms and had lasting effects in our lives. It took us a few years to work through the damage done to us, but thankfully, we both survived and enjoy being sisters.

May life be nestled deep in your soul. May you walk in the shadow of our Creator's wings and find the hollow of the rock to rest in awhile. Skip rocks on the water, laugh in the wind, and ride the hope of the setting sun.

Chapter 7

Brother dearest,
Wobbling icky mind of idiocy,
Trained like a monkey to perform,
A glass full of hate embedded,
Mine shards of brokenness,
Castaway of violence,
Climb the wall, wail in anguish,
There is no door to the hate that claims,
Silence is the enemy,
Stealth is your game,
Locked in decades of incest,
With the tolling bell, a destroyer!
Tears, brother, tears,
No regrets that I've won!

1965-69

My brother, Samson, began working with Aaron on the Beaver Dam Project as soon as he got out of high school. They also worked at various sawmill jobs around the area cutting timber. Samson liked to drive fast; he lived on the edge of destruction. He began to drink, gamble, and hang with an undesirable crowd. He finagled buying an old 1949 car as a means of transportation. He was still living at home under Aaron's authority at twenty-one when I left for Draughon's Business School.

Ruth shared with me Samson had tried to corner her after I left. Aaron had made a wooden ladder to use to get up on the roof of the blockhouse. She and Ezra Joel would use it to get away from Samson. He would climb up after them and they would jump from the roof to escape. Finally, in desperation, after the ladder was chopped up, they learned to shimmy up the bathroom vent-pipe to get away from him.

Ruth would go up first and then pull Ezra Joel up out of the way of Samson.

She said they stockpiled rocks, sticks or anything they could throw at Samson after they got up on the roof to keep him from getting to them. They would rock him until he gave up and went away. Then they would carefully come down from the roof. What a way for my young'uns to have lived. It broke my heart as Ruth shared these facts with me over the years. We can now laugh at the picture of Ruth and Ezra Joel defending their rooftop fort where it was safe.

> *Little boy, little boy,*
> *Thinking what a big man you are,*
> *Small is your mind,*
> *Mean is your middle name,*
> *Rape walking,*
> *Spittle flying,*
> *Man, O, Man,*
> *What are you?*
> *A bastion of emptiness!*

Ezra Joel shared with me Samson started abusing him the night I left. I cried my heart out. Our parents were devils', but Samson was even a worse monster. Ezra Joel was forced to sleep in the same bed as Samson, thus enduring his horrific abuse and evil. Samson's abuse carried over to his own children.

Ruth says she managed to outrun Samson and can't remember if he ever hurt her or not; she suffers amnesia about much of her childhood. I believe she did not escape Betty's abuse or his. She didn't understand Ezra's fear of Samson nor did she know Samson was molesting him night after night. She only knew her own fear and hate. Our physical suffering couldn't be repaired, but our faith in God has grown and given us strength. We murdered our emotions to survive the torment done to our bodies and our souls. Our erected walls of protection are in place and we only let a select few into our "circle of protection".

Samson began dating. He would find a girl, falling in love after the second date and, if they broke up, he stalked her and her new boyfriend for weeks. He hid in the woods, watching them through the scope of his rifle. He made elaborate plans to kill them and then describe what he was thinking with Betty. She told him to catch the girls and bring them to her and she would show him what to do to them. When I was home, I could hear them planning where to hide the bodies if he carried out his bizarre plans. Samson terrorized several young women for five or six years.

Samson slowly worked up to leaving our parents for a few years. Aaron blamed me for his leaving. He told me if I hadn't left home, Samson would have stayed on the farm. I was their favorite scapegoat.

In 1970, twenty-six year old Samson Russell married sixteen year old Mary Catherine Stewart. Then he had a young wife to bully. They had an extremely troubled marriage. She was a sexual abuse survivor and he was a rapist. He was abusive to his wife and children. In their confiding to each other about things in their lives, Samson disclosed having sex with the animals and molesting me.

Betty's obsession turned into tormenting their marriage and hating Samson's wife. Her unhealthy sexual desire for him lasted until her death. Ruth, Ezra and I were never important.

Samson finally succumbed to the stressors and pressure of his wasted life and, without a viable way to make a living, returned to live on Pap's property. By moving back, he put his three children in harm's way. Aaron demanded total obedience from Samson if he was to stay on the farm.

2015

Samson is very ill, a diabetic at this juncture in his life - dying. He is a man of rage and filth. He does not believe in God and demands to know why he is still living. He yells, "Why can't God just kill me?" Even worse, for years he wanted to know why Aaron wouldn't die so he could sell off the farm. Aaron is dead! Samson has had a stroke and is confined to the home care of his daughter, waiting to die – and as I understand, can't speak. The farm is valueless for him except to be used as a bribe for his care. It is a miserable existence. I feel a deep sadness knowing he has a death wish, yet won't get his life in order to meet his Maker. I believe he sinned his 'day of grace' way. God does not forget justice and vengeance is His. Repentance for wrong still requires consequences. Samson has chosen to curse God and die.

After Samson returned to the farm, he spent several years terrorizing the Hollow. He patrolled the Madison County Road, which ran through Aaron's property, on an ATV. He carried a rifle and a pistol. He stopped people, threatening them, yelling with filthy cursing, sometimes holding a gun on them. He told them he owned the road, and they were on his property, even though the county had a road right of way and maintained it. Samson's life choices got him banned from many Madison County businesses because of his nasty mind, foul mouth and dangerous attitude toward women. I banned him from my life long ago.

Samson is seventy-one years old and has corroded

from the inside like a sinking ship without a rudder. He is the product of our parents' beatings, hate, and sexual abuse.

Samson faces God without any mercy from his siblings. I remember him as an innocent child and pray God will be forgiving during his final hours. My sister says her prayers gave out a long time ago for him and our parents; I can see her point. I promised Grandma Russell I would call the names of her children and grandchildren in prayer as long as I as I live. I am trying to keep my promise.

Climb a mountain, leave fear behind, look through the windows of life and throw open the door. Follow the road that leads to your dream. Pave that road with life. What is your suitcase filled with and where will you travel? Does your life plan include a bucket list and are you working on it now?

Chapter 8

Mind games,
Those ugly little things called consequences.
Where could a child run, who could save them?
Nasty, nasty, games of secrets that destroy.
Closet full of despicable lies,
Leeches attached to the flesh,
Threats vile, full of dirt and guile!
Who will sweep the cobwebs down,
Opening the window of despair,
If not I, who then will stand, bold and proud?

My grandparents, John and Lillie Russell, had a great influence on my life and much of their story is shared in my first book. Their love for me was unconditional. They had a hardscrabble life and Aaron was abusive to them.

Growing up with them caring for me, I am sure, preserved my life and gave me the strength to become who I am today. Their prayers sustained my faith and gave me hope. They lived what they preached. It is hard for me to reconcile that my grandparents, who were godly people, raised a passel of unruly children who were hell-bent. The sinful ways of their children grieved Grandpa and Grandma and affected their grandchildren. When I lived with them that last summer, I would hear them lifting their voices in prayerful supplication to God to have mercy on their family, their children and their future children. They wept bitter tears for the redemption of our family from the blight of domestic violence and incest.

I know very little about their child-raising years or why many of their children used religion as an excuse to rape and abuse others. There are a few odd occurrences I want to include in the following pages. Aaron had a sister, Daisy, who was a Holiness preacher, shouting, praising the Lord, and saving souls.

Aunt Daisy used to buy me clothes and shoes to help me stay in school. Much to my shock, her granddaughters informed me how she would be driving along the highways of Madison County and see something she wanted. She would shout, "Praise the Lord! God just spoke to me and that piece is to be mine." She would make the girls go back and help her steal whatever it was she wanted from someone's yard after dark! She raised the girls when their mother abandoned them and was wonderful to them. Aunt Daisy died just short of 101 years old in 2013.

Her granddaughters spoke of their mother, Ruth, and how she would have old men come to her place to "visit", paying money to her. She threw parties, but she was the only woman present. She was a sex addict. She would make the girls wear dresses, without panties on, and sit on the old men's laps. She would say, "Now you be nice to Mr. So-and-so as he is giving me good money." I was saddened to see the look of pain in my precious cousin's eyes; yet like me, they loved their mother, but must live with the effects of sexual abuse. Incest makes familial ties almost impossible to break – and if the ties are broken – there is no bridge back into the family. Any kind of attention, even if it is bad, is better than no attention at all and is sought after by children of incest.

Aaron had another sister, Aunt Nancy, who is in her early nineties, who presented a pattern of sickness and deceit in the family. She would shout and praise the Lord with the best of them and firmly considers herself on the road to heaven. Most folks believe her to be a rare sanctified Saint of God. She has thirteen children. She would make the girls run around naked even though they were developing physically. She said, "Why wash clothes when I don't have to? Besides, I don't need many clothes this way for all of them to wear."

Aunt Nancy's girls were put out in the bushes to pick blackberries naked as the day they were born with their breasts exposed to the elements. She and her children are angry with me for writing about our family and told me, "I don't know why you are doing this to all of us. God made men in the family to teach their daughters how to have sex. I know my sons had sex with my daughters and there ain't nothin' wrong with that. I don't know why you are so mad that Samson had sex with you. It is only 'natural' that the boys practice on their sisters." She stated I shouldn't be mad at my brother or my parents for using me sexually as this was the will of God.

She claimed to have proof of her point of view from the scriptures. I have never found that scripture after fifty plus years in the ministry. Excuses are varied and rationalized excuses range large for abusers in incestuous families. Aunt Nancy's second oldest son raped his daughter. My aunt told her the same thing, "Why should she be upset as it was natural for a father to teach his daughter about sex." This precious cousin suffers from depression and Post Traumatic Stress Disorder and has cut herself off from her family. She was left with no other choice than to protect herself emotionally. Many in my family are dysfunctional adults with varied disorders. Survival has not been easy for the lost children who suffer as adults.

As you can see, my immediate family did not stop the incest for my brother, my sister or me or the many others harmed. One of my younger Russell aunts left the family having very little contact; I now can understand why. There are no healthy relationship boundaries in any of our families. Secrets lived and grew in the silence of incest.

My great-grandpa, Stephen Russell, raped and abused Aaron's oldest sister, my Aunt Mary, who was a source of great support to me until she died. She often talked with me and urged me to expose the incest in our family. She never married nor was able to trust in a sustainable relationship. She became a clinical psychologist in Bakersfield, California. She was sure Grandpa Stephen raped her sisters or others in the family. She called me every weekend until 1991-96, when she became too disabled. She encouraged me to stand strong and write our family story.

There were three brothers and sisters of the Carter and Russell families who married each other and thus produced three sets of double cousins. We were raised to be suspicious of each other and not allowed to play together. As one of my cousins stated during my writing this book, "A big ditch was dug to protect the family secrets. We were kept away from each other because if we had been allowed to be friends, we would have found out each other's secrets. We could have banded together to do something about it." Fear is the gatekeeper of sexual abuse and incest.

Grandma Russell's brother, Uncle Tom Carter, attacked my Aunt Mary near a country road. He had almost raped her when a neighbor heard her screaming and beat him off her. She said it was awful and she was very frightened. She believed Tom and Burton Carter raped all of her sisters and others around the county. Tom was a smooth-talking, handsome fellow who was a land surveyor with access to many children through his job. Grandpa shared with me that he didn't have a virtuous daughter. The Russell girls were known to be "wild as March hares."

In 2011, my beautiful cousin, Tom Carter's granddaughter, revealed he began raping her when she was a little girl. She endured his rape and abuse for many, many years. Her grandmother knew, as well as her parents, but they forced her to go on drives with "Pa" and told her she was his little girl. My sweet cousin stated, "Couldn't anyone see what 'Pa' was doing to me? I was afraid of him and just knew everyone could see what he was doing to me. He would take me to another room away from the family, attack me sexually, and then force me to mingle with family again. I wondered why they didn't notice the dirt he left on my body. Why didn't someone protect me from his abuse? I felt so dirty and ashamed." She has become a beautiful human being who lived through a dark period in her life, but overcame it and is a survivor.

W. T. Carter, her father, raped her sister. All I could do when we were in college together was hold my cousin's hand as she told me how horrible it was to know her father was her rapist. Neither of us knew how to stop the rape in our family. My cousin died in a car wreck in the mid 90s. She had found a measure of peace before her death.

We had another great uncle, Burton Carter, who raped many women, young girls, boys or anyone he could secret away – he raped me as a small girl. He was the epitome of what Samson has become –evil and vile.
He was living with us on the Old Pharis place and Aaron caught him raping me. He was forced off the place by Aaron when I was around two or three years old, but nothing was ever done to make me safe or understand what had happened to me. I was blamed by Aaron as having caused the attack. I was like my

cousin, why couldn't someone see the shame that I felt?

Rape and incest weren't confined only to the Carter and Russell families. Betty was around three when her mother, Catherine Mead Walker, died from tuberculosis. Coleman Walker brought his daughters to live with his mother Frances Reed Walker in Madison County – the family had a live-in rapist. Betty's Uncle Hubert Walker raped her and her sister, Helene, shortly after they were brought home to Arkansas from New York. Betty and Helene, in turn, sexually abused all of their children. A generational heritage doesn't stop. It has affected numerous lives destructively in my immediate family.

Conditioned members of my family are confused, angry and unproductive because of the incest and are abusers themselves turning to drugs and alcohol. Five to six generations of incest move forward with a legacy of hate and abuse. I am praying my exposing the incest in my family will have a cleansing effect.

Continuum

Bookmarker of the silent,
Crypt of the living,
Dying of the soul,
The living of the dead,
Dread,
Fearsome beholders,
The fearing and the bold,
Takes and deceivers,
Division of the giving,
Keeping of the selfless,
Faceless,
The monster most feared,
Looking back from the pool of life,
Shiftless idioms of realms best left alone,
Continuum!
The defender, less defendable,
Conspicuous choice, easiest out.
Easing the conscience, rubbing away,
Touching the motionless,
Melting, denial so strong,
Of the thing most feared,
The reflection but a glimpse,
The truth in the seeing,
The monster that lurks,
The saying in the telling,
The hardest to face,
Is of the self.

Life is either filled with disaster or a bucket full of
gumption. What is in your bucket? You are just
as brave as you dare. No one can steal your
dreams if you fill a sack up with them.

Chapter 9

The Dancing Clown, limber and lean,
Jangle, jangle goes his bangles,
Ah, if you believe his painted on smile,
You will join his dance,
Peek around him,
See him for what he is.
Clown in disguise, stealing the show,
Pretense is his middle name,
He places with smoke and mirrors,
You will never see who the clown is,
From his toes to the bells on his funny hat,
Watch his show, join in his chorus,
A partying he wants you to go
But, alas, he wears many faces,
Painted face aglow, hiding the in the midst,
Look, look, look and see!

1965-70

The next few years were the happiest of my life. Much of this time is my own and is not for sharing. I got to go places and see things that were wonderful. I went home with many of my friends from college for all of the holidays. I became active in Chi Alpha, a college outreach program of the Assemblies of God Organization. I preached often for the churches in our area and was happy to find another outlet to serve the Lord and stay entrenched in my God-calling. I saw many lives changed through the love of God. I believed in the transforming power of my Heavenly Father. I grew in my spiritual walk, but was emotionally stunted by my past. I worked toward getting two college degrees: Business Education and Speech and Drama. I learned to prepare better sermons as I progressed in my classes which were life changing.

If I returned home, I weathered beatings and abuse which intensified as I got older. The beatings were to intimidate the young'uns into being obedient and subservient when I wasn't there.

I knew the young'uns stayed hungry since I wasn't there to cook so I saved all the extra boxed cereal, chips, and packaged cookies I could from my meals at college and took them home for the young'uns at Christmas. I worked in the cafeteria to pay for college. I received grants and took out loans. The years of stress caught up with me and I developed ulcers, painful urgent holes in my stomach which kept me in its grip for hours.

My back muscles locked up when I was a junior in college. I was hospitalized and put in traction. I couldn't return to the classroom so I had to withdraw from college for the semester, returning to the Hollow.

The stress of my existence was killing me. After the hospitalization, Betty put out the word I had been raped by an assailant so when I returned to church I faced many invasive questions and stares of condemnation. Betty just stood and grinned at my horror. It was untrue and why she did that I couldn't fathom except to cover her own immorality in case I voiced accusations against her. I can only believe she thought she was getting revenge against me for stopping her sexual abuse.

I was put on drugs for the pain and became addicted to the Methadone. I quit cold turkey. My mother beat me daily, telling me that I was a lazy, good-for-nothing, and I was not going to live off them. I endured. Finally, I found a job. I got enough money to return to college, but I was a wreck.

I became a perfectionist with obsessive/compulsive tendencies demanding I succeed and do things correctly. I left myself no room for any margin of error. This obsessive/compulsive need drove me most of my life. If I could be perfect, surely I would gain my parents' love.

In 1969, my sister, Ruth, graduated from Kingston High School. I had been waiting for this day a long time. Finally, my baby sister was going to be legally free of Aaron and Betty. I was so worried about her.

I returned for her graduation. Thank God she had survived. She was bitter, scared and angry with me for not being there for her. She was so fragile; if a good wind came up, she would blow away.

She knew she had to leave, but how was she going to do that? I understood she didn't know whether to trust me or not. I told her if I could make it, she could too because from now on, I could at least offer her what help I had. I had nothing but determination and grit. I tried to emotionally shove that into her heart. She was smart. She was beautiful, but the cowed look in her precious eyes was that of a wounded dove. I could see in her eyes the fear of going into the unknown; she was terrified of telling Aaron she was leaving.

She had applied to Arkansas Tech and had been accepted. She was going to try out for their basketball team, but as small she was, I didn't think she would make the team. She lived and breathed basketball. I feared she would be disappointed in that arena. I talked it over with her and decided I was the one to take on helping her get away. I opted to confront Aaron about her leaving and demanded she was going to live with me in Springdale. I fought with him for a weekend, standing up for Ruth. Aaron and Betty raged, "You ain't takin' Ruth. She belongs here on the farm. We need her to do the chores since you left."

"There isn't any way I'm leaving her here for another year; it isn't going to do you any good to argue. You've almost killed her by all the hard work you've piled on her. She isn't your slave. She's my sister and I'm taking her with me. She'll be eighteen in October and I'm taking her now so she can start college this fall." Ruth stood as if turned to stone, fearful that Aaron and Betty would turn on her as they did to me. I could tell she was ready to run for the hills if Aaron made the slightest move toward her. I took his knockdown as my due for fighting for her, but I wasn't going to stand down for them at any point.

I emphasized to him how small she was and had very little physical strength. She was just too smart and too little to be of any value to him on the farm as a helper. He knew she couldn't do much as she hadn't been able to keep up with many of the chores since I'd left. "You can bellow and scream all you want, Aaron, but I am taking her even if I have to have the sheriff come and take her away for me." Ruth's shrunken eyes were as big as saucers.

I knew she couldn't ever remember me standing up tall and talking back to Aaron the way I was. I had gained a bit of strength. I was taking her away from the Hollow with or without his consent. Aaron woke me up during the night to resume the argument, slapping me around. Ruth rolled over against the wall and curled up in a ball.

I am sure she felt like a cornered rat. I did too, but I wasn't going to leave without her. I didn't dare let Aaron see my fear or I would lose the battle for Ruth's soul. I knew if I did lose, she would never escape, so I spit right back in his face, yelling, "We're leaving in the morning. I'm going to take the pickup." It was now or never! It took Ruth some time to accept that I had freed her; now I had to quit being her mother and that took time. She had a crock full of resentment toward me for leaving her, but she was alive and I was so full of joy over that fact.

Betty chimed in the argument and said that they needed the pickup to drive to church and get groceries. I could see Aaron's mind was bent around me taking the pickup and using it for us to get work that summer. God had heard my prayers before I set in to wrestle Ruth free.

Betty whined how ashamed she would be to be seen riding in the logging truck to church. Aaron turned on her like a cornered badger, "Well, ya' just get used to it, my mind is made up, and I'm willin' to help Catherine this one time so Ruth can get to Tech. She is the smartest one in the family. My Mam helped my sister Mary get away for an education, (I had pulled out that 'gun' and used it heavily. The bullet of Aunt Mary had sunk into his skin), and I am goin' to let Ruth get one." I could have shouted with joy, but acted all appreciative and bowed and scraped some for him. I figured my pride was not in question here, but Ruth's freedom.

Ruth just sidled around and got out the door on the run. I found her and Ezra out in one of our favorite places. I told her to get her things packed and in the pickup for in the morning, we were out of the blockhouse and she didn't ever have to return! I tried to explain to Ezra why I was taking her away. His big eyes were haunted with unspeakable things he was enduring. He acted like a zombie. He looked like the children of the holocaust I had studied at Arkansas Tech. My heart almost failed me. He wanted to go with us, but I told him I couldn't live off campus until I turned twenty-one and I had no place to keep him with me. He was skinny, dirty and I swore something broke in his heart that day. It did in mine. How could I forget my sweet brother, knowing he was in hell the minute we drove away in the pickup? I did manage to go get him one time that summer and took him and Ruth down to Hot Springs to the alligator farm and to see the sights. He was such a kind-hearted little boy, but his torture got worse from that day on.

As Ruth and I drove away, Ezra Joel was left completely alone. I couldn't afford to take both Ruth and him. He was a lost soul without us. We didn't know how to rescue him. We figured we had made it, he would one day make it also. Ruth was just glad to get away from doing all the washing, cooking and taking care of Ezra. She seemed to feel no regret at leaving him behind. She was just glad to make her escape. He has been bitter and angry at Ruth and me down through the years for abandoning him. In our abandonment of him, we gained freedom, but Ezra lost his soul.

We had to leave him standing by the side of the road, tears running down his dirty face. He didn't speak a word, his eyes were dead and his heart closed. I cried as I left, but Ruth just seemed numb as if she couldn't believe she was getting away. She has told me over the years, if I hadn't come back and taken her way, she didn't think she could have escaped on her own.

I rented an apartment for Ruth and me from Anna and Fred Berry who had been one of our neighbors in the Loy community. Ruth's move went smoothly, but she was a prickly pear to deal with. She wanted to drive the pickup, but didn't have a driver's license so I refused. I had just gotten mine a few weeks earlier. She got a job as a carhop at a drive-in restaurant and started her working career. She was able to eat two meals a day on the job. She had never had such wonderful food – hamburgers and fries when she wanted them. I think she must have eaten a ton of them, but she loved the milkshakes best! Her boss told me she was a hard worker. I went in and helped her after my job when the restaurant was short-handed. I never liked waitressing, but Ruth took to it like a fish to water. She said it was sure easier than milking all of those cows. Besides, she got good food which was in short supply at Aaron and Betty's house. How wonderful it was for me to be able to keep my promise to her from August of 1965. The joy on her face at leaving Aaron's house was worth my defying him – and defy him I did.

She blossomed that summer and we got to do a lot of fun things. It took her another fourteen years to overcome her resentment of my leaving – she saw me through the eyes of Betty and Aaron and their hatred for me. I just stayed steady; loving her as she was, trusting God and knowing she would accept the truth when she was ready. She was and is the best sister ever.

I spent the summer sewing clothes for Ruth. I made dresses, not knowing she hated dresses, but she soon outgrew them due to her eating good food – and she later told me she was so happy to shed those dresses. She was so tiny and fragile when I rescued her, and she began to grow at seventeen. She grew into a wholesome beauty. I had a hard time letting go as Ruth's mother. Guess I still haven't accomplished that even at my age. At times, she still calls me 'mommy'. It sweetens my heart. I always told my children, she was my first daughter.

Ruth didn't make the basketball team at Tech, but she got involved in tennis and became a star player for the college. After she left college, she continued to play tennis in Arkansas. She was an exceptional tennis player and if she'd had the money, could have progressed to the national level. This was her life for many years. She still loves a good tennis game.

In the spring of 1969, I met a young man and fell in love. I was so happy inside, but didn't know how to share with him that I was one of the walking wounded and a victim of incest. Gary and I were talking about marriage. He was my heart's desire. I thought our love would last forever. We were planning a future. Dating was an interesting idea for me. I could actually talk to Gary and he didn't act like I was an idiot. I finally felt like I had found someone who would love me for me. I wanted to be needed and loved. He was all I dreamed about finding in a man, sweet, handsome and a hard worker. His mother and father thought I was as wonderful as I did them. They were country folks and loved it because I could eat a mayonnaise and onion sandwich! They were proud I wasn't a city slicker. They welcomed me into the family with open arms of love. We talked and dated for about a year. He was an army MP and had to finish out his enlistment.

My first cousin, Uncle John's daughter, was engaged to Gary's brother and they set a wedding date. Just days before the marriage, she cruelly dumped him. Laughing in his face, she stripped him of any dignity he might have held. She did this to several other men.

Unfortunately, Gary believed I was cut from the same bolt of cloth as my cousin. He thought I would do the same to him so he suddenly dumped me. I was nothing like my cousin. I was heartbroken, destroyed, and hurt beyond words - shattered. My world spun in crazy circles and gut-wrenching pain. I had never loved anyone the way I loved Gary.

My cousin gloated how dumping her fiancé felt good; she never acknowledged any of the turmoil she left behind. "No," I replied, "You have destroyed not only your boyfriend, but my relationship as well." She thought it fantastic she could do what she did and found nothing wrong with her actions.

Our break-up hurt Gary's parents who loved me as no one ever had besides my grandparents. They were crushed. I was beyond hurt and pain as I was living with the heartbreak of being rejected. I was too ignorant and full of pride to talk it out and try to see if we could get around the problem of my cousin and his brother. I was too proud to beg him to reconsider his actions.

In anger, I rashly vowed to him that I would marry the first old man who would have me. My heartbreak almost destroyed my fragile being. I have never known another love such as I had for Gary

When I went home, Aaron beat me almost to death, telling me I was a bitch and no man would ever want me because Gary sure hadn't wanted me. Aaron battered my mind with Gary's rejection. He tried to make me move home and quit college.

I found out later Gary only needed me to say I wanted him, but being young and dumb, I didn't know how to react except to hide inside myself as I had learned to do against Betty and Aaron. I walked away with my heart in shreds. Neither of us knew the words to say to repair our hurt.

Since then, over the past ten years, we have become good friends after both of our failed marriages. We both are afraid of commitment, but it feels so wonderful to have him as my friend. I still love him very much and we have healed a lot of hurts. He is my handsome prince, the light of my life and best of all, my friend. Maybe someday he can see the wonderful man I know him to be and he can recover his fragile self-esteem!

At that time, college was all I had left. I was not an outstanding student, but knew if I were to survive outside of the Hollow, I must finish my education. I laid aside any dreams of having a loving husband, and mourned for my lost love. Heartbreak is not a kind taskmaster when you are vulnerable. I made many mistakes because of my impacted upbringing and abuse, but life never promised me roses. Instead, I got the thorns.

In spring of 1970, after all the stress of my broken dreams, I contracted trench mouth and was forced to leave college because of medical reasons as it was contagious. Ruth and I had been roommates. She stayed in college alone and then found her own roommate which in reality was much better for her. I returned home again for the remainder of that semester and endured the familiar daily beatings. When I was able to return to college that fall, Ruth had married and quit college. I got to see her very little after that time until she was in her early thirties. She was just so relieved to be out from under the chaos and on her own without hearing or seeing our parents.

The chaos and heartbreak in my life left me vulnerable to being preyed on by Noel Snow. I didn't realize until later he had researched anything and everything about me before pursuing me. He used my God dedication as a weapon and a way to convince me that we could be a couple even though he was many years older than me. I am sure he could detect my loneliness and eagerness to belong.

Shadow Diviner

Unmasking the face, that shadows hide,
Veiled secrecy of the dust and dawn,
The in between time that grayness fades,
The unlatched matters that always follow,
Following no matter where footsteps run,
These trailing veils that cloak willing,
sights and sounds
Boundaries taken, banished apart,
Tossing all secrets aside, one veil at a time,
Swept, these secrets, by whisk and broom,
The crumbs, that crumbles with sanctities pride,
Masked and veil no longer in place,
The ripped aside truth, the face.
Life trudges, mirrors of the soul,
Steps taken, results, these shadows hide.
Visage reflection scintillated,
Dawn upward, shadows gray, the light diviner,
The face, it bares all, this unleashing of the veils,
Effrontery choices of life assurance,
Impudence shackled, trampled veils beneath,
Left faces, the shadows,
the grayness, mask intertwined.
Dance, dance, it is a turn I am needing to find.

Weeping in the sand will not add one drop to the
ocean. Tears are the window washers of the soul.
Plant your feet in the sand and laugh into the wind.
The ocean has no tears, but the sounds of time float on
its tides.

Chapter 10

Give me a twirl,
I am looking for a girl,
Any girl will do,
Shape, size, looks, doesn't matter
Just a vessel is all I need,
Come dance, be 'the man'
Show me how it is done.
Hold the world at bay.
Come dance, Hat Man.
I can overcome, but I won't let you die,
Do my bidding, hear my voice,
Listen to all the voice, they are right!
Let them lead you into my light!
Know my voice is the only voice that guides you,
I am, the reason, I am your rod and staff.

The Shadow snorted at the thought of 'The Man' getting married. He thought the fellow had learned better from his last marriage debacle. Who needed marriage, as there were too many "freebies" out there? He knew 'The Man' was a liar and would not limit himself to the marriage bed – what a laughable concept! The Shadow's hiccupping laugh resounded around the lonely barn. 'The Man' liked children too much. Yes, ah, the new bride; she was young, twenty-three years younger than 'The Man,' but she would never keep his interest for long.

He was a selfish man, liking to have his way, lazy and indifferent to the tender needs of a woman. The Shadow detached from 'The Man' knowing that it was futile to fight against what was becoming the stronger persona in the relationship. Lift the whip high, Man, wield it just right, and pop it on their backs. Then they will listen and appreciate your dominance. Oh, yes, a new bride in the house. She'd better learn to scurry like a mouse quickly.

Chapter 11

Oh, foolish woman,
How blind you are!
Can you not see the monster?
Looking back at you through yon window?
Peer quickly, see the reflection,
Can you not see the evil coming against you?
Run, run away, do not a bride become!
Lasting commitment do not make,
Run, run, and hide in your hidey place,
Do not do this deed!

Noel Snow was a forty-seven year old blonde, charming man with a charismatic facade hiding an evil soul. I was a dumb, naïve twenty-four year old and still did not understand the world of normal sexuality. My world had consisted of brutal sexual abuse, hard work, and the Hollow captivity. I met Noel through his oldest daughter, Aileen, from our college Chi Alpha Club. She would take me to church at one of the local Assembly of God churches and bring her father along.

Noel began to pursue me relentlessly once he found out I had an apartment in Russellville off campus. He would show up early in the morning, smilingly brightly, as if I were the next best thing to white bread. He'd inform me he was lonely because and his oldest daughter, Aileen, and her husband were out of town. He thought I was a good influence in his daughter's life and Aileen was lucky to have me for a friend. He just needed a 'friend' to talk with and listen.

He sang praises about how wonderful I was because I was a good Christian girl. He complimented my cooking, ensnaring me with words of need and created a sense of intimacy. Being a sucker for a sad face and not a good judge of character, I invited him in for breakfast – a great start for his manipulation. He looked so hang-dog, wearing an expression of woe and I fell for his line of idiocy – I was a sucker because of his praises.

He confided in me how his first marriage failed because of his wife's infidelity. He cried because his mother never loved him and how his father had been abusive. He told me I was beautiful. He helped me do the dishes. We went on walks together. He was solicitous and exhibited fine manners towards me. He asked me out to ride horses on his farm in Johnson County. I made a horrible mistake that day…I went!

He immediately purchased a 1970 white Chevy Malibu, telling me he wanted to give me the very best. He was living in an apartment in Dover, Arkansas - a very nice place compared to where I'd grown up. It was clean, but what I didn't know was that his mother and sister had cleaned it and furnished it for him. He spent the next three days visiting me.

He figured out I was exhausted, alone, isolated, and extremely needy. I was looking for anyone to accept me, believe in me, and want me for me. (He was an old man – and I had promised Gary that I would marry the first old man to ask me, hadn't I?) He preyed on my weaknesses, telling me how he would take care of me and let me rest and get my health back. He catered to me.

He got down on his knees and asked me to marry him, shaking like a leaf - I was a fool and agreed. Looking back in retrospect, I believe he was scared to death I hadn't fallen for his lies. I would have been wiser to flee and live under a bridge or on the street. He explained he'd talked with Aileen and her husband and had their approval to ask me to marry him. In reality, they hated me. I'd tried to call them and received no answer. Dear God, if I'd only gotten hold of them on the phone when I called! I wouldn't have made the mistake I made in marrying Noel if I had found out they would despise me for marrying him.

I was pathetic!

I was frantic for someone, anyone, to love me.

I wanted to believe him hook, line and sinker - I did, oh God, if only I hadn't.

I was physically bankrupt and at the end of my rope. I didn't want to have to return to my parents to live again – so I made the fatal mistake of my life. I was at rock bottom, with no one to care; I was tired, worn-out, desperate and afraid. I thought perhaps he would be the answer to all of my prayers - *and I was keeping my sworn promise to my ex-boyfriend. I dwelt on that fact like a rung-out dishrag!*

I was very naive, not understanding love - he wasn't the man he claimed to be. Lust is ugly no matter how it's wrapped and presented. I believed in lasting love; this was a lethal mistake. I thought he was choosing love and happiness with me; but in the end, he turned out to be my worst nightmare.

I just wanted him to be proud of me as I worked tirelessly to help us become successful for our future. I wanted to believe!

It was painful when I discovered he didn't love me at all! We could have had a good life, one which could have been the envy of others. Finding love shouldn't have been hard, but I didn't know the full story yet!

I thought anything, or anyone was better than my parents; I could dream, couldn't I? I was a foolish innocent! I'd worked on my education, learning all I could about business so my life could be better, hopefully for a future family. The hell of the Hollow and the abuse was being put behind me, but the pattern of horror, hellish torture and abuse moved in with me. I thought my education had given me wisdom. Oh, how the Devil must have been laughing!

I was raised as hillbilly white trash, dirt-poor and taught to believe I was nothing. I grasped at anything and anyone who made me feel like I mattered. The real problem - Noel was a creep who played on my insecurities and vulnerabilities with the precision of a sidewinder toting a screwdriver corkscrew.

Oh my, I was easy prey for the manipulative smooth-talker reptile. He sank his fangs deep into my soul. There was nothing special about me; I was passable in the looks department, overweight, worn to the bone and desperate, but I had a quick mind to learn. Learning to be married shouldn't be too hard. I didn't believe there was much physical attraction on his side, but I could learn to satisfy him.

I was looking for love and thought I had found it in church of all places, in Noel, but I soon found out he was a son of perdition! His spirituality didn't even ride in his hip pocket. There were no identifying marks revealing his deceit.

I was naive, believing if a man was in church, shouting, and praising God, he had to be a decent man. I forgot all about Pap doing the very same thing. I was so wrong – I should have asked for verification from God in writing! Somehow, Noel sensed I would be a woman easily dominated.

Noel was determined in his seduction, skilled and captivating with a charming personality for an unskilled, green hill girl. I was ripe for the plucking – and he plucked me like a grape. I had never been allowed to date while growing into womanhood, so I was emotionally stunted in the love department store in such matters.

He was not a Sears Roebuck catalog mail order groom, his packing was damaged and he wasn't returnable! Going through the heartbreak of losing the man I'd loved slid me into the reckless mire of mistakes – and I hoped - a way never to have to return to the Hollow.

Even living through the rejection of my parents and their hatred, I believed I could handle the future I faced. I knew nothing. I was determined to have the good life I had prayed about for so many years. Noel convinced me he would love and adore me - and I would do the same for him. He swore on everything holy in God he would treat me better than my past had treated me. If only wishes were horses, I would have been assured a ride to heaven. So foolishly, I agreed to marry Noel Snow.

We shopped for a wedding dress in Little Rock, but Noel claimed he was just not feeling well enough to continue. How my heart yearned to marry in a white, frothy dress. Little did I know he was leading me by the puppet strings? When we bought the license from the Pope County Courthouse, Noel tried to convince me to have the County Judge marry us immediately, but I wanted a church wedding before God.

I shrugged off the feeling of doom lying in the pit of my stomach like a lead ball – the warning signs of common sense fled before me. Instead of the white dress I had always dreamed about, I wore black. Oh, how fitting that was! I tugged my dress down as if the length of my dress could cover my trembling knees. If only I listened to the gut feeling in my innards! I would have turned and fled the church and kept on running - there was nothing wise about my decision. I followed the wisp-o-the-will temptation that rose like fog amongst the Hollow trees. It all was a pipe dream.

With bravery in my heart, and hope for a better future, I stood before Rev. Terrell Brashear in Russellville, Arkansas, joining my life to a man I barely knew. As I stood in front of the preacher, the old wives' tale rang in my head, "Wear black to get married in and you will spend the rest of your life wishing you were back. I never got to wear my white dress, but chose an old filmy black dress that matched Noel's brand new, shiny black wedding suit. I thought how cute, we are a matching pair!

As I said my vows I thought Noel was a man who would stay with me forever, cherishing me and being good to me as I planned to be to him.

The Wedding, August 1971

"Catherine, do you take this man, Noel Snow, to be your lawfully-wedded husband to live together in marriage?

"Yes, I do," I replied.

"Do you promise to love, comfort, honor, obey, and to keep him for better or worse, for richer or poorer, in sickness and in health, and forsaking all others, being faithful only to him as long as you both shall live?" asked the minister.

"I do," I replied.

"Will you do your best to make this marriage honorable before the Lord, your God?"

"Yes, I promise.

It was a promise I made in honesty, to do my best to be a good wife. I was finally going to have someone to call my own. My new husband declared he loved me and desired to be decent to me. He was adamant I must promise one thing in the wedding ceremony - my obedience. I was young, desperate, so I gave my solemn word I would 'obey' him. He assured me

before the preacher and his mother he would never lay
a hand on my body, nor harm me in any way, so I
swore to 'obey' him.

I lifted my left hand for the cheap thirty dollar,
plain wedding band to be slipped on my finger. I lifted
my face for the kiss of a stranger. I was stubborn and
my pride would see me through the grim thing I was
doing. My health was on the brink of ruin. I had
worked too many years; I had ulcers and I had faith.
My doctors told me to take a break from the stress in
my life or I was facing collapse.

There was no one at my wedding, except Noel's
mother, Bertie. Bertie, my future mother-in-law, stood
in grim-faced silence, a witness to a wedding she
seemed to be objecting to by her stiff stance. If I had
only foreseen the hate she carried in her heart for any
woman that came near her son, I would have run away.

Bertie was a woman bent on vengeance; she
carried many long-standing grudges and demanded her
pound of flesh in return – I soon become the object of
her hatred. What a pity Noel's mother wasn't honest
about her dislike of me before our marriage. I found it
out too late. Her hatred brought suffering into my life
beyond belief. The week after our wedding, Bertie
bombarded me with her hate of anyone and everyone
she and Noel knew – especially his former wife.

Who was this man I was marrying? Why was I
the object of his desire? Why did I garner his
intentional pursuit? What was in me causing him to
want me as a wife? Was I only an object - and a future
punching bag? These are the questions I have spent
the past forty-four soul-searching years for the
answers.

I tried to call several friends, but everyone was out
or still at home during the college summer break. It

would be three weeks before my friends returned to college. Perhaps someone would have stopped me if I had managed to connect. I didn't comprehend I was very foolish - and logically should have been committed to the nuthouse, but I chose the fatal path of marriage.

It was my deadly blunder believing his lust was love. His lust was a powerful motive – though love was not in his equation. Noel had a chance to be happy with me, but in the end, he turned against everything I held holy. I believed he would learn to love me enough to be happy because I was tireless in being the woman I thought he wanted! I should have launched him to Mars instead of taking him to my bosom.

In reality, he only wanted a galley slave to take care of him, do his laundry, have sex with him, keep a roof over his head, and put good food on his table. He said he knew I was excellent at working, cooking, and knew how to take care of children. I was his chosen bride, oh, yes, as in Frankenstein's Bride!

We spent our wedding night at his apartment, with his mother just down the hall. I was scared to death about having sex. He shyly swore to me, "I don't know whether I can last very long. I haven't had sex since my divorce." It was a wonder his pants didn't catch on fire for lying or the jaws of Hell open wide and swallow him, but oh no, I didn't know yet, he was the Son of Perdition!

He seemed hesitant, with a gentle look in his eye, so I thought how bad can this be, but that was before the end of the night. There was no foreplay, no sweet words, and no kisses to prepare me. He rolled onto me, forcibly thrusting inside me without any gentleness, grunted a few times and was finished. I was awakened again during the night for a repeat of his behavior. I thought, "Isn't there more to marital sex than this?" I couldn't grasp this was the beginning of a painful psychological abyss in my life.

Noel brought a mantle of evil to our marriage bed, wrapped it around me in my unwise joining with him. He created a destructive soul wind of mega-magnitude proportions. He left me reaping a harvest of rotting silence filling our marriage with demonic forces I couldn't combat. Even though the doubts and fears set in immediately after our wedding night, I had nowhere to flee.

After a week, we took his mother to his sister's in Morrilton as he told her this was his time with his new wife. I had hoped for a daughter/mother relationship with her, but my hopes never materialized in spite of all I tried.

Noel's sexual appetite in bed was overwhelming for a green girl; I mistook his lust for love – I even wondered if it was more than Machiavellian lust – but a need to brag to his buddies how many times he could copulate. He insisted I walk, ride horses, and exercise. He immediately began grooming me to control my every movement, suggesting if I would lose the weight, he would buy a horse trailer and let me participate in rodeos, which he knew was a dream of mine. He had several beautiful horses and I was crazy about riding. I believed his every promise so I lost the weight. I had a compulsive need to believe and sought a reason to go on, but I was worn down to a nubbin of hope.

After six weeks of "wedded bliss," my world crashed. I told Noel I didn't know how my parents would react toward our marriage. I tried to prepare him for how abusive my parents were to me – thinking he would be my defender. I believe he thought I was exaggerating the truth. I took Noel up to Madison County to meet my parents.

I faced my parents with trepidation and trembling, but thought surely Noel would be with me so they wouldn't dare abuse me. I was supposed to be the dutiful daughter, stay at home, continue to work as Aaron demanded, and take care of him and Betty. What was it in him causing such hate of me and not wanting me to marry or have a life? Was it his perverted sexual desires? I put on a boldface, determining I was going to be truthful and trust in Noel's protection. My sister, Ruth, was already married and they hadn't objected. My brother, Samson, was married and they had attended the wedding, but Aaron had forbidden me to marry. Ezra was still a teenager at home and his life was hell.

Wham! The blood spurted as Aaron slammed my head into the hallway wall of the old blockhouse. The instant pain was a life-long familiar circumstance. I begin to sink into darkness, as I cried, "Dear Heavenly Father hold me close."

I saw the Red Bird hovering in the attic opening, fluttering in horror.

"Aaron," I screamed, "I am married; you can't do this anymore."

Aaron screamed right back at me, "I own you - you bitch. You are mine. I will do what I want to you anytime, anywhere and you can't escape, never, never!"

"Please, Aaron, don't hurt me anymore, please stop!"

Aaron bellowed, "You stupid bitch, you have married a man who was married before, didn't you!" His fist knocked me against the wall again.

"Dear God, help me! Noel, make him stop

beating me! Please help me." He only stood there
smiling. I could see it in his face; Noel Snow was a
yellow-belly coward. He was a suck-face, puke-filled
certifiable coward!

Aaron didn't listen to my pleas as he was in a
blind rage. Why was he angry I had married?

He grabbed me by the hair and slammed me back
into the wall repeatedly. Blood was streaming from
the back of my head, dripping down my neck. My
upper lip was slashed from a blow to my mouth, blood
dripped from my tongue and down my chin. I could
feel my eyes begin to swell.

"Please, Aaron, you have got to stop this madness.
I am married now. I don't belong to you anymore.
You can't keep beating me like this. I am twenty-four
years old," I whimpered.

He roared in rage, paying no mind to my beaten
condition!

Aaron had always been domineering and
tyrannical toward me; his physical, mental, sexual and
emotional abuse had known no bounds. Aaron
screamed, "You are my legal property and I certainly
never gave you permission to marry." He snarled he
could do as he wanted and it was his prerogative to
beat me. I had defied him in marrying. He saw me as
a vagina he had a right to sell to any man for profit.
He had not chosen my husband, so he wasn't giving up
the rights of ownership.

My father was beating me senseless; I had
anticipated I married a man who would defend me.
My new husband swore he would love me just stood
there, not three feet away, and smiled at my terror as
my father slammed me into the wall, cursing me, and
calling me a whore. Aaron hit me repeatedly in the
stomach, slapping my face and accusing me of being
pregnant and having to get married. He demanded to

know how many times I'd had sex before we were married.

I screamed, "None. We waited until we were married. I didn't have sex with him." Some god-sense in me gave me the knowledge to wait until marriage to engage in sex with my husband, though Noel pressured me the entire time. I didn't want Noel ever to be able to accuse me of being unfaithful to him. I was frightened of having sex because of the rape I had endured, but I was determined to learn what was good for a marriage. Grandma had shared marriage sex in a loving marriage could be wonderful.

Aaron hammered me with each fist as he slapped my head back and forth until my ears rang. Blood was running from my nose. Where was I to run? He said he was going to make sure if I were pregnant, I would lose the bastard's baby. I screamed out in despair for God to deliver me. I fell to my knees weeping uncontrollable, crying out to God, "Father, I commit my soul into your keeping. Let the angels carry me to you." Eminent death felt close.

The Red Bird, my only friend, who first started coming to me in my dreams as a very small child during beatings and other troublesome times, appeared in the attic, diving through the opening to me. I lay with the Red Bird tucked into my breast as the beating continued.

My new husband was doing nothing to protect me from the brute that controlled my growing up years; I was helpless. I was in a nightmare! My father spent the night berating me, beating me, and yelling obscenities at me. My husband never defended me, but he did demand sex from my battered body when Aaron finally gave out and went to bed.

Oh, God what had I done?

A demohad crept into my bed, demanding

obedience; a Bluebeard in disguise and establishing his reign of terror early in the boat of my desires for love and happiness.

Surely, this was just a nightmare! When would I awaken?

Dear, sweet Red Bird, what am I to do? I had nowhere to run.

> *Sing sweet Bird, sing,*
> *Wipe my tears with your feathers bright,*
> *Let me hear your golden voice in my despair.*
> *Show me the light that I may be where you are,*
> *Able to fly, able to see,*
> *Hold me sweet bird, hold me tight!*

The evil person I married never shared his family discord with me before our wedding. I wasn't prepared for Noel's hatred and manipulation. From the beginning of our marriage, his family and mine set a course to destroy me.

His three sisters often laughed at how they would destroy doctors or neighbors whom they believed had wronged them or their mother. They would pretend to be a girlfriend, calling their wives, telling them exaggerated stories of having sexual affairs with their husbands. I was up against the queens of liars. My marriage was soon to be besieged – how did I think I could escape them?

Noel's mother and his sisters bragged over the years how they had made sure that Noel's first wife, Clara, had been destroyed. I finally got the message. I faced destruction if I didn't do as Noel wanted. Noel's parents' unhealthy marriage hadn't taught him healthy boundaries or anything about Godly love for one's spouse. They were social outcasts like my own family. Their constant bickering and hatred of each had created deviant personalities in all eight of his siblings who exhibited abusive bizarre behavior toward those whom they disliked. Their actions were as bad as my parents.

Ignorance isn't blissful. Being beaten black and blue is a crime. You have a right to be treated kindly and with respect. Demand it! As a survivor of domestic violence, you are free. Without humiliation, you can break free like a butterfly and soar. May you seek the dignity of life and be an impact wherever you live.

Flame Shadows

Truth, like the lit fire of the darkness,
Burst forth into eternal flame of light,
A beacon seen from the far hillside,
Breaking, shattering the illusions of the hidden,
Flames casting far shadows,
Dancing candles in shadowy circles,
Bouncing back, against the serum of truth,
Fasting the night away into the day's light,
These flames burning the dross of the soul,
Catharsis of mind truth, hidden, now seen.
Shadows of the mountain made illuminated and seeing,
Far reaching is the light of the past,
present and future burning flames,
The beacon high, high for the reason of truth,
Hoary frosted, dusted ashes as touched by time,
the ashes of truth,
Time revealing what thoughts where hidden,
purified by heated time,
Darkness is but the veil of truth,
Thrust aside by burning shadow's illusionary flames,
Lit forever by eternal beacon of hope.

Catch the wisp-o-will of hope and cling tenaciously to
it. Hope is the window of yesterday and a glimpse of
the future.

Chapter 12

Power, the key to power,
Piece by piece,
Stolen, solving the puzzle,
Is noticing, watching,
Lying in wait,
Finding the solution,
A man holds the world,
Blind faith of the innocent,
Laughter of the jester,
Dancing on a string,
Hilarity of the damned.

"Tick Tock said the clock, run around the circle, go round and round," chimed the Hat Man.
"I am now in control," laughed The Hat Man.

He chortled, "I have a new woman, a new life. The old one isn't the future, the past or the present. I have been given the light from my *Father* how to control her. I have taken the key!"

Doing a jig of delight, he chortled, "I am who I have become. Ah, the joy of seeing her father take control. I was given a wedding present better than pure bliss. HER! I am the Hat Man and she will dance to the tune of whatever Hat I am wearing."

He loved seeing the fear on her face, "I can come out and play in the dark and she will never know I have played." He gave thanks to his power, "I love the dark, and I love to play!" Her father made him happy. "I am The Man! I am supreme. I rule! She will cease to be innocent! Laugh, oh, laugh in the darkness, have your way! You are The Man!" Triumphant!

Sing into the fan that goes round and round.
Voice your rage, let the world know the perpetrator!
Silence tills the field of despair.

Chapter 13

Innocence can cease to exist
When there are no tears left.
Life can be grimmer than darkness,
Run, girl, run far away!
Catch the flyaway road,
Follow its track to nowhere,
Cry, baby, cry,
I like it when you cry!

When we returned home from the brutal parental introduction, Noel immediately began watching my mileage on the car and accusing me of seeing someone else as I went to my college classes. Who? I don't know. I was in a nightmare! Life was as if I still lived in the Hollow.

I thought myself wise in escaping the Hollow, but I had found worse.

"Noel, I want to know why you didn't protect me when Aaron beat me so badly."

He gave a big belly laugh, shoving me back on the bed, his intentions clear.

"I just wanted to see what kind of a girl you were so I waited until I met your parents. Your dad showed me what to do to you if you don't *mind me.* You are just as I thought, not much, but I reckon you will do for me, as I haven't had anyone to have sex with in a long time. Now roll over and give me some." His abuse was heinous, as it was done in the name of his 'love', sworn to me before God and the preacher. He was a non-discreet Phalanx bent on destroying our marriage before it even got started – a debaucher of my soul.

Noel believed it was his right to use force to have sexual intercourse with me. It didn't matter if the sex was without my consent. He took!

He believed Aaron's treatment of me gave him the transfer right of ownership of my person. I grew up in such abuse and hoped in marriage perhaps his treatment of me would be better than my parents. Like Aaron, he believed his ownership of me gave him a right from *God* to use my vagina as he saw fit, as God had made woman just for a man. I had no rights so I bowed my head and trudged forward. I knew how to adapt; I had a lifetime of training.

Before we married, I shared with Noel that stress and the abuse had caused the state of my health. I slept sixteen hours a day. I had labored and deprived myself of anything except the bare necessities for twenty-four years. I suffered; I am sure, from Post Traumatic Stress Disorder. I developed peptic chronic duodenal ulcers. I needed to rest, live quietly and regain my health. Noel swore to me he would give me loving care. I let my guard down with him and believed in his promises – but it seemed fate, destiny or whoever had given me a man with an obsession to destroy.

I didn't last very long as his "dumpling of desire" as he'd sworn in front of the preacher. His holy allegiance bounced out the door quicker than a hound dog after a biscuit with sausage gravy! Each day brought a new crisis to our marriage. The troubling course of his treatment was like a storm shadow in my heart – my efforts to love were new and precarious at best. He'd become a beast, but I was not a dragon slayer. Our marriage was raining teardrops of fearful failure. It was a poignant river, running in disaster; I just didn't know which paddle to use in escaping.

After a few weeks of this, and demands of sex in perverted ways, he told me it was either him or college. Being extremely foolish, whipped, and betrayed, I quit college just nine hours short of graduation. The desperate need to have someone love me was an addiction in my blood; I *needed* him to love me.

Noel carefully laid out a rational argument how he was much more sexual than I because I was so ill and he'd been without a woman too long. He informed me either I gave him all the sex he wanted or he would find another woman to satisfy his sexual appetite. It was my fault I was ill and wasn't satisfying him; he laid a guilt trip on me thicker than cane field molasses. He became violently jealous and cut me off from all of my college friends, isolating me in the name of teaching me the things a new bride should know. I never did finish that long list of demands.

The next three years were spent in doing exactly what I was told, how to do it and when to do it. I kept thinking, in spite of my lifelong abuse, I would find the recipe to satisfying his unnatural hungers - or maybe because I was raped for so long, I just didn't know how good sex was supposed to feel. As long as I would ride his horses and accommodate his sexual fantasies, I was not shaken, shoved, slapped, or squeezed in a bear hug which left my ribs hurting. He was a silent batterer, making sure that he hurt me underneath my clothing so the marks were covered and out of sight.

Noel was a domineering, older man who found nothing wrong using obsequious and hypercritical behavior claiming he knew what was best for me – often this behavior was exhibited bizarrely in front of others. He would bow and scrape and act ingratiating – I called it his enslaving mode as this act seemed to quiet many peoples' questions about him. He was sly as a wolf dressed in sheep's clothing. I lived in the silence of my tears with his blasphemy. Noel wanted me to buckle, but I refused to oblige him. I set my teeth in the leather of nothing and pulled forward.

Oh, how I craved to be loved! Maybe if I gave up the essentials of myself, he would love me, as my parents hadn't. I tried anything and everything he suggested, hoping he would *love* me if I didn't complain. I kept a perfect house; I walked, rode horses, and got in good shape. I looked nice, dressed nice, but then the jealous rages began.

He became a demanding screaming shrew! For who had I lost the weight? Why was I glancing at that man in the grocery store? Who had I met on my way to the store, or wherever?

Within six weeks of my quitting college, I woke up during the night with him raping me. He thought I was asleep and was forcing sex on me. This happened for the next twenty years. I could never acknowledge I was awake when the rape was occurring, or I would pay the consequences with a severe chest squeeze.

He would whisper, "Stay asleep, this is how I like it! Sleeping is a good thing." If I moved, he would lay very still until he thought I was back asleep, then resume the sexual assault. I was on birth control pills because I didn't want children too early in the marriage. He fought tooth and nail to make me quit the pills, but I refused, stubbornly holding that one line in my marriage. I knew a couple should take time to learn about each other rather than bring children into the equation. I wanted time for myself as I had been raising children for far too many years already. I longed to confide in someone, but there was no one to listen.

Not long after our marriage, he took me into Clarksville pretending he wanted to buy me some shoes. We entered a shoe shop just off Main Street. In the back of the shop were racks of magazines. He took me over to some of the racks and told me to pick up a magazine. The magazine cover contained sickening vulgar pornography. I had never even heard the word before. I didn't know such things existed. Ignorance was not bliss. He asked me if I had ever thought of doing some of those things with other women or with him and another woman that the magazines were displaying. I was so shocked I ran from the shop in shame. He followed laughing at me all the way to our car. He pretended he just wanted to show me those things existed. I was so dumb; I didn't know he was grooming me to go into a world of perversion. It was a world of destruction which, in the end, almost destroyed me.

In the next months, he would slowly suggest a new position, a new humiliation, and a new idea and tell me if I truly loved him, I would accommodate his fetishes. He asked me if he could share me with another woman. I was mortified, answering with a resounding, "No!" It was not the last time he would make that suggestion.

He never kept his marriage vows, but found other women he could intimidate, fornicate with, or rape. He fanaticized what would it be like to have another woman and man in our bed with us – me a Christian with moral values – I was mule stubborn steadfastly refusing his request! I didn't walk into his sexual desperation, or let him triumph by manipulation in this area. There was not a book of rules for Noel's madness. My marriage was full of lethal deadfalls built with Noel's mind traps; I never learned the grounds rules.

Noel had a chance to be truly loved by me, I tried everything my church taught in being humble, caring, loving, and in submission; nothing worked. I worked tirelessly in the church, ministered, visited, helped the widows, and held a full-time job. I was never good enough for him, even though I actively participated in our sexual joining. He proved he was neither constant nor committed in our relationship. He never gave anything to our relationship of any substance or any merit as a marriage should have contained.

I entered the marriage hopeful for the future, but was disappointed repeatedly with the results of all the hard work I poured into the relationship. Unless there is reciprocity, there is no relationship.

I was in love with love - convincing myself surely Noel would love me. I sought the happily ever after, truly believing it would surely be mine if I just found the right key to unlock my door to his heart. I didn't know the difference between affection and sexuality. He added fuel to the feelings of my inadequacy by his insidious remarks and suggestions – *if only I was this or that* - and I was deathly afraid of abandonment and the loss of belonging. In addition, I carried enveloping guilt over not being able to satisfy him, nor save my brother and sister from their abuse.

I didn't trust anyone; thus, with this inability to reach out to anyone for help, I was locked in a prison of his making. I was internalizing the shame and the heavy guilt by his persistent god-like eminence. It was too bad, but I found it easier to take on the sins of others, apologize, and take responsibility as I had for Pap and Mam's abuse and for every wrong they committed against me.

I felt responsible in my marriage for everything and nothing. Noel's attitude, treatment, and narcissistic self-absorption continually laid waste to any mature of hope for me to reconstruct our marriage into a building of love and mutual respect. I just didn't seem to grasp it took more than one to construct a home of love. I could cut, trim, nail, and place one board at a time, but I needed help to hold the hammer that drove it all – love.

After several months, Noel decided to go to California to visit his family. He had been bragging he had married a 'young thing' and the rest of the family needed to meet me. I suppose this was my reward for becoming skinny by his showing me off! I could have done without being a trophy!

We killed a deer during the hunting season, so I fried enough of the meat for meals to get us through to California, put the food on ice, made biscuits, eggs, fried pies, no-bake cookies and packed our bags, ready to leave the next morning. That night, I dreamed I was to take my next-to-the-youngest stepdaughter with us or she would be dead when we came back home. I told Noel about the dream. He sure didn't like it when I insisted we get in touch with her mother and get her consent to take his daughter with us. Well, I wasn't much impressed that I had dreamed that dream, as this was to be my honeymoon trip. But I had learned one thing over the years; never ignore a warning dream from God. I demanded we take her; Noel threw a mad fit, yelling and storming all about. "This was to be our time! Now why do you want to take her along?" I said, "She will be dead when we return and I won't be responsible to God or any of you." For once, I wouldn't give in. I declared I wouldn't go if we didn't take her; he needed me to help do most of the driving. He finally agreed and I called her mother to ask permission.

The trip was long, tiring and not quite comfortable having a teenager with us, but we did manage to make it through. We even had a bit of fun seeing the Petrified Forest and a few things, but I was extremely embarrassed he wanted to have sex with me while his daughter was in other bed in the motel room.

When we arrived in California, his sisters weren't

happy we had brought his daughter with us. Old family arguments flew to the surface airing past dirty laundry. His mother and sisters were out to punish this young girl for the sins of Noel's first wife. It was horrifying. Noel beat her badly. His beating reminded me of what Aaron had given me weeks earlier. I was terrified he was going to turn on me. I had already learned my lesson about interfering with anything he did. Interference would get me twice the whipping he was giving someone else. His sisters and mother were berating her and calling her mother a whore. It seemed they took joy in seeing Noel beating her. The family fights progressed to the reputation of her second older sister. His family accused the sister of being a whore and the baby she was carrying a bastard. I had no doubt the older sister was innocent of any wrongdoing. I stated it would be easy to tell whose the baby was after birth.

I didn't mean I was supporting his sisters' viewpoint, but that was how my stepdaughter took it. Well, the situation was more volatile than ever. The daughter thought I was siding with her aunts. It wasn't what I meant all, but I shut my mouth. I was sickened that these so called Christian sisters-in-law were punishing my precious stepdaughter for her mother's sins. None of this finger pointing should be happening in front of the teenage stepdaughter. I thought I had walked into a dungeon with no way out. I had to sit and listen for hours to all of them ranting on about how I didn't know anything about how bad Noel's first wife, Clara, had been. They just didn't get it; I didn't care. They were informing me of all their remembered sins against Clara. They proved they were as bad as Aaron and Betty.

We got into the car to go somewhere else and Noel again beat my stepdaughter. It was horrifying to see his violence against his own child. He was more violent than I could possibly know.

Then Noel faked getting sick, grabbed his chest, pretending he couldn't breathe. He said it was his heart; he refused to go see a doctor. This was my first experience with his manipulation. I was frightened to pieces, as I believed he was very ill. He was mumbling about how the stress of his first marriage was killing him. He wanted me to know how things were, and if I loved him, I wouldn't take his daughter's side. I felt so bad for my stepdaughter, she was young and innocent, but I was powerless. All of my stepdaughters weren't bad girls, just normal young women with unhappiness eating at them because of their father. I hadn't seen 'bad' out of any of them.

When we came home and took the daughter to her mother's house, they came out of the door and the first thing out of her sister's mouth was, "Last night all of your best friends died from a gas leak."

I felt frozen inside. What if I hadn't listened to that voice in my dream?

I didn't know how to comfort her. Out of my ignorance I had wounded her soul without meaning to do so. The sister that was being accused of having an affair and having a baby by another man was screaming in a rage. His ex-wife was throwing a raging hissy fit, Noel was screaming. All I wanted to do was to find a safe place away from them all and hide, licking my wounds. I was just too scared and didn't know how to get her to understand her sister had heard wrong. It was a hard lesson to learn about keeping my mouth shut in a family feuding.

Can you catch a whirlwind as it passes by you? Do
you ever dream of riding the wind through a mountain
pass? Where will the sunbeam dance during the
misting rain of tomorrow's hope?

Chapter 13

Death Mask
Penetrating behind the face,
Lifting evil from the wind,
Clinging to the past,
Seeing into the future
Bartering for the soul,
Winning or losing, it doesn't matter,
Owned by the Devil.
Cream of death rising to the top,
Brush plated lies,
Tempters of the righteous,
Stealer of holy vows!

Not long after we returned from California, we were out riding and Noel challenged me to a horse race. The horse I was riding was a green broke filly. I slapped leather and she was off - running like crazy, one mile, and two miles and headed out on the third one.

He kept yelling, "I am going to beat you, woman. I can outrun you on my horse. I will show you how a real man rides a horse. Can't you make Veronica run any faster?" His horse was pounding up behind me. He was hitting the horse each time it took a stride.

Suddenly, my horse's chin-strap broke, she was running free, wild-eyed and I was desperate. I was beginning to lose leg strength to cling to the saddle. I had never ridden a horse that could run so fast. She suddenly turned up a driveway into a neighbor's yard. He ran out in front of her saying, "Whoa, whoa!" She stopped, her sides were heaving – I almost flew over her head. The neighbor quickly looked her over and then looked me straight in the eye, stating, "Your horse's chin strap has been cut. You are in danger.

Someone did this deliberately to this bridle." I felt the earth move under my feet, but managed to stay upright. By that time Noel arrived, acting as if he was so worried about the horse running away.

Oh, yes! Noel was so repentant about the filly running away with me, and convinced me someone had gotten into the building where he kept the tack and cut the chinstrap. I was not even suspicious of his motivation at this point. He was so abjectly sorry about my narrow escape; he put on quite a show in front of Mr. Pharis. He paid special attention to me for several days. He worked hard at convincing me of his story. Years later, he admitted he had cut the strap hoping I would die. His family had convinced him in California he needed to rid himself of me anyway he could. His plan almost worked, except I was a good equestrian - and very lucky – I knew God had held me on that horse during her wild run.

Why would a man who had just married want to murder his wife? What sin had I committed within weeks of our marriage to cause my death? Was it because of Aaron's treatment of me in front of Noel?

Later, I learned to become an even better equestrian – it meant my survival. Why did I make excuses in my mind this was the only life I deserved? My soul was conflicted; life was a heavy burden. Did Noel have some kind of evil malice in him desiring to bring death to those who loved him the most? Was it a need to see someone almost die, so he could play the hero and step in with his big white hat and save me? On the other hand, was it a more sinister compulsion to let harm happen and then swing into savior mode to the rescue so he could look like a big hero in the community?

Several days later, he took me over to the Wilson Hole. It was snake-infested, but a lovely hole of water tucked away on a neighbor's property. We were trespassing, but he didn't care. While I was tying up the horses, he had stripped naked and slipped into the water. He cajoled me into stripping and going skinny-dipping. He said, "Come on in, Honey. The water is fine!"

I asked, "Is the water warm?"

"Oh, yes," he hollered, showing me the sexual effects of seeing me standing naked on the rock. It was a beautiful fall day. I didn't want him to think I was a prude and not wanting to share myself in the marriage.

"Oh, yes, it's wonderful." I had never stripped naked out in the open before. It was funny to see him laughing and joking for once with me. I jumped in and the water was frigid! He laughed himself silly, thinking it was a wonderful joke to convince me to plunge into the cold water. Just then, a big snapping turtle slid down the bank of the creek into the water close to Noel and headed straight for him. He screamed and jumped out of the water running buck naked through the brush. He didn't think that was too hilarious!

I didn't get his practical joke with me jumping into the frigid water, but I thought the snapping turtle's behavior comical! I never undressed "au naturel" again. That was one cold dunking, but it was somewhat funny. I figured God let the snapping turtle come into the water at the right moment. If I'd had any sexual turn-on by his attitude, the cold water killed it, but at least he attempted to be funny, I think!

I adopted a black kitten shortly after our marriage and named her "Booger". She was the smartest cat, dainty, cute as a button, and loved me unconditionally. She seemed almost human and was my shadow. She would lie on my arm just like a child at night. She would take a bath when Noel or I did. I thought he liked her also. She traveled to California with us and was leash trained. When we got back from that trip, she disappeared out of the apartment one day. I cried my eyes out; I loved that cat and she loved me. After six or so weeks, I gave up on her ever coming home. Noel told me to "buck up" that someone had stolen her.

One night, around midnight, I heard this pitiful "meow" at the back stairs of the apartment. I jumped out of bed, and sure enough, it was my Booger! I was so thankful to see her! Her feet were bleeding and her fur was filled with filth and dirt. She had found her way home to me! She was skin and bones. I gently gave her a bath, and she cried the entire time. I fed her, wrapped her in a blanket, and took her to bed.

I could tell Noel was very angry with me for having the cat. Later, she came into her heat cycle. He had a horrible old bird dog out at the farm. He told me if I got rid of my cat, he would get rid of the dog. He pressured me for days, telling me that I should love him more than the cat. He badgered me day and night. I finally gave in. I cried all the way to the pound. My kitty was reaching through the bars of the cage and crying for me.

He laughed as he got rid of the sorry dog and told me, "Now I have you all alone like I wanted." I hunkered down like a cornered rat, knowing I was whipped. He had done this deliberately and I asked him, "Did you haul my cat off?" He laughed and said, "I knew you were a smart girl and it worked, didn't it? I just didn't figure on that cat knowing how to come home." He was no better than Pap.

Anytime I got a pet, from that day on, unless it was his choice, my pet was killed, stomped to death, shot, or hauled off. I learned to act as if I hated

whatever pet I wanted to keep.
He would take them to neighbors, or give them to
passing strangers, it didn't matter if I cried, and he
thought it was funny to hurt me this way.

I asked him once several years into the marriage,
"Do you love me, Noel? What am I to you?"

"Why, nothing," he stated! "Hadn't you figured
out you are only a receptacle for my sperm? You were
young and I figured I could get some more kids on
you. Why are you always asking me to love you? I
married you didn't I? If that wasn't enough, sorry!
Women aren't to be trusted."

It was a brutal destruction of my idealism and a
blow for my bruised and aching heart. Because of my
poor health, I was trapped in a situation that I couldn't
fix. Noel's pounding, conditioning and further damage
to my low-self-esteem was never ending.

I truly found out giving someone your love is not a
guarantee you will be loved back.

I was brainwashed as a child and now the physical
and verbal abuse was added in a marriage where I'd
had unrealistic dreams. I actually believed I needed
Noel to survive. I could not see myself outside of his
definition of who I was. If I had not had God, I would
have lost all meaning in life. God was my rope and I
was hanging on by the frayed edges with no room to
tie a knot.

Because I had never taken time to heal from my
childhood abuse, I made a poor choice in choosing my
husband. There weren't any excuses; I searched for a
man who would nurture me and want me to belong to
him. I picked a man who was like both of my parents
and had not one nurturing bone in his body.

Noel was obsessed as badly as Betty about wanting
more children. Betty constantly demanded more children
from Aaron. I knew how hard it was for me to help raise

the young'uns and I didn't want a big passel of children starting my marriage, one in my belly, another one hanging to my skirts so I resisted having children. I would have loved to have several children, but after being married a few years, I knew I didn't dare bring many children into the world, so I tossed out a few more of my dreams.

I left no stone unturned in trying to be a good wife, but my work turned into vanity. The first few weeks of our marriage, Noel was the perfect hold-the-door, treat-a-woman-right; old fashioned kind of man, but that didn't last after the first six weeks. Nothing in my marriage was to be real – he was a silent assassin. How could I fix a marriage full of holes like a flour sifter, holding nothing, giving nothing, and taking every drop of warmth I had in me?

After we were married a year in 1972, Noel decided we would move out to his old farmstead. The house had been built in 1867. It had cracks in the walls that you could throw a cat through. The old, wretched windows gave off very little light and let in air freely. It was more like a barn than a home. After four years back on the farm, we still hadn't accomplished much on refinishing the old house. Noel had not lifted a finger to help remodel, but made plenty of excuses. He was badgering me to have children. I was not going to have children until we had a better home for them. I decided to get a book to learn how to remodel a house.

I ordered a *Reader's Digest* self-help book about building. I had a hammer, a level and an old Sears Craftsman skill saw. I believed I could learn anything so I started to work. Noel became upset because I was going to rebuild the house, so he went to the VA hospital in Little Rock. I took the opportunity, tore out all the old windows and installed new windows. It was immediately warmer in the house. I needed lumber to rebuild many of the walls in the house.

Noel granted me permission to tear down the old Snow barn. I was able to salvage a lot of good lumber out of the old barn. He helped me a little each day working on the old barn. He was happy I was tearing it down and using the lumber for the old house, but he never lasted long on helping me with anything around the place. He was very talkative about the violence in the barn and how he was glad to tear it down and burn the memories. While we were working on the old barn, Noel disclosed how his father had raped him there. He took to his bed of affliction.

I finished tearing the old barn down and then burned the rest of it – ashes leave no memory after a good rain or two.

I rebuilt, tore down walls of the old house, employed a carpenter to teach me what I didn't know, hired a rock mason so I could learn the rock mason business and then I finished the house inside and rocked it outside myself. I loved learning the building business and have been in it for the past 30 years. I have subdivided and remodeled several properties as a licensed contractor.

It took Noel being a lazy man to force me to learn the trade. He never helped me on another property after the desultory start on the old farmhouse. In fact, he was insanely jealous because I could build and remodel and he couldn't. His anger would go from calm to out of control in a matter of seconds. He might take a hammer and tear down what I had just built for spite, especially if I didn't stop building for sex. I had hoped he would like having a nice home and want to help me get it all fixed, but I was wrong.

The swaying treetops whisper in the wind. The wind rides
the pull of the tide in and out, day after day, into the future.
The future is an empty box that we push forward, filling it
with what we will. I dared to fill my box with God's good
things that He whispered to me in the stillness of my soul.
The box is taped shut, memories are all that linger in the
beauty of His love.

Chapter 14

Escape is impossible,
I am strong,
She can't run fast enough,
I will find her no matter where she hides,
She is mine; nothing can change that fact,
Stupid, stupid woman,
Can't you get it, you are owned,
Mine! Mine! standing still,
Standing still, face unreadable,
You are mine,
A frown here and there,
Her fear is palpable,
She doesn't seem to learn,
Cleaning, cooking; she is mine.

The woman will never learn. When will she understand that I am in control? She is unwanted. I am having fun. I hold the keys, the chain and the bars to her soul. She will comply or die. I am dancing and singing in the darkness of the night; this is just the beginning of her sorrows. I am strong, in control. She will bend! If she doesn't learn to bend, I will lead her on a leash like a dancing bear! She will dance on command, sing like a birdie, all just for me or the lash of my anger will burn her. Tandem dreaming and believing in a powerful God will glean her soul nothing. She offers prayers constantly for a loving marriage. Bah! I am in control. She will learn or die!

Let caution be your guide! Walk your path. Be choosey in
your faith. Prove God! He will answer in the whisper of
your soul and he lingers near just because!

Chapter 15

Dance, Hat Man, dance!
Do a jig for your supper.
Smile through the lies,
Laugh with the best of them because she is desperate.
You will never be me,
But I will be you.
Dance, dance, it is a turn I am wanting to hear.
Give me a twirl,
I am looking for a girl,
Any girl will do.
Shape, size, looks, do not matter,
Just a vessel is all I need.
Come dance, 'be the man'.
Show me how it is done,
Hold the world at bay.
Come dance, Hat Man.
I can overcome, but I won't let you die.
Do my bidding, hear my voice,
Listen to all the voices, they are right!
Let them lead you into the light!
Let my voice be the only voice that guides you,
I am the reason, I am your beam.

1975 Making Babies

I decided I would have to get a job. I got a
bookkeeping job at the Clarksville Wal-Mart Store #66 in
1973. I had to pass a background check and was bonded
for one million dollars because I helped handle a lot of
money through the daily sales. Preston Goode was the
manager. The job was challenging and a wonderful break
from the stressors of home. I worked for two years before I

became pregnant.

I met Sam Walton within a few days of beginning my job. Mr. Walton was an insightful man with a retail dream for America. I learned more from him than any other person in my business life. I began noticing all our damaged returns were being thrown out the back door. I had a meeting with Mr. Walton and told him I believed I could get each company Wal-Mart dealt with to give him a refund on the damaged merchandise. He scoffed at first, but I challenged him to let me work on building a relationship with his suppliers and keep track of all the returns for one year in our store.

I got all our suppliers in the nation but one on board to give us merchandise return credits. Mr. Walton came down to meet with me after the year was up. I had the spreadsheets ready. Steve Thornton was the manager at this time. He told me I was going to shock Sam Walton with my findings. When Mr. Walton sat down at my desk and looked at the spreadsheet tallies, he sucked in his breath stating, "Well, girlie, you sure showed me!" He had 66 stores at this time, plus the new ones just opening during the year. If we averaged out all those stores, attributing across the board a set amount to each store, he had allowed thousands of dollars to be wasted. The program I developed became the forerunner for all of Wal-Mart's return polices, eventually leading to the best and biggest return policy in America.

Steve Thornton was Bob Thornton's son. Bob was one of Sam's earliest men collaborating with him in the hierarchy of Wal-Mart. Steve was a tremendous smart manager and aggressive in his climb up in Wal-Mart. His wife, Judy, was brilliant and gave Steve help in personnel building. They were the best husband and wife team in the first few years of the Clarksville store.

One Halloween, Judy helped Steve and Ricky Russell dress up as Bonnie and Clyde. When our bosses came to work with a toy machine gun and held us up, no one knew who they were! Holding a toy submachine gun on me, they 'kidnapped' me as I walked in the door for work and escorted me to the office. I was frightened and still didn't recognize them. Steve was dressed in a black wig and a dress wearing a padded bra and carrying a purse. They sat me down in a chair, ordering me to open the cash drawer. I refused, shaking like a leaf and both of them started laughing hysterically at how they had fooled me! I laughed my heart out with them because, if they had persisted, I would have been on the floor in a faint. It took our customers and other employees quite some time to figure out they were our bosses. Evidently, Duane Steele, Clarksville City Police Chief, was also in on their foolery. Wal-Mart was always full of life and hilarity with these two men at the helm of my store. I looked forward to the job each day.

They treated me as an equal. I learned much from Mr. Thornton's guidance as the store manager and our sales skyrocketed from Steve's directorship. I had the most fun with these two bosses of any I have ever worked with. Steve's wife, Judy, helped throw the grandest parties for the employees and put on skits that kept us in stitches. Steve died suddenly while I was a pastor in DeWitt, Arkansas. His untimely death broke my heart for his family. I counted Mr. Walton as a mentor and friend, as well as Steve Thornton and Ricky Russell. They gave me 'carte blanche' to succeed. I was named Wal-Mart's number one bookkeeper the years I worked there. I loved Wal-Mart and Mr. Walton's business philosophy in creating the giant retailer. He was a wonderful man.

Noel's anger began to take a sinister turn. His reasoning didn't make sense. His VA doctors in Little Rock told me he had done the best that he had ever done while being married to me. They tried to get him to see I was a woman of my word and I did care what happened to him. He had nice clothes and food on the table. I had a good job, but he was insanely jealous of me. I would look down from my office and he would be standing there staring up at me; he had been watching me for hours. It was creepy.

Noel made my work life at Wal-Mart miserable. It seemed to give him a feeling of power and being a "real man". I never was a man-hunting woman so I never worried about him spying on me, but it drove my bosses crazy. In the twenty years of my marriage, I never considered breaking my marriage vows, but I know Noel broke them repeatedly. I dreamed often of somehow convincing Noel I did love him and I was honoring my marriage vows, but it was impossible. I desperately searched for chemistry in bed with him, but he never understood lovemaking was a shared responsibility for both of us.

When I came home from the office, his first question would be, "What took you so long to get home? Why are the miles not right?" He would write down my mileage. I had to call him from the office before I left so he could time me getting home. If I had to go to the grocery store or stop for any reason, he just "knew" I had been seeing a man. What made it horrible was Pap had been suspicious, always accusing me of being out and having sex with some unknown man. I was as trapped and controlled in my marriage as I had been as a child. I still couldn't figure out how to go against the dictates of my Pentecostal upbringing of being in submission to my spouse. Noel wore many faces with his Jekyll and Hyde personality.

Noel was obsessed with having sons. He defined his masculinity by male offspring. He wasn't a man if a woman couldn't bear his sons, sons planted by his sexual pillaging. It was all a woman's fault in not receiving sons from his loins because his sperm was top choice.

This was the topic of many of Noel's conversations at the barbershop or after church with men. It seemed this had been his obsession for many years, even during his first marriage, but he hadn't bothered to share these insecurities about wanting so many children before our marriage. During his first marriage, he had grown his beard long and shaggy, declaring to the community he wasn't going to cut it until he had a son with his first wife Clara.

After four years of marriage, I finally agreed to get pregnant, so I went off the pill. I decided it was time I had a baby and maybe this would help Noel want and love me if I could give him a son. At least I would have someone else to share my love. I had lost the weight so I was physically prepared to have a baby. It took about six months for me to become pregnant after a lot of praying on my part, but not for the lack of his trying. His pregnant making efforts were worse than a rabbit in a briar patch!

When I missed my period, I went to the doctor asking him if I was pregnant, he told me, "There isn't any way you are pregnant. I have told you before you will never have children. You just have too many health issues." I was devastated as I desired a family, but I had faith the size of a mustard seed. I knew my Heavenly Father was the giver of miracles.

I sought God for a child much like Hannah did in the book of Samuel in the Old Testament. I didn't take the doctor's word for it not to happen, but I believed in the unknown by faith. I stayed busy with my praying. I had been working at Wal-Mart as a bookkeeper and serving as the part-time pastor for the Lee's Chapel Community Church in Johnson County. I asked the church to pray with me.

I felt the call of God to preach at age sixteen and had been in the ministry for twelve years. I had a dream one night of giving birth to a blue-eyed, blonde boy. I knew I was pregnant, so I returned to the doctor, asking for a pregnancy test. He agreed to a test to get me out of his office. He was flabbergasted and told me there was no way I could be pregnant. I was already nearly two months along.

I told my church I was pregnant and going to have a little blonde, blue-eyed boy. I had the most beautiful little boy God ever created. He came crying, "Mama". The doctor spanked him a time or so more, just to hear him cry, "Mama!"

"Doesn't that beat all? This one came out talking!" the doctor stated.

They laid my son on my chest and his gaze connected with mine. He was the best of me. How my prayers were answered, I was full of joy. What a wondrous baby! Noel bragged he was "The Man" and he could father sons.

I fell in love with my baby! Oh, my, he was precious – my baby son. The fulfillment of years of longing to have a child of my own was simply overwhelming. I was in heaven - and he was my dream little boy. The doctor tried to get me to agree to have a tubal ligation, but I refused. His partner intervened, telling me due to my health, I should wait only six months, and try to get pregnant again. He thought that way I could have two of the children I longed for. I loved being a mother.

My wonderful son began talking at six and a half months. He adored me. I was crazy about him. He was walking by nine months and talking in full sentences. He was exceptionally bright and he was my delight and joy. He was the fulfillment of my empty heart's dream. I believe my steps sang as I went about my bookkeeping duties at Wal-Mart. I was so happy to have this wonderful baby in my life. He was my own little man-child.

Noel was extremely jealous of our son and resented the time I spent caring for him. After my son was born, I had plenty of milk for him and he was a joy to breastfeed. There was just a special mother-bond with him and being able to nurture him as centuries of women before me had done for their children was totally fulfilling.

Unfortunately, Noel began to demand that if I was going to share "his" breast with "my" baby, he was going to be breast fed also. He began trying to nurse on the opposite breast while my son nursed. All of a sudden, my breasts were his erogenous zone for a feeding frenzy. I was appalled by his actions and his trying to force me for his selfishness. I couldn't stand the thought of his nursing like a baby; it was a total turn-off for me. I did not find it sexually stimulating or an indicator of womanhood. It was difficult enough to suckle my baby as my breast nipples were raw from the new experience. Noel bit my nipples for revenge until I could barely abide nursing my son.

I told him, "No, get away from my breast, I am not going to do this; it is a sick idea." He had a bullish look on his face. I knew I was going to pay for my rebellious action.

He was a grown man able to eat at the table and I wasn't going to be dragged down by sharing the breast milk with him. He gave me a pitiful story about supposedly how, John D. Rockefeller bought breast milk to live on and I should think as much of him and let him have the milk. I didn't buy that story at all. I was punished. I was sent up to my parents to "discipline me". What a hellish week that was. I didn't change my mind either. There were some things I would stand up for because my baby was the most important little man in life. My son needed what milk I had; we couldn't afford to buy formula.

I didn't understand how insanely jealous Noel was of my body parts being touched by our baby - *his* baby! He would pinch my breast until I would have bruises because I was refusing to let him nurse. He would squeeze my breast until I would pass out from the pain and then rape me, trying to force another baby on me before I was ready. I kept reminding him the doctor instructed us to wait at least six months. Fortunately, I had an overabundance of milk so his abuse didn't stop the milk flow.

Oh, yes, he did try the old song and dance with me, that if I let him nurse several times a day, it would save on our grocery bill! Oh, my, did he try to justify me breastfeeding him. I was totally turned off by the whole idea. I absolutely couldn't do it. It made me gag just thinking of him nursing at my breast. I thought it was a sick idea and told him so.

It was a war I won, one of the few. I refused to accommodate him in this manner in any way. It was a tiny victory. It was just too gross and gave me reminders of Mam and when I was young. In the twenty years I was married to Noel, he never once considered my well-being or what would make me happy. If I had understood what a narcissist represented, I would have seen that he was totally concerned with only himself. I refused him sex only two or three times in all the years we were married.

He was a selfish and stunted individual. He would get angry or plan revenge on someone and could puke on demand. He could turn on the anorexic and bulimic behavior when he wanted something if his family or I didn't give in to him. He would look so pitiful until we gave in to his demands. He could starve the weight off himself in a matter of weeks. There was absolutely no excuse for his behavior. He was a sadist. He would demand in a funny voice, "I am 'The Man' and you will do what 'The Man' tells you to do and when he speaks you are to obey." I learned quickly some part of my body would get a fist, if I didn't do as he said. I often prayed for him to gag on his food, fall dead of a heart attack or incur some other catastrophe. I found myself wishing him dead.

He would pretend his heart was suddenly hurting if I asked him to help with anything around the house or on the farm. He mimicked the worst chest pains and I fell for his line of 'hooey' for several years until I realized he was faking it and just simply was a lazy worthless man. He would trundle off to bed and stay there until I was done with a project and then demand sex. I should have told him that if he was too weak to help me, then he certainly was too weak for sex, but I didn't dare. Noel's behavior became so bizarre I never knew what to expect from day to day.

If someone came to visit, even if he had been in a rage, he would open the door calmly saying, "How nice of you to visit, come in and the woman will get you something to drink." Turning to me, he would order, "Honey, these folks haven't had a meal; cook them something." Unfortunately, like a docile cow, I would cook a meal and listen as he bragged loudly on what a good cook I was. I was his chief bottle washer and sexual object; he owned me and he wasn't afraid to remind me of my place after people finished their visits. I lived an invisible life.

,I began to notice how Noel never took any responsibility for any of his actions, offenses, or wrongdoing. He would rant for hours against his first wife, Clara, and the 'supposed sins' of his children. According to him, his children could never do much right. He'd blamed everyone but himself for his shortcomings. He was a would-be assassin on the prowl. He held years of rage against people he thought had done him wrong, especially his mother and first wife. If I made a mistake, I was not allowed to forget it. The next time he got angry or was in one of his spells, he would rehash the perceived wrongs repeatedly and could keep me up weeks on end without adequate sleep. I functioned like a zombie. He'd say, "Mother and my sisters never forgave anyone. I ain't ever going to forget the lessons I learned from Mother."

Yet, he would go to church, shout, dance and sing victories to Jesus and come home like the Devil incarnate! Oh my, how this man could shout in church, and sing, dance in the "Spirit" and talk in tongues. He could make the rafters sing with his fervency. He made people believe he was really walking the walk as one with God. Angels couldn't have done a better job of acting as he did. I, at first, thought I had married a godly man. He would pray with me, as I like to pray every night and offer thanks over my food, but after about few months, his praying stopped at home. I was no longer welcome to share a Bible reading with him and he stated I was being too religious. He would get mad at my praying, but I never quit. God was all I had; there was no question that I would ever give up God as He had never given up on me.

I began to realize Noel was a religious fake. When others were praying, I watched him; he was keeping an eye open sneaking a peek at those near him. I was shocked, but eventually faced the truth; he had tricked me into marrying him by his pompous religiosity.

My life was a mess. Noel took care of our son while I was at work. He became increasingly angry about it, but had agreed to babysit before we had him. I had talked with him in depth thinking he was in total agreement to care for our son. My Wal-Mart boss had been wonderful in letting me take a lot of my work home with me, so I could breastfeed my son.

Noel was still insisting I have more babies. My son was eight months old when I became pregnant again. I hired the next door neighbor to babysit my son after Noel began refusing to keep him, rather than give in and quit working. Noel, who was fifty-one, claimed he was too old and too ill to care for him. Funny, he hadn't been too old to have sex. We needed the money and insurance to afford a second child. My second child was born in 1977.

What a beautiful baby girl! I had a difficult pregnancy and delivery, but nothing was too hard to hold my own princess in my arms. She was ill when she was born and I

almost bled to death after her birth. I thought they were
going to have to do a hysterectomy to stop the bleeding. I
didn't have an abundance of breast milk for my daughter as
I'd had for my son. For six weeks, I fed her with a syringe,
dribbling my breast milk in her mouth after pumping my
breast, but then I had to switch over to bottle feeding.
During the pregnancy, I developed a thyroid goiter and I
am sure that contributed to the non-milk factor.

While I was working in the Wal-Mart office, my
bosses smoked several packs of cigarettes daily. When I
went on pregnancy leave, I began craving cigarettes. I
could have eaten an entire can of Prince Albert Tobacco. I
learned I was having tobacco withdrawal symptoms. The
doctors believed that was why my baby was born so ill. I
carried her nearly to ten months before the doctors induced
labor. They thought she would be a ten-pound baby, but
she was born with skin hanging all over her body and
weighed only seven pounds and four ounces. She did not
gain weight easily.

My joy cup ran over. I loved my children fiercely. I
laughed through the day caring for them, and thought my
life was good. After my pregnancy leave was up, I had my
neighbor begin caring for both my children so I could
return to Wal-Mart. She was a good neighbor. Then when
my daughter was several months old, I found her bleeding
vaginally one evening after picking her up. I called the
babysitter, asking her if she noticed the bleeding. She told
me she had given the baby a bath and perhaps she had
rubbed her too hard. Like a fool, I believed her.

Nearly twenty-three years later, she told me she knew
Noel was molesting my children but was too afraid to tell
anyone what he was doing. She feared he would murder
the children and me and kill her and her entire family. One
of my pastors told me the same thing, saying he thought
Noel would kill him or us if he told me about his
suspicions.

My neighbor thought perhaps Noel would be satisfied in marrying me, as I was so much younger than he and should be able to keep him sexually satisfied. She told me Noel had made overtures to her and tried to force another neighbor woman into having sex with him – possibly raping her. She had been afraid of him raping her. Oh, how I wished she had told me her suspicions! What my children endured, God only knows! My guilt has been a heavy burden and a battering ram to my soul in the darkness of the night. It was Noel's sin, but I was their mother and somehow I should have known he was a sexual predator. Unfortunately, I never dreamed of such an ugly thing in my own home. I had been a ripe grape just clinging to the vine, waiting to be picked by Noel.

I thought I had the world by the tail and was living the life I wanted. I created a semblance and an illusion of a normal life, or so I believed. Five months after delivery of my second child, I had to have a total thyroid and parathyroidectomy. It threw my body into a tailspin. The doctors warned me not to become pregnant after the parathyroid removal and possibly, I might not live more than fifteen years. It was terrifying.

Chapter 16

Who knows the madness of insanity?
Who will pay the piper?
Where does the dark cloud hide?
How is humanity to understand?
Glaring eyes,
Evil intent,
Hopelessness offered!
Captivity of the damned.

Noel began refusing to pay his child support for his older children while I was working at Wal-Mart. We had gone to court a time or so getting the amount reduced as his children aged out. The Johnson County Clerk, Armil Curran, came to Wal-Mart to see me. He told me Noel was going to be arrested for non-payment. I went home and talked with Noel about why he wasn't paying his child support. He blew up! He didn't want his ex-wife, Clara, getting his money. I tried to reason with him that the money was for his children. Child support had nothing to do with the custodial parent; it was for the welfare of the children. Then he decided we were going to flee the country to Canada or Mexico. I refused to go. I should have let him go to jail; instead, I began paying his child support myself. I was not going to be a party to his selfishness. His children did not deserve his sorry insane attitude. It was a bad situation for me to be in, but he didn't care I was being blamed by his children for his non-payment. He thought it great fun to brag to people that I worked in an office and brought my paycheck home and handed it over to him.

Noel was getting more and more aggressive with his sexual demands. I felt more and more like a cadaver. His perversions were branching out. I wondered if he was visiting the pornography room in Clarksville to come up with ways to intimidate me. Anytime Noel wanted sex, I provided it in any manner I could because I wanted to be a good, loving wife. No one knew I was black and blue beneath my clothing.

Mother knows best!

For seven years, I tried to be a good daughter-in-law. I sent Bertie flowers for each holiday so she would know she was remembered. I wrote her faithfully each week as Noel refused to write to her after our marriage, but insisted I write. I thought I could win her favor by being nice and she'd accept that Noel married the right woman. I hoped her attitude would change since our wedding. Bertie claimed to be Christian, but her way of thinking certainly precluded her salvation declaration! I offered her my forgiveness, but received hatred in return. So much for a Jesus meeting. Noel's bed was between us.

Noel's mother, Bertie Snow, came for a visit in the fall of 1978. She'd not been for a visit since our marriage. I looked forward to having her in our home. I wanted to bless her as my mother-in-law. I faced her visit with trepidation, but thinking she would be happy to see her two new grandchildren. She was diabetic so I planned special meals for her. Do you think she appreciated the fact I offered wonderful meals for her to share? No, anything I cooked she rejected even though I was a good cook. She insisted I buy extra so she could cook for her and Noel, telling him I didn't know what he liked. He had certainly liked my cooking before her visit.

She hadn't been with us long until she began insisting that Noel go for walks with her. I worked hard to remodel the old farmhouse and it looked wonderful. I kept it spotless. She had never seen Noel living in such a nice home. One day, Noel had to go for his VA appointment in Little Rock, so I stayed with her and the children. I could tell she was unhappy about something. I let the children play quietly near her so she could enjoy them. I hoped she would love her grandchildren. My youngest was fourteen months old and the oldest one was thirty-one months old. Both were sweet-natured children. I got them to 'color' pictures for her. She didn't to want to be close to them. She acted as if they were tainted leprosaria offspring.

The youngest one kept trying to get her attention, playing close to her feet and standing by her knees. When Noel came home, his mother was so angry. She told him I had urged the children to hit her, beat her legs, and slap her. My babies were gentle children. They'd played quietly all day. They each had tried to get their grandmother to play with them. Before I could react, Noel grabbed both the babies and harshly spanked them. He insisted they had beaten their grandmother. I was horrified. I got between him and the children. I thought she was a wonderful, godly woman and found out she was an unbending sneaking, snake hypocrite! I was an idiot. I found out she was telling Noel I was having an affair with my boss. Poppycock! I was horrified.

She kept at Noel during her visit, demanding he walk with her and when he returned, he was violently angry with me. I insisted neither the children nor I had done anything wrong. I was exhausted, so I called a motel in Little Rock and took us all there the night before her flight, thinking this might appease her.

Once we reached the motel, Bertie was angry as all get-out. "Noel," she bawled, "These children aren't yours. There just isn't any way you could be man enough to get such beautiful children on this woman." She began embellishing on how Clara had cheated on him and I was the same kind of woman as Clara.

I gaped in shock in clock-choked silence! I shook my head, unsure I had heard her right. I gulped and got the courage to speak. I told her she was full of clear-cut delusions and she was finally unmasked. She was the culprit in Noel's first failed marriage. I emphatically told her, "These are Noel's children, I am a Christian and I haven't been whoring around, besides sexually satisfying your son is a full-time job. I have been working a job full-time, pastoring a church, and got two children at home. When would I have the time to fool around with another man as Noel is at me all the time?"

I turned to Noel asking, "Noel, what is going on here? Why are you mad at me? I haven't done anything wrong. These are your children," I cried. I should have remembered he was a yellow-belly coward and mama's boy!

He told me, "I know nothing of the kind. If Mother says you are a whore, then you are a whore because she knows everything."

He slapped our son across the face and Bertie smiled the most beautiful smile. I thought, "Oh, God, she is getting a high out of Noel abusing us as Betty used to do."

"Noel, you know I haven't been with another man in our marriage," I wept in outrage.

She began to insist even louder I was a whore. I looked at her with pity, "You are a sick woman, Mother Bertie. I have respected you and given you honor, but you are a woman without any honor. It isn't me being a bad woman, but you."

Noel shoved me onto the floor and told me, "Quit disrespecting my mother." I looked at him with pity, "Noel, you are the one disrespecting your children's mother. I am worth at least your defense."

My children begin to cry from the anger erupting in the room. I had slept on the hard floor with the children through the night so Noel and his mother could have the beds in the motel. I was exhausted.

I asked Bertie, "How could you believe such things about me?" She told me she "knew" about me and I was mean to her son. She accused me of having affairs with the same men she and his sisters had accused his first wife. I almost vomited at the thought of such accusations, but it didn't stop her. The Red Bird hovered close to me as I lay on the floor. I whimpered in despair for my children and me. She did as much mental damage to Noel and our marriage as she could until she boarded the airplane.

I finally got her and Noel to the airport. She refused to hug the children goodbye and told me they weren't her grandchildren and weren't any kin of her family. My little ones looked at her and said, "Grandma, we love you because Jesus loves you, too."

I was flabbergasted and affronted as she told my children to shut their mouths. Hurt, angry, and sickened from all of this, I felt such despair. I had a moment of premonition of sorts of what the future would hold. I hadn't any warning about any of this. It blew my mind. I should have remembered how she treated my stepdaughter in California. I had forgiven and forgotten, but it would be the last time. Mother Bertie was unmasked as a female villainous wretch.

After his mother left, I never had any kind or hope of a relationship with my husband. His hatred of the children and me began to escalate proving the lack of masculine honor in his soul. He refused to go to church with me. He started leaving the Bible on our dining table open about a whorish woman, Proverbs 6:26.

He began to exhibit an obsessive desire to have more children, insisting he wanted enough to have a baker's dozen. We didn't have the income to support any more children and the doctors told him I mustn't get pregnant again. Bertie telling him he wasn't man enough to have gotten our beautiful children on me fermented in his mind. Her suggesting they belonged to some other man drove him to the far plain of insanity. It seemed to have pushed him over reality's edge. I was very ill with the thyroid disease.

My hair fell out, leaving me with a bald band around my head. I was running a daily high temperature.

However, I began exhibiting pregnancy symptoms a few weeks after Noel's mother left. I was scared. I knew I might be pregnant from his many sexual assaults.
I went to the local Dover doctor, Dr. Walter Lane. He told me I was about six weeks pregnant. He thought my life was in danger if I kept the baby or it might be malformed, and mentally retarded because of my thyroid dysfunction. He gave me something to abort the baby. Noel started an abusive cycle I thought would kill me. Again, I marked it down to his being mentally ill. I went into Post Partum Depression because an abortion was against my faith, but my children had to come first. Noel tried to force unwanted pregnancies on me for many years. During his vicious assaults, the Red Bird huddled close by offering what solace it could.

Noel watched my every movement. I went to more than one Assembly of God pastor seeking help, but I was told there was something defective in me or my husband wouldn't have a need to rape me. I sunk into despair. I was trying to respect God by staying in the marriage, but there was no honor in my heart toward Noel. I had two small children, and was too ill to work. Would the vicious cycle of my life never end or would I die first? Had there been a preventive factor I could have used to stop the abuse and salvage my marriage?

I thought when I married Noel he would be the kind of man who would be proud I was a minister, as he had claimed before our marriage. He promised he would stay through thick and thin and the bad and ugly of marriage, but when better turned to worse, he failed every natural test of marriage. He wasn't a man with any kind of backbone or staying power.

I preached where I could, as this was my only outlet. Noel hated me for preaching.

The Sherrillville Pentecostal Church above Clarksville asked me to become their pastor. I later found out when Noel got the men alone and he would hug them and kiss them on the neck – even the little boys. Evidently, he was trying to groom them and see if he could have sex with any of them. I was told they loved me, but didn't believe my husband knew God at all. It was a sad day to hear of his treatment of my church people. I was not surprised, though, with this news.

It hurt to find out I hadn't seen through Noel's evilness and lies with the dread of what he may have done to children in my pastoral work. I was a licensed Pentecostal Church of God Minister, preaching revivals, appearing to the community to be in a normal marriage, but living a life of hell at home.

After seven years, the VA doctors finally explained to me Noel was a paranoid schizophrenic along with other mental complications. They shared with me that sometimes a change of scenery was good for this type of mental illness. I hadn't been told any of this from his family or him. Noel was in a bad place mentally and I read everything I could on his mental diagnosis, but as an abuse survivor, I was ill-equipped to deal with him. He started stalking the neighbor women again not long after his mother's visit that fall. I don't know if the community women knew he was fixated on them or not, but I knew he was unhealthy in his talking about them and their bodies when we were having sex.

I thought perhaps Noel needed a change of surroundings away from the family feud and memories stirred up by his mother's visit and his own abusive past. I hoped a move might facilitate his healing or at least give him relief from the pressure being exerted by his family. I hoped if I got him away, he might find peace. I took a pastorate down in Southern Arkansas just outside of

Stuttgart for the Pentecostal Church of God in DeWitt. It was a troubled church and would take a lot of focus to rescue it from the brink of closing, but it would be a fresh start.

We only took the things needed to live in the small parsonage, but left everything else in the farmhouse. We planned to spend only part of the week at the church. We could drive back and forth, have the best of a pastorate, and still keep our farm critters cared for. I took over the duties of pastor for the little church in southern Arkansas. At first, Noel liked being the new pastor's spouse and getting attention, but that quickly changed.

DeWitt was a delightful little community, but the Pentecostal Church of God had garnered a bad name in the community. The former church pastor had run off with the church secretary. Together, they had stolen what little money was left in the church treasury, sold off some of the church furniture and purchased many things on the church's credit from businesses in town. They took all of those purchases and vanished. The church was left with the debts and the town had a nasty taste of evil in their mouths.

I hoped Noel understood I could pastor churches, thus giving me a spiritual outlet to use God's calling on my life, make a living, and still be at home with him and the children. They were two and three years old. We still had a few years before they would enter school. His family continued their phone calls and badgered him to conform to what they wanted our lives to be – and that was sequestered back on the farm. He became so angry and did not want me to be in the preaching business. I believe it was because I was getting all the attention instead of him. Noel could not appreciate the call of God in my life and my ministry had to be done in secret.

I began visiting each member of the church listed on the church roll. Most had become disenchanted or offended by the Church's handling of the situation or moved on to another church Most of the Pentecostal Church of God ministers were undereducated. Many of them had little training in working with people in need, thus this was the highest contributing factor of the failure. The internal control and oversight of the national organization was lacking. So many hurtful things were being done in the name of God. I heard many heartbreaking stories from former members. My pianist was the town drunk who stayed sober as long as I was the pastor and played in the most beautiful way possible.

One former member took after me with a chainsaw yelling, "I am going to whack you into little pieces. How dare you come here and ask me to church." I managed to jump his fence, made it to my vehicle, and fled. It was an interesting time seeing and trying to restore the faith of many who had been wounded. I never did restore my husband's faith to a place of healing. The church people didn't recover so I recommended the church be closed as the former pastor had destroyed their faith.

I helped all the town business people get their money and the church debts paid off while I was there, and in the end, the town business community took up a collection helping me finish paying all the debts. It was a business community of integrity. The church people were too wounded to recover, but I felt I had been able to do some good.

I saw God do many wonderful things in people's lives in DeWitt, but had to resign after a few months and return home because Noel became worse.

The melting pot of the world is filled with empty promises, but we can change that by our choices! It is up to us how we filled our share of the world. Do we pay forward or are we takers. To be a great individual we must be unafraid to stand alone for what is right!

Chapter 17

The drummer was drumming.
More children are needed.
Pesky little things,
But necessary vessels,
To pass along the learning of the past into the future.
She isn't important,
Remember women are pussies and betrayers.
Give her no thought,
keep my abilities I have given you close.
You are 'The Man'.
Invisible, indestructible in all that you do.
It is children that are needed.
Come, be a man, you can do this.
Slinking in the shadows gives you power.
I am the Hat Man in control. I
Will be content if I have more children.
Vessels of fulfillment, stars of brilliances,
They are all mine.

1977-79

I had the thyroid surgery in October of 1977 just months after my daughter was born in May. When the doctors told us that my health was in danger and would take me some time regain it, Noel went to bed and pretended to be ill. I carried his bucket of poop and pee for all those years. I was desperately ill, but he got sicker in his pretend world. I had two small children and him to care for. It was the hardest thing I was ever called on to do. I bathed him in bed, and wiped his bottom as if he were a baby. He was helpless, but when he wanted to go hunting,

glory be if he didn't have a miraculous cure and out the
door he went. If someone came who wanted to go ride the
horses, out of bed he jumped, just feeling like he could
make it to saddle a horse. He would go ride horses at
anytime, anywhere, and then it was back to his bed of
sickness. I was just so glad to have him out of the house. I
was still working full-time for Wal-Mart, now I had a
husband in bed and two small children to care for. It was a
heavy load. I felt dragged down, but I still believed Noel
was very ill.

He could grab his heart, turn white as a sheet and hit
the ground if he didn't want to do something. One could
believe he was dying - he was a masterful actor. I lost all
hope of that ever happening, though I did ask God to help
him out a bit in that department and prayed for God to
strike him dead. This behavior stayed consistent.

It seemed the more out of control Noel became, the
more my parents were right there encouraging him and
participating in my degradation. Betty claimed she also
had a bad thyroid condition after I had my surgery in Ft.
Smith. She insisted she wanted to see the surgeon who had
done my surgery. I called him and told him I believed she
was faking it and asked if he could see her as a favor to me.
He had heard the sense of urgency in my voice so he agreed
to see her. He told her he would like to put her in the
hospital in Ft. Smith. He wanted to run a test on her to find
out if there was anything wrong with her.

I brought Betty to my home before the scheduled
doctor's appointment. I took her into my Wal-Mart office
thinking that she would be proud to see where I worked. I
was blindsided. My boss, Steve Thornton, came up to me
and I introduced her to him. She boldly looked him in the
eye and up and down, crafty as a fox, "So you are the man
my daughter has had her babies by. Her husband isn't man
enough to produce such good-looking children. They look

just like you." I was so humiliated; he almost slapped her. "Are you insane, lady? You ought to be ashamed as a mother. Your daughter isn't the kind of woman to look at other men and besides, I am a happily married man. She has a husband who is the father of her children. If she weren't my best employee, I would fire her here on the spot, have you arrested for threatening me, and sue you for slander!" Mr. Thornton was livid, but Betty wasn't giving up. I wanted the earth to open up and swallow me! How mortifying could she be?

She snickered and said, "If that is the way you want to play it, I can tell when a man is whoring with a woman."

He ordered her out of the store and told her never to set foot in it again. I was mortified and in tears.

I had a mother who was continuing her abusive ways and a mother-in-law who was essentially just like Betty. Both were demeaning and evil in their intent to control and harm me. I was so appalled and embarrassed.

Betty was hospitalized the next day. The doctor called me the next morning laughing hysterically. He said, "If I didn't know you claimed this woman was your mother, I wouldn't believe you were related." He was very embarrassed and told me so. "You won't believe what your mother has done here in the hospital."

"Oh, God, now what has she done?" I moaned, knowing it could be anything. He stuttered all around the answer. So, I asked him to just spit it out! "She has propositioned three of the doctors I sent in to see her. She started telling them how good-looking they were and that she would be happy to spread her legs for them. She asked them to line up and get at it. She grabbed one of the doctor's genitals asking him for sex."

My doctor friend had sent in three psychiatrists to examine her after seeing her himself. He was suspicious of her actions and her obvious hate toward me. Not surprisingly, she was diagnosed as a sociopath. He was

horrified people like her and Aaron had raised me. I
assured him I wasn't upset with him, and shared with him
some of what my parents had done to me. He told me she
needed to be on psych drugs and institutionalized to keep
society safe from her. I told him my parents were ignorant
people and my father didn't believe in psychiatry at all. He
would never commit her, which is what she really needed.
In fact, he considered any doctor who worked in the mental
health field to be in tune with the mind of the Devil.

I dreaded Aaron's reaction because I knew he would
be in a rage. His ire would be directed toward me, instead
of Betty getting help.

When the phone rang at 2:30 a.m., the next morning, I
thought long and hard about not answering it

"What do you think you're doing, you low-down
bitch?" He yelled. Yep, Aaron was in fine form. I rubbed
the sleep out of my eyes, knowing I needed my senses.

"You're trying to take your mother away from me," he
screamed. This was his reaction after she had called him
and told him about the doctors' diagnosis. "I'm going to
kill you. I will hunt you down like a dog for doing this to
your mother."

"What is it you think I have done?" I questioned
Aaron. "I have no power over any doctor. Betty was the
one wanting to go to the hospital, claiming she was ill. The
doctors have found there is nothing wrong with her
physically, but she is sick mentally. She needs help and so
do you." I knew it was the wrong thing to say, but it needed
saying.

He continued to scream and threaten me. The doctors
wanted to send Betty to Little Rock to the state hospital, but
Aaron was killing mad. "All them doctors want to do is
have sex with your mother. Why, she would never do what
they said she's done. She is mine, and I will never let them
do anything for her," he said furiously. He was fit to be
tied! Threats continued to roll out of his mouth.

"You ain't no daughter of mine anymore. I will see you in hell before I let Betty take any kind of medicine for her mind," he bellowed. "I am going to get you for this; you are a dead woman! How could you do this to such a good woman as your mother?"

At that, I laughed uncontrollably. I reminded him again, "She was the one who demanded to go to the hospital and I wasn't with the doctor and had no control over her diagnosis." I couldn't help but remember all the years he had accused her of sexually being after any man that wore pants.

I got up my nerve and told him, "I am done being your daughter. I am glad the doctors have found the truth out about Betty. I've had enough of you both and I never want to see you again." It was a relief to say those words - "I'm DONE!"

I got one more phone call and it was from Betty in June 1979. "I have finally got you where I have wanted you all these years; you are out of this family. I wish I could kill you myself. You have lost," she boasted. I quietly hung up the phone, glad the past was now over. My course was set against them.

I wondered what it was she thought I had lost. She, Aaron and Samson had taken my childhood, ruining me sexually. They stole my good years when I should have been a carefree child. I was a punching bag for her and Aaron. I lost all hope for her and Aaron many years before, but what troubled me so much was she was evil and no one recognized it in her. Oh, thank God, the doctors had found her out and I knew the truth! I had peace at last, in some measure, knowing she had a real diagnosis and I wasn't the crazy one. I did not see or hear from my parents after July 1, 1979.

Finally, in self-defense, due to Noel's insane jealousy and abusive attitude, I quit my position at Lee's Chapel Church and my job at Wal-Mart in April 1978. It broke my heart as I loved pastoring and working for Wal-Mart. I became a full-time mother and a homemaker.

I had the time now so I fought through the VA system in Little Rock and got Noel his full VA compensation. John Paul Hammerschmidt, our Arkansas congressman, and the VA doctors in Little Rock helped me get his 100% disability back through the system. Noel's sisters and mother fought me every step of the way in getting Noel's 100 % VA compensation. Noel went to the Little Rock hospital kicking and hollering all the way, but he did stay at the doctors' insistence, until they restored his benefits. He actually, for once, did the right thing for his family. Securing Noel's VA benefits ensured all of his children would draw a monthly stipend to attend any college of their choice. The doctors said it should have never been taken away, but Noel had voluntarily given up his benefits because his family was ashamed of his mental disability. They didn't want his first wife and children to benefit from his military service. We now had Champva 80% health insurance coverage and I didn't plan for more children. I thought perhaps if I stayed home and took care of him, he would get better. I started building fences, clearing brush and repairing what we had. Noel was babysitting the children an hour here and there. I took them with me when it was safe when I worked outside.

Chapter 18

Run, girl, run,
'The Man' owns you and you don't even know it.
Bribe the briber!
Pay the penalty for hate.
Rise on the flood of ire.
Rush downstream with all of the bramble and brush.
Your life is owned.
You are nothing.
'The Man' is rising on the tide.
He is getting stronger, you are becoming invisible.
His hatred is real. Run, girl, run!

1981

My son started school in Lamar, Arkansas, excelling in his studies. How I adored my wonderful children. I worked hard at being a good mother, attending school conferences and classroom events, taking cookies or helping in any way that I could. I worked with his teacher, insisting the school start the first program for gifted students. By the second grade, he was reading at 12th grade level. I took joy in hearing the teacher exclaim, "Mrs. Snow, your child is the brightest and the best student in school." How proud I was of him! Being a homemaker and full-time mother did have its rewards! Noel very seldom went to any school events. My daughter was a year behind him in school and exceptionally beautiful and bright also. They were my full-time joy.

There were Christmases I couldn't provide much for the children, but I made wooden cars, stick guns, crocheted doll blankets and space critters for them to sleep with. My son was a Star Wars nut. It was fun watching my children grow and excel. I wanted my children to see a bit of the world so I planned a trip.

I planned a trip to California with Juanita Ragsdale, who sang and traveled with me in the evangelistic ministry. She was Clara's cousin and an excellent guitarist and gospel singer which enhanced my revival meetings. I appreciated her walk of faith with the Lord. The children loved her like a grandma. I wanted to go on to Idaho as I thought it would be good for us to relocate with a new start away from Noel's bitterness and past. I was excited about heading to Idaho where we had a revival meeting scheduled. Noel agreed for me to look at land in Idaho and Oregon. It would be closer to California for him to visit his mother and dad.

We traveled with a car full of laughter and joy. My children had fun seeing a lot of things and places. I was hopeful a new start away from Noel's and my bad memories might soothe the beast living in his soul. It was a great sentiment. I was trying to appeal to his masculinity. Even after all his meanness, I still sought to find the goodness surely hidden deep inside him.

I swung by Bakersfield, California, on the way to Riverside where Bertie Lambdin lived so I could meet my Aunt Mary Russell for the first time. What a shock! I was looking at myself! It was fun getting to meet my look-alike. She was a clinical psychologist. She had a counseling office in her home. She was articulate and very bright. We had a good three-day visit. She knew what Aaron was like, and wasn't surprised by the doctors' diagnosis of Betty. She was sad because if she had known how mean our parents were to us children, she would have taken us away from them and raised us herself. She was the only one of Aaron's sisters who got an education.

She'd heard Aaron's version of events about the psychiatrists diagnosing Betty and agreed the doctors were right. I had begun writing to Aunt Mary in the fourth grade and kept up the correspondence all those years. We continued keeping in touch, but now we each had a real face to put to the other one. She was one of the only people in the family who encouraged me to continue fighting on to do the right thing in life. When she died, she believed she was the oldest practicing female clinical psychologist in the United States. After leaving Aunt Mary's, I headed to Riverside.

The visit with Noel's family in Riverside was hideous. I should have been cautious after Noel's mother's visit in1978; my life became a living nightmare. Malevolence doesn't recognize boundaries or distance. There is no way to counteract lies or people who practice self-deception. If a man chooses excuses to become immoral, it is his journey alone. Evil is an insidious current that weaves webs which become entangled and enmeshed in the fabric of a family through incest secrets. Incest is like the sticky, nasty sickening feeling of putting a hand in the black widow's spun web. A deliberate cover-up of sexual sins destroys not only the family, but also the community of faith which encompasses that family. Such was and is Noel's family. The trip unmasked them. They were out of the closet and there was no going back to my ignorance.

Just before I left for California, Noel took a stab at mowing the yard behind the house where my son and daughter had left their outside toys. He deliberately ran the lawn mower over my son's truck and tractor that my brother, Ezra Joel, had given him for Christmas. He never offered my son an apology. He came inside as the day progressed and took my daughter's new doll and ripped it apart. He was smiling the entire time. The children were in tears. I shuddered at the face of evil.

When I returned home from California, Noel had bought a new truck for my son and a new doll for my daughter telling them he loved them best. The children rejected his toys. He was furious, threatening me for teaching the children against him. I didn't have to say a word, the children knew their Papa; he was doing the teaching all by himself! It was a terrible situation, but I taught the children Noel was mentally ill and we should be kind to him, so we all continued to try to believe.

It was not long before his sisters concocted a scam by which they would keep me in their power on the farm - and at Noel's mercy. They made plans to kidnap our children. According to Noel, they were going to sell them in Mexico. He told me he was going to get me declared an unfit mother, because his mother 'knew' I was a whore. I started getting kidnapping threats delivered by Noel if I didn't do what he told me to do. He was diabolical in assisting his sisters in this sociopathic threat. I have always wondered if he aided them in the threatening muffled phone calls at all hours of the day warning me to walk the line or I would never see my children again. I had awakened early one summer night with the urgency to go right then and check on my children.

Thank God, I did! I was so tired I decided to lie down in the bed with them. If I had not been in the bed, they would have been kidnapped. I loved to watch my precious little ones sleep, but I believe my being there was a God thing. I had almost dozed off to sleep. It was a hot sultry night. I had the windows open in their room. We couldn't afford any kind of air conditioning and only had one fan, which Noel confiscated.

As I lay there, suddenly the window screen popped off. I sat up on the side of the children's bed wondering what in the world was going on. I got up and leaned out, picked up the window screen off the ground, and put it back. There was a chimney flue next to the window. I lay back down in the bed with the children trying not to be scared. Suddenly, I realized there was no wind blowing and it had to be someone who pried window screen out of the window. I jumped up, ran to our bedroom and woke up Noel. He pretended to be all upset. He grabbed a gun, threw me one and we stepped outside. He went one way I went the other.

All of a sudden, someone jumped from out behind the chimney on Noel's side. The person fled across the yard, down through the little barn I had fixed together, and on down the road onto the back side of our property. Noel did not fire a shot. I always wondered about that fact. I believe he knew who was trying to steal the children, and probably had set it up.

I told Noel I wanted to call the Sheriff's Office. He stated, "Oh, no, it's just someone fooling around and you just imagined them trying to get the children. I told him, "You just wait. If it is someone bent on kidnapping the children, they will be driving down by the road in front of the house in a bit with their lights off." Sure enough, there came the car in about twenty minutes – no lights. He still wouldn't let me call the police. I knew he was acting funny about what had happened, but I didn't know the depth of his deceit for many years.

I wept in fear and didn't understand why he didn't want the sheriff involved. I cried so hard he finally told me that his sisters didn't believe I deserved to have such beautiful children. Because they believed his mother that the children weren't his, they plotted to kidnap my children and sell them! I lived with the threat of kidnapping for many years.

Evil incarnate lived in my bosom! I prayed often and my loving friend, the Red Bird, stayed constantly in my sight.

Once again, fear was my living, breathing companion! Noel's mother and sisters were intimidating me by threatening to call Child Welfare. They claimed they could prove I was an unfit mother because I was so ill. I didn't have sense enough to know my church people in the community would have had a very different story to tell

Law Enforcement or Child Welfare. However, when fear is ruling one's life, it is hard to think clearly. It was a very difficult time as I loved my children, they were my life, but I felt defenseless and hopeless. I didn't realize his family actually had no power.

Chapter 19

Free enterprise,
The joy of money,
The sound of those clinking tunes,
Rasping against the shovel of hard work,
Bend that back, swing the pick,
Forty hours a week, a paycheck,
From sunup to sundown,
Sweaty brow, hardened hands,
Coal mining is the life!

In the fall of 1979, I took a job as a bookkeeper for a coal mining business, Go Cat, Inc. in Coal Hill, Arkansas. The mining company was out of Oklahoma. I had about fifteen to thirty-five employees. All of the men were strong drinkers, hard workers and cussed a lot. The company CEO's son was running the company. The son was acting as president of the mine. They'd run an ad in the local newspaper wanting a bookkeeper for the site. I thought it sounded interesting. We needed the money, so I applied for the position against Noel's wishes, but our need for extra money outweighed his objections. When I arrived on the job, the site was in the middle of a strike and a wage dispute.

Tony Alamo and his trucking crew were from Alma. Alamo and his wife were TV preachers. They had a cult following and a TV religious service going each Sunday morning. Many young people were following them, working for food and a place to sleep, but no money, giving all their wages to the Alamos. They were one of the mine contractors on the job hauling coal with their eight-wheelers to the barges at Ft. Smith on the Arkansas River. The mining company's CEO hadn't paid the miners or the contractors. The Alamo outfit was striking and out for blood. They brought in many of Alamo's trucks and were blocking the entrance and exit roads and generally packing big sticks and guns. These men were bent on trying to prevent mine employees from coming in or going out. There was a lot of yelling, threats, and anger. There was about to be bloodshed on the site as the miners and the trucking outfit were at war with each other. Hot words were flying and rocks were being thrown.

This was my first day on the job. What an introduction! I stepped out into the middle of the road coming up to the office. Alamo's truck foreman was carrying a club big enough to slay a dragon. I was the only damsel in distress and there wasn't a white knight riding to the rescue. I was shaking inside, but I wasn't going to back down. I needed the job to get away from my home life. They told me they were coming through me and shutting down the operation. They intended to ruin the equipment, which was top-notch and leased. I had already called the sheriff and he was on his way. I told the foreman who I was and this was my first day on the job. They said, "We are going to take down this outfit."

I spoke quietly, but loudly enough for them to hear me. "You all will have to come through me and I won't go down without a tussle."

I raised my hands and said, "Let us pray." I had more gall than good sense!

I bent my head in prayer wishing I had big visible angels standing with me. I believe I did.

"Dear God, we are in a mess here at this mining site. We need you to intervene and give us wisdom how to help these men. These truckers and these farmers all need their wages from the coal mine. God, come and stand here beside me, let these men see your mercy and grace. Now, I ask you in Jesus' name to give us peace in the midst of all this anger and hate. Give me wisdom to help all of us to find a solution. Amen!"

I took a quick peek at the men in front of me and heard

the stirring of my crew behind me.

The shock on their faces and the gasp of my men behind me let me know maybe a good old hellfire and brimstone prayer just might have quieted the situation down.

I needed to keep stalling to give the sheriff time to get to the site, so again I bent my head in prayer.

"Heavenly Father, I bring this angry bunch of men to you, in Jesus' Name as you know I can't do anything at this point. Quiet their hearts and let them know I will do my best to find out the truth of what is going on. I promise to do my best, Lord, if these men will be honest with me." I stretched out the prayer with a few more supplications as long as I dared. I backed the Alamo bunch back to their trucks and got them off the property. It was a tight moment or so, but prayer turned angry men into decent working folks at that moment. I put the employees back to work. I appointed one of the older men to act as temporary foreman. Finally, I heard the siren in the distance.

The sheriff arrived and he said the look on all those men's faces was priceless. He had seen Alamo's men going down the road. He guffawed when I told him I had been praying. "Only you had guts enough to pray in this situation, girl!" He grinned and winked.

A few weeks later, the owner's son pulled over a neighbor of mine. I was with the son as I acted as his manager on the mine site. We had to tend to some banking business in Dover. He pulled up beside her on a lonely country highway, flashing his badge at her. He motioned to her to pull over as if he was a sheriff's deputy. He asked her for her license and told her that she driving erratically and speeding. The incident scared her and me both to death, so I turned him in to the County Sheriff's Office. He was arrested for impersonating an officer.

I fired him from the job and his father told him to 'git' as did the sheriff, or go to jail.

It was one exciting thing after another happening on that job site. Mayhem ruled night and day. We were set up to run with floodlights all over the site 24/7. One of the miners working for me broke into my office and stole several blank checks. He wrote a few hot checks on the new account, forging my name on them. I had my name and telephone number on the office wall just in case someone needed to reach me. He didn't know how I signed all my personal checks. My personal signature was nothing like my office signature. I had my reservations about the job situation and refused to sign any payroll checks when I took the job. This young man had forged my name as it was on the wall on all the checks and cashed them in Clarksville. Businesses began calling me, saying, "Why have you written a check to us and it has bounced? We are turning you over to the Sheriff."

This was my first knowledge the checks were stolen and my name was on them. I told all the businesses I would get back with them shortly and see what in the world was going on. Many of them knew me from the years I had worked for Wal-Mart. I hadn't written any checks on the account, but I began to suspect who might have.

I notified the owner as well as the State Mining Board Office. The County Sheriff knew me from Wal-Mart and recommended me to the Mining Board. The mining board representative vouched for me to the businesses. The State Police lifted one of the miner's fingerprints off the checks. The other miners remembered him and his wife coming to the mine shack during his off hours. He was arrested and charged with forgery, theft, etc.

The check forger obtained the services of a close lawyer friend of mine by lying to him. The young man told him I recommended my friend to defend him. When my friend came in to court to defend him on the charges and he saw me there as a witness, he said his stomach sank. He told me he never wanted to go up against me as a witness in court again. The man got two years' probation and a fine for the charges.

One morning I hadn't been at work long when I heard this loud rumbling noise coming down toward the mine office. Men were screaming, "Run, Ma'am, run! I made it outside the door and there came a huge twelve-wheeler coal truck which had lost parking brake and was driverless. It headed downhill toward the office. I lifted my arms in prayer, knowing my end was at hand! Just as I thought for sure the office was going to be wiped out, it veered to the right and plunged down into a soft pit of dirt, stopping with a bang. All the miners were scared witless, but said they could hear me praying above the runaway vehicle for God not to let anyone get hurt. God provided safety again! The men did seem to respect my prayers after that!

Another morning, I got to work to open up the office so the men could sign in and go to work. A loud rat-a-tat knock sounded on the office door. I yelled, "Come on in, the door's open." In stepped a man, tall, slender with a sidearm under his suit jacket. He asked me if my name was so and so. I stood up and told him, "You are either FBI or DEA. He pulled a badge out of his jacket pocket and handed it to me. He was from the Firearms Division of the Treasury Department. He told me, "I am here to arrest you."

I laughed, and said, "I don't think so! You first will have to tell me what I am supposed to have done." He got a funny look on his face at my laughter. I told him I had never stolen anything on any job yet, and hadn't started on this one.

I said, "I will call the County Sheriff, and he will vouch for me as I can't think of a thing I may have done wrong on this job." I called the sheriff's office and got hold of the sheriff. After talking to him and explaining the situation, I handed the phone to the Treasury Agent. They talked a few minutes and he hung up the phone.

"The Sheriff says he will vouch for you, but I already knew who you were through the State Police and an FBI check. They say you are a good woman and an honest one, so I was just checking out how you would react."

"Whew," I stated, "I am glad it is not me you're after and it's a relief to know that."

I offered him a seat and asked the men to get started working. I asked my foreman to stay in the office with me as we could use his insight.

The FBI had called the man to come to my job site. I was amazed how bad news traveled so fast and I had known nothing about it. He told me the mine dynamite bunker had been broken into and dynamite had been stolen over the weekend. He asked me to take a count of the blasting caps and sticks of dynamite in the bunker. I agreed quickly, thinking this was a nasty situation. I called my two demolition men, Billy Williams and his sidekick to come in to work and verify what the Treasury Agent was telling me. The agent informed me someone had called in a bomb threat. The man stated he had some dynamite from the mine and was going to blow up the Clarksville High School.

The Fed knew about the stolen checks and my having worked for Wal-Mart for several years as a bookkeeper. I had been bonded there for a million dollars and had passed State Police and FBI background checks on that job. They knew who I was professionally.

"I believe I can narrow down who this might be as I think it is probably the same person who stole the checks." I was right. They ran prints on the bunker door and it was the same guy. He was arrested and admitted he had stolen the dynamite. He got several years on the Federal charges.

The mining job was winding down after the visit of the Federal Agent and the bomb threat. My mining employees began calling me at night saying there were shots being fired on the mine site. I felt the men were trying to draw more hours. The employees were claiming it was the Alamo men doing the shooting. I drove up to the mine site about nine p.m. without letting any of the men know I was coming. I made the men on watch build a huge fire outside of the office and posted guards at four checkpoints.

I had Noel stay up on the hill above the site with his shotgun. Noel was too scared to join me around the fire with my employees, as he just knew an unknown assailant lurked in the darkness. The men were scared to death of Noel, afraid he would shoot them so it was a standoff amongst cowards. I didn't bother to inform them Noel was as much of a coward as all of them. He would only shoot them in the back or tuck tail and run over the hill toward home. I took our big blue tick hound and he bayed at the moon, but his howling impressed the men around the fire, as they just knew the hound dog was on to them.

I made them change shifts around the fire every two hours. Before the night was over, I assessed the situation. I fired two or three men over the incident proving it was them shooting rather than Alamo's men terrorizing the mine site. The employees were causing the fracas to get more working hours. I spent two nights on the job site. There were no more calls to the sheriff's office or to me in the middle of the night. Sometimes, checking out people's stories sure can stop trouble. After all the trouble, the State Mining Board wanted to shut down the mine.

After the mine president was removed, the forged checks settled and the man arrested for the dynamite theft, the employees settled down. The State Mining Board of Arkansas agreed the mine could stay open. I agreed with the owner for the state to take over the management of it. The owner and the farmers, along with all the employees and the truckers readily agreed. I was able to get the rest of the coal out of the site and put the land back according to EPA guidelines. The farmers, the employees and the trucking companies were happy to get their money. The

State Mining Board concluded the job was done, according to Sam Rice, State Mining Inspector. All debts were satisfied.

The job ended on March 6, 1980.

Chapter 20

"Suffer the little children to come unto me,"
Jesus told his disciples.
Where do children run?
To whom can they turn?
When no one can see the hidden darkness
creeping up on them.
Are those shadows lingering in and near?
Who will cleanse the homes infested with incest?
Who is there for the innocent?
Where do they hide?
How long will the children endure the torment?
Oh, the heart of the innocent child,
Bludgeoned, with no champion!
Ride, Oh, Knight of the Round Table, come to the rescue.
Where is the white charger that you ride?
Come, come, O, Savior of the innocent?

1981-1985

I made many allowances for Noel because he had
gifted me with my two precious children. My son was a
very healthy baby when he was born, and then contracted
various illnesses. He was my constant source of delight. I
was doing everything I could to ensure that he had anything
and everything to eat, but something was wrong. I
constantly prayed for him, and even his doctor was
worried. His fever would spike suddenly and I would have
to rush him to the hospital. I was frightened for his
survival. He had grown and flourished being able to nurse
at the breast, but when I become pregnant with my
daughter, I had to stop nursing him. The doctor hadn't
wanted him to gain any more weight because he had

weighed twenty-six pounds at nine months old. The doctor put him on cows' milk. At two, he started getting pneumonia. Much later, his therapist told me that she believed his father had been molesting him at this early age.

Finally, I got him tested for allergies at four years old. We found my son was allergic to all wheat, dairy, dust and molds. It was very difficult to find things he could eat and we could afford. He craved bread, especially store-bought bread, which was made with wheat by-products causing him to get pneumonia after ingesting it. He had constant ear and lung infections.

I found out Noel had been encouraging our baby daughter to get the bread down when I was out of the house and give it to her brother knowing the bread would cause a severe allergic reaction. He would whip our daughter as if was all her fault our son was eating the bread. She was only three years old. It was a wicked thing to do to the children. How could a father be this mean? I had to hide the loaf of bread from my son or his little sister would hunt and find the loaf while I was out working in the garden and take it up to their attic playroom. He would eat the entire loaf of bread and then, in the span of a few hours, I would have to rush him to the hospital emergency room with double pneumonia. Hindsight tells me Noel had a fetish for making the children ill so he could step in and be a hero in rescuing them. I let Noel's mental illness blind me to his harmful treatment of us all.

One time my son's temperature spiked and he stopped breathing. He fell on the floor, lifeless and turning blue. I worked with him trying to resuscitate him. His teeth clamped onto my right hand and I couldn't get my hand out of his mouth. I knew first aid and began trying to administer chest compressions, but because of his teeth being clamped on my hand, I wasn't successful. I couldn't find a pulse. I screamed for Noel to help me get him out to the car and to the hospital. I was praying and begging God not to take my baby from me. I was seven months pregnant with my next baby.

His teeth were still clamped onto my hand. He was lifeless in my arms, eyes fixed and dilated. I kept screaming for Noel to drive faster and faster, and for once, he did what I asked. I rushed into the ER, praying and weeping. My son's teeth were still clamped onto my hand. The doctors couldn't find a pulse. They couldn't get him to let go of my hand. I was still praying.

"Oh, God," I begged, "You gave me my precious son even though the doctors told me I couldn't have children. Please don't take him from me now. Sweet Jesus, I need my precious son. I love him. I have tried to do my duty to you as your servant." My tears rained down my face and onto my son's face. The Red Bird fluttered helplessly near my baby.

The doctors were talking about declaring him dead. All of a sudden, he turned loose of my hand and sat up. "Mama, why are you crying?" Oh, how I wept in Thanksgiving that my son wasn't taken from me! No sweeter words than those ever crossed my ears, before or since.

His fever spiked at 104 plus. The doctors put him in a tepid bath and broke his fever. They diagnosed him as having double pneumonia and he was admitted to the hospital for a few days. He was put on antibiotics after several hours of observation. The doctors stated they were ready to pronounce him dead. They also informed me they believed something had caused him to have a seizure, thus the clamping on my hand and not being able to loosen his jaw. Neither the doctors nor I ever imagined sexual abuse.

I had to take my son to Children's Hospital for additional allergy testing. He had pneumonia and ear infections so many times this was deemed a necessity. He was not thriving as he should and the doctors were worried as to why. My sweet little boy thought I was punishing him by having those needles stuck in him. He hated the tests. He was allergic to so many things. Later we found out it was not only an allergic reaction, but also anxiety attacks causing him to have to be hospitalized so much. It was a scary time for me. I stayed alone in the hospital with my boy, making excuses why Noel couldn't come to the hospital and help. He was at home claiming to be in bed ill, but he wasn't.

That same year, my baby girl took sick with violent diarrhea and was hospitalized. It was a year of battles for my children's health. She almost died from the dehydration and vomiting. Ten and half years later, my youngest daughter did the same thing. They couldn't find out what was causing the diarrhea and why my children were so ill.

Noel's youngest son had died from the same symptoms in 1968. Again, in the aftermath, I realized what a fiend I had married and how very blind I had been. I forced myself to love him and taught the children that Papa was just mentally ill. We had to take care of him. He betrayed my trust and love.

None of the doctors thought to check my children for sexual abuse. I was so naive, I didn't even suspect that the children's problems were stemming from sexual abuse.

Noel was in and out of the North Little Rock VA Mental Hospital. His brother and sisters began to interfere with his hospitalizations. I was supposedly after his farm, but when we married, I insisted he have his farm appraised. He had twelve hundred dollars cash and the farm appraised for a thousand dollars. I had nothing but a strong work ethic and willingness to work. He later stated he knew with my education and drive, I would be a money maker. The VA doctors in Little Rock had a long association with Noel and offered him help. It was a struggle to be supportive as he was so abusive. I hung in there trying to survive after quitting work full-time.

His brother and sisters were meddlesome with our decision to sell the farm. They cajoled and threatened us. Their kidnapping threats increased as they tried to intimidate us. All the turmoil worsened Noel's paranoid schizophrenia. I bore the brunt of his wrath and his sisters' lies. As angry as he was, he stuck by his decision and went against his family. He was still determined to sell the farm. He thought maybe they would leave us alone if we moved away. Not once did he openly stand up to them, but was passive-aggressive. He wanted to sell the farm, but pretended to them it was all my idea.

He finally put the deed in my name in self-defense, not wanting them to get anything out of it. When we married, his house was unlivable until I remodeled it so I didn't feel like I was taking anything from Noel by having my name on the deed. I remodeled the house, cleaned up the land and it was worth something. It turned out to be a nice old place when I was done.

I made a large garden each year, canned hundreds of quarts of fruits and vegetables, and helped Noel hunt so we would have food to eat. It still didn't make a difference. I raised corn, green and shell beans, beets, carrots, salad, potatoes, tomatoes, various kinds of squash, pumpkins, radishes and peas. These things fed us all summer and through the winter. I made jams, jellies, relishes, and anything good. Noel ate the best he had ever eaten in his life, as did I.

I raised a fattening hog each year on the goat's milk. Around Christmas time, I butchered it with some help from Noel. He would shoot the pig and help me gut it. We would have a large black kettle over the fire full of boiling water. I would place burlap sacks over one side of the hog pouring boiling water all over the burlap sacks. I would let the hog hair soak for a few minutes, remove one sack at a time, then scrape the hair off the hog. Noel always became very ill at this point and fled to his bed of affliction. Once I got all the hog prepared, I would have to roust him out of bed to help me hang the hog for quartering the hams and shoulders, and then I would take out the tenderloin along the backbone. I cut the backbone into stew pot size or to be baked. I had to cut the bacon into usable sizes. I took out the liver, heart, kidneys, and cut off the feet, all of which were considered delicacies. Noel would go back to bed. I was left to finish butchering the hog by myself (I found I was thankful Aaron had at least taught me something). I build a saltbox in one of our small sheds. I salted the meat down with sugar cure and hickory smoke cure. Those were some of the best hams and bacon, and no, I didn't keep the meat for company like Mam had when I was a child. I fed it to my family.

The son-in-laws told me it was some of the finest meat they had ever eaten. They were good about hunting deer on our property and sharing the deer meat with us. They were good to my stepdaughters.

I cooked everything from scratch, making bread, cakes, and pies daily because Noel wanted it done. I had seven stepchildren and eight grandchildren. Often I had my stepson and stepdaughter come to be with us on the weekends, even though it made Noel furious. However, I stuck to my guns, and took them on trips with us to places I thought would be fun for them. They were his still children and I would not deprive them of that right. They needed to feel cherished and valued, but Noel didn't have a clue. I loved to cook for them. They were caught in a bad situation and it wasn't their faults, nor was I going to be party to depriving them of a parent, such as he was.

My stepchildren had an uneasy reconciliation with their father after our marriage. They came for meals when I would cook. I was determined to have a family even if it angered him. We rode horses and hunted a lot. I was raising beagle dogs and the son-in-laws loved to hunt with them and listen to them run. I had several outstanding bitches and an excellent male sire. I guaranteed them to run deer and to hunt rabbits. I was an avid hunter like Noel. This was something he did seem to enjoy doing with me. If I killed a deer, he liked to brag to the men at the barbershop how his wife was a great hunter. This praise was better than nothing.

This was a pleasant year for the stepchildren until they found out Noel had put the property in my name. This was the end of the reconciliation.

Our children were normal children, but his mother and sisters took every opportunity to demean them as not his. Their childish exuberance in play set Noel off into a frenzy of anger and days of ranting. He began sleeping with a loaded pistol to my head for days on end. I was careful in how I approached him or got in and out of bed. I never knew what might tip the scales of his madness and make him murder me or harm the children.

The children and I became adept at living in the attic for weeks, shutting down the door and laying things on it so he couldn't raise it without waking me up. I feared for our lives. I would slip out and get food for us, cooking enough to leave in the fridge for him to eat so it would placate him. I got the children off to school on the bus each day. How they excelled in school, I don't know. I was living a nightmare at home. His doctors were telling me Noel had been in the best mental health he had ever been according to his records. What had he been like at his worst? Apparently, I was doing a good job with him. My marital situation was on shaky ground, but I was determined to stand by my man.

With his worsening mental decline, one situation stood out that year.

I remember January 19, 1982, as being an unusually bad day with Noel. He tied our horse, King, up to a good-sized metal ring hung from a strong tree branch. He was trying to put shoes on him, but King was a skittish young two-year old horse. Noel's yelling made him act up even more. I could horseshoe King by getting him to lay his foot in the hollow dip of a cement building block. He wouldn't fight me. In fact, he adored me. I loved him back. Because King was scared, he jerked his foot away from Noel in fright. Noel began beating him with his hammer and shoeing tools. Of course, King reacted badly. Noel began to scream for me to come out and help him 'hold' the horse.

The young horse was huge and when frightened, he could do some serious damage to a human being. I stepped out the back door. Noel begin yelling and beating the horse. "This is your entire fault. If you would have held the horse like I told you, none of this would have happened."

I tried to calm him down by telling him, "You know that the children are too little to be left alone in the house and need one of us to watch them. Could you not have waited to shoe him until our son was in school? We could have stood the baby up in a box or the back of the pick-up where we could watch her," I said.

"Get out here and hold this horse. I am going to kill the sorry thing," he screamed.

I enlightened him, "You're too mad to be trying to shoe the horse. You have him scared to death." I tried to reason with him, but it did no good.

He shouted, "I will show you scared!" He hit the horse between the eyes with his hammer. Oh God, he was killing my horse! I saw my Red Bird flutter between King's ears. I knew death was near.

I was frantic. Noel was screaming obscenities and hammering King in the forehead. He roared, "You are an idiot, nothing, do you hear me, you bitch? You're nothing!"

I tried to mollify him. I kept telling him I loved him and didn't want him to get hurt or hurt the horse. I begged him to calm down or he would have a heart attack, as he was so mad. I asked him if we could work out the shoeing after he got in control of himself, but nothing was working. I was praying again, seeking God's divine help and intervention. The Red Bird was all fluttery motion between the horse and me. I needed an angel to show up on the spot, preferably with a big sword in his fist and fire in his mouth to save the children, King and me.

Suddenly, King reared up, fighting back with all of his horsey heart. He stood six foot at his withers and weighed about 2,000 lbs or more. He rode like a dream from being part gaited American saddle horse. He rose up on his hind feet, flailing about trying to break the rope tied to the ring and avoid Noel's hammer. I knew if I got too close, I would get hit with the hammer or King's flying hooves. I felt faint from the blood pouring from King's head wound. I saw the Red Bird fluttering near King's ears. Fear kept me on my feet, but I didn't know what to do. I stood there whimpering like an idiot for King, powerless to stop the beating.

King finally managed to break the rope. When the rope broke, the ring swung high and hard and caught Noel in the mouth, breaking off two of his front teeth and splitting his upper lip. King stood trembling and shaking badly, still trying to stay close by as a good horse should.

Noel came at me with the hammer, but I ran. He was yelling, "I am going to get the shotgun and that horse is dead."

I screamed for King to run and hide. I managed to hold Noel off as best as I could. That horse did exactly what I hollered for him to do. He took off to the back forty running flat out in fear. Noel shoved me aside as if I was wheat straw.

Noel ran into the bathroom to see the damage done to his mouth. When he saw himself he began to bellow like a bull. He was enraged, snorting every breath. He took a swing at our son with the hammer. I grabbed the boy out of his way and told him to run upstairs with his sister and hide.

I kept trying to get Noel calmed down without him doing damage to himself or killing me. He grabbed me by the hair, dragging me into the bathroom forcing me to look in the mirror at the damage. He kept screaming, "Can't you see what you made that horse do to me? You put that horse up to doing this to me. You want me ugly."

At that moment, I believed him to be one of the ugliest human beings I had ever seen. His anger turned to sexual assault. I prayed the children would remain hidden upstairs until he calmed down. His rape was brutal. All I could see was the torn lip hanging down with blood dripping onto my face. Sex always calmed Noel down.

I talked him into letting me take him to the hospital. He later informed me he thought about telling the doctor I had done this to him in a domestic violence scene. He laughed and said his sisters told him to take every opportunity to use against me in any situation to get the children away from me.

However, unbeknownst to him or me the doctors had the nurses interview the children. Our son told him about how Papa was 'beating up' the horse and threatened me with a hammer and "Mama hadn't hurt Papa at all." Thank God for children's truthfulness! The doctors informed me privately the children's story was the same as mine. I knew I was in trouble for sure with Noel; trouble seemed to flow from him like an avalanche traveling at breakneck speed down a slippery slope mountain. All I wanted to do was to survive. I didn't know where to run for freedom – I'd been conditioned all my life to accept my position as *normal*.

When we got back home, Noel took a bucket of feed

over to the back forty and caught King, bringing him back to the house. He tied a thick rope around his neck so when he fought, he would hang himself. He tied the horse to a high huge limb of the walnut tree. It would be impossible for King to break loose from that rope. I could hear the rhythmic thudding of the club Noel was using to hit the horse. King's pathetic squeals echoed in my brain. I knew if I dared beg this time around, the club would turn on me or the children. I hid in the shame of my cowardice holding my two children in my arms. We cried together knowing we would receive our punishment next. Noel had King almost beat to death when James and Clara Williams showed up from our church. They said they had felt an urgent need from God to come to our place. They came, as they were, having dropped everything and drove like crazy to get to our place.

The man quietly walked up to Noel and said, "Hey, Brother, it looks like you are having a bit of trouble; let me help you with that horse. Say, Noel, isn't this your young horse you have telling me about? He looks like he is in trouble and suffering. Can I help you get him up and get him steady on his feet?" King was beaten to his haunches, his front legs were shaking so badly, and he was choking to death.

Suddenly, Noel was calm, cool and collected as if he hadn't just been in a killing rage. He was acting as the perfect horseman, being solicitous to King and his injuries as if someone else had beaten the horse.

Mrs. Williams came with me in the house, solicitously asking what was wrong. I cried so hard and told her what had transpired. She said they knew God had wanted them to come quickly to our house. They had laid the rubber to the road to come our place. They knew how Noel was, but never had experienced the need to obey God in such a manner. They came in time and were the most unlikely angels.

Noel helped get King up and agreed to turn him loose. The poor horse limped away. He didn't come back for a month and a half, hiding out in the woods recovering. I slipped him food when I could.

Noel came in the house, hollering, "Honey can you get these folks something to drink?" You would never have known he had just been in a killer rage just minutes before. This kind couple visited until dark and gave Noel an excuse and time to calm down. The fellow later told me Noel would have killed the horse if he hadn't arrived when he did. He said as he drove up he could tell what was going on and told his wife to get in the house with me and let him see if he could calm Noel down.

Again, God heard my cries for help. How often I had to beg God for help and he never failed me. I often wondered how God had such patience with me – a cowering coward. I loved my beautiful horse. He never let Noel shoe him again. I had to do the job. King would let me carry both the children and ride him. He would walk as if he was walking on eggshells. He had the most pleasant gait of any horse I ever had the pleasure of riding.

I loved the farm; I had turned the old farmhouse into a lovely country home. I kept it gleaming, but there seemed no way I could polish my marriage. I knew my son needed goats' milk, so I purchased a wonderful nanny goat. The children dearly loved old "Pet." We had our own 'pet milk' so to speak. She was a Toggenburg-Alpine goat cross and gave a tremendous amount of milk. At last, Noel had a source of milk rather than nagging me to nurse at my breast. He and the children would have a continuous supply of milk. He couldn't complain he wasn't getting any milk because the children were taking it all. I learned to make goat cheese and goat butter for my son. He loved the goat cheese – and he said the chocolate milk wasn't so bad. At last, he was able to have cheese again.

I began to buy other goats by justifying them to Noel

because they could eat the brush off the forty acres. We were trying to sell the farm so it needed to be spruced up and look like a producing little acreage. The goats would follow me all over the property and as long as I cut the brush, they would eat it and stay right with me. The children got to have fun with the goats. They had new pets. I loved buying the goats, milking them and then guaranteeing them as having sound udders, dehorning them, and breeding them. I quickly had a large business. I would buy a pickup load of goats within 150 miles of our farm. It was interesting, and gave me a job from home. I was able to make extra money this way. I eventually began learning other uses for the goat milk and I loved the goats. The goats were reminders of the old Nanny that I'd had as a youngster at Mam and Pap's. After getting in the goat business, things picked up around the property. It was looking mighty fine.

I had two of the best son-in-laws who lived close by. Noel wouldn't help me cut wood and we didn't have the money to buy firewood. The children and I were about to freeze to death. I asked one of them to train me how to use the chainsaw. He was an expert at it. He was patient and kind about teaching me. I was never again to be without firewood to heat the old farmhouse. I am indebted to him for helping me. It made Noel madder than an old wet hen because I was cutting the wood, but he was laying in the bed – too lazy to even help load it. I had no choice. I managed to split the wood in small enough pieces that the children could carry the smaller stuff to the pickup. A good chainsaw was a lifesaver.

I began attending estate auctions to buy stuff and resell it. Noel could see proof of how much profit I was making so he did do a good thing for me. He built a very nice cattle truck rack for the pickup. I was able to buy a huge truckload of items at auction and resell them. This was one of the few things he ever did for me. Of course, Noel enjoyed seeing the profits.

I begin collecting antique dishes and had a great selection of them. It made up for so much of his mean-spiritedness. This outlet provided me with the "pretties" I had craved as a child. It was a puzzle to me because he did have some good qualities, yet he chose to let his evil outweigh any of his good. We could have had the exotic ingredients for a sweet May/December marriage and have been joyful in our togetherness, but it never happened.

A friend and I met two or three times a month on Saturdays in Dover where we had a huge rummage sale on the Dover Supermarket lot. We always cleaned up and left things looking good. We were allowed to do this for several years before yard sales were popular. The children and I had a lot of fun. I caught Noel spying on us a lot. My friend would say, "Don't get scared and don't look, but Noel is hiding behind such and such vehicle and watching you." She said, "Doesn't he know by now you aren't chasing any man?" I reckoned he didn't and his sisters and mother kept persisting I was a whore. No matter how good I was, or how hard I worked or what I turned my hand to do for extra money, I was supposedly always out looking for a man. He was just like Aaron. And I never did find that "mail-order" man in the mailbox, either!

Proverbs 20:19 A short tempered man must bear his own penalty; you can't do much to help him. If you try once, you must try a dozen times! (The Living Bible - Paraphrase)

Chapter 21

Clean until you sneeze,
Dust, and make it all right,
Don't expect any thanks,
Being Cinderella isn't awesome,
Hidden in the corner,
Sitting on a toadstool,
Gets you nowhere,
Finding hope in the bareness,
Tis' a pipe dream, no substance,
All is smoke and mirrors!

Noel's forty acre property was neglected for years. He was too lazy to keep the brush cleaned off it and the fences repaired. I began work on the house and property in 1972 and finished it by 1985. After remodeling the house, I had a small barn built and a hayshed. I mended the fences, piling and burning the brush. People often stopped by to tell Noel how nice the property was looking as if 'he' was cleaning it up. He thought it was funny he was getting the praise. I was doing the backbreaking work, but it was my dearest wish to have a lovely safe place to live, enjoy, and raise the children so I didn't mind.

There were several old junked cars and tractors sitting on the property near the house and the pile was an embarrassment to me. The overgrowth and briar patch were an eyesore and a snake pit. Noel kept imagining he was going to fix them up and sell them for big bucks. I offered to help him 'part them out for sale.' I told him I was going to sell them; he pitched a fit, but went to the VA hospital with a *mad nervous spell*. I called up a local junkyard man who paid $350 per vehicle. I made enough to fund the building of two porches onto the house, a barn and sheds. He never forgot or forgave me getting rid of his *expensive* cars.

The place was looking wonderful so I developed a second garden patch where the old cars had sat. I bought a donkey to break and plow the garden. The children loved old Kate. She was patient with the children, but if I wanted to plow her, I had to ride her three miles. Sometimes, Noel would do this, but by the time he got back to the house, he was just too sick to help me work in the garden. I didn't care; I was strong, young, with two children and him to feed. I hooked her up to the plow and my garden flourished. I raised a big garden, canned and kept the house nice. I could put one of the children on to ride her holding on to the harness hames. Old Kate would let one ride her and the other one lead her through the garden rows as I plowed – the children loved it. At least I didn't have to pull the plow as I did as a youngster. I was actually thankful I knew how to plow the garden and had a good donkey to work. My children never had to work as I did. I wouldn't allow it. I wanted them to have the freedom to be children.

There were so many things I thought were much better than when I was at home with Betty and Aaron. I convinced myself things were really far better for me in being married. I was an idealistic idiot and a fool. Ignorance was not wedded bliss. The fact I was having legal sex and married only complicated the problem of what was being done to me under the sanctification of marriage.

I was blinded by the years of abuse and Noel's mental and sexual abuse of my children. When Noel's sexual abuse of them started, I don't know, but I suspect it was very early on in their little lives. I tried to hide his abuse of me from them, but my tears and fears affected them, I am sure.

I was becoming well-known as a minister in the area

Holiness and Pentecostal Church of God churches in Pope and Johnson County. I was invited to preach services within a hundred mile radius. I preached often for the Assemblies of God and held revival meetings in both churches. I tried to keep my sermons honest, honor God and be who I said I was. Noel wouldn't go with me much, but the children and I went. The children enjoyed the attention of being the visiting preacher's children. They got a lot of positive attention as well as I. It was a good spiritual time for me, growing in the grace of God.

Noel just wasn't strong enough to stay away from his family who were manipulative mean snakes. I'd hoped when I broke away from my parents in 1979, he might see my strength and do the same. His family didn't want him to have anything nice. He'd lived like an animal and made his first wife and children live in dirty, nasty conditions. I had grown up in poverty, but I refused to live like that again. I'd had a bit of sense before I married him insisting we would live in a clean, nice place. He had agreed. I held him to his promise, but I made a huge mistake. I told him if he ever beat me and people noticed, I was gone. I didn't understand what I'd set in motion until the 'silent battering began.' He solemnly swore he would provide plenty of water and wood for me to use. I didn't know it would be water in my eyes and wood on my back. I was in a no-man's land with no place to run or hide.

Apple pie and grandma! Old maid flowers, zinnia's waving in the wind! Tree frogs chirping in the gliding evening darkness. Sitting on the porch listening to the crickets is something that weaves through my memories. Cinnamon smells of yesterday and the gentleness of grandma's love!

Chapter 22

Hiding, hiding, hidden deep,
Scratch that dirt, build a roadway!
Problems that don't run,
They stay, or move with you,
Run, girl, run, hide far away,
Catchy, catchy, goes 'The Man'.
He is hiding; you just can't see his face,
You have to see under the mask.
He is a divided man, one of many,
Walking cat-paw quiet,
He is a fouler and a liar,
A puzzle of pieces,
None fit together,
Run girl, run,
You never will detect his sins!

1985-1986 Texas

While we were in the process of trying to sell the farm, Noel drank some Purex mixed with water I had sitting in a gallon jug to disinfect it. He knew I disinfected all our pots, dishes, and water jugs with Purex. I used the disinfected jugs to hold my distilled water. I had to use water from an open well, which was a few feet from a stock pond for our drinking water. The pond water leached directly into the well producing dangerous drinking water. I took special care of the water, distilling it to kill the bacteria. We lived as if we were a third world country. Oh my, one would have thought I'd planned to murder Noel. He puked, screamed and threw a hissy-fit. I called the Poison Control Center. They told me if he had vomited, he should be just fine. While I was on the phone party line, a neighbor heard me telling the Poison Control Center what had happened. She immediately called Noel's family in California, informing them I had just poisoned Noel. They just knew I was a murderess in the wings waiting to kill Noel. The Sheriff called me because he had gotten accusatory calls from Noel's sisters stating I was trying to murder Noel. I explained what happened and told him he was welcome to come on out and check out what I was doing. He knew Noel – and me. He told me he would call Noel's sisters back and tell them things were fine.

Noel was a grown man and could smell the strong Purex water. His family used this incident to drive another nail into my marriage coffin. I never knew if he actually drank any of the Purex water or not, but I gave him strong soapy water to drink and he did vomit. I drove him to the hospital and the doctors doubted he'd suffered any harm. They couldn't even find any Purex residue in his vomit; I'd had sense enough to save his vomit.

I had to use the well water for our laundry and to bathe the children and myself. We had no other source of water. I had a wringer washer and a double set of rinse tubs. I hauled the water up to the back yard each week to do the wash. At least I had a way to haul the water rather than having to hand carry it as I did as a child at Mam and Pap's. I had four ten-gallon milk cans to fill up with water and haul to the house in the back of our car. I felt I was very modern with my washer and tubs. I air-dried the clothes on lines strung between two sets of trees.

The real estate market was very depressed and we lived a long ways from town making it harder to sell our property. It took us five years to sell our forty-acre farm in Lutherville. We moved to Texas in the spring of 1985. Noel apparently didn't mind the move to Texas because my sister needed me.

My sister had married a man from Kingston after he

returned from Vietnam. They could find no compatibility for a stable marriage. She divorced him three years later. Her second husband, Charles 'Bud' Hansell was very good to her. He died after two and a half years of marriage and left her with a baby son to rear alone.

My sister became suicidal after losing Bud, the love of her life. She desperately needed family close so I told her I would come if the farm sold. It did. I convinced Noel I could buy a house there, fix it up and sell it in the Texas market. Then we then could go on to Idaho after a few months. I had tuberculosis and was on INH medication and Vitamin D for a year. I thought I'd picked up the bug when I worked for the Health Department in Madison County while in college.

After moving to Carthage, I continued the TB treatment in Tyler at the Texas Tuberculosis Hospital until I completed the prescribed course of action. I had to coordinate with the local Texas Health Department. The year's treatment took a toll on my health.

When Noel found out about my TB test and subsequent x-rays, he immediately began coughing and spitting as if he had TB too. He did this for the next six years even though his skin test was negative. He would cough, spit in his hands and rub his spit on the outside of his clothing. By night, his clothing would be slick with his spit. He alleged I gave him TB. He punished me by holding me and rubbing his nasty spit all over me. It was extremely difficult to live in such a bondage relationship, but I believed the VA doctors about mental illness diagnosis. I felt it my duty to care for him.

Noel kept demanding more children, come hell or high water, with no consideration for my health. He understood the risk I would be taking if I became pregnant. I found myself in a loveless marriage, a receptacle of punishment rather than a cherished wife. He abandoned what could have been a marriage of precious friendship for each of us.

I tried conflict resolution, he laughed. I begged, he snorted. His emotional put- downs and abuse were soul poison. He began a campaign to convince me I was crazy and I was the one imagining things. When he got mad and began shoving, pushing and hitting me beneath my clothing, he would tell me if I would just get it right, he wouldn't need to punish me – but punish me he did. He insisted I asked for trouble and said, "If you would just do as I say, things would be just right." I was the cause of him getting angry. I deserved to be slapped because he was sure better to me than my parents. The food was never good enough, although he sure did love eating my cooking. His emotions would yo-yo back and forth. I never knew what angered him, and if I thought I had it figured out, I would try what had worked the day before or maybe even an hour before. It was always the wrong thing. Somehow Noel evaded the *Honeymoon Cycle* in his abusive behavior and his madness would start all over again in a day or so manifesting itself in bizarre ways I couldn't predict.

We finally sold the farm and purchased a 2 bedroom, 1 1/2 bath home in Carthage, Texas with a garage and carport. I started the remodeling job immediately. I turned the garage into a master suite and turned the half bath into a full bath. It turned out beautifully. This was my third remodel. I had remodeled the Dover apartment for part of the rent. I had rebuilt the old farmhouse. I loved remodeling and making things beautiful and I found I was good at fixing what other people misused. It was a shame that I couldn't fix my marriage.

The children loved the Carthage School District. I'd have liked to stay there, but my husband became fixated on my sister. He would turn up at her home, telling her he wanted to 'comfort' her and make her feel better. He told her that she could turn to him since her husband was dead. He assured her how happy he would be to give her solace.

He even hinted at giving her another baby. He wanted her to know he was available. He frightened her. I was petrified, but what was I going to do?

I shared with my sister how Noel was raping me. I didn't know how to stop him. I put the house up for sale and left. My sister didn't need me adding to her burden in life. I still believe Noel raped my sister's little boy who was two and a half years old. He came very close to harming my sister. She became very afraid of him and his sexual talk. Noel would get a smarmy look on his face, hitch up his right knee and get as close to her as he could. He tried to convince her to let him get his hands on her, *wink, wink*. It made her sick to her stomach. I was her sister. We made excuses for him because of his mental illness. We shouldn't have, but ignorance is not hindsight.

My sister often told me that we had a good relationship even though our parents tried to teach her to hate me. She stated, "We are like an old patchwork quilt with a lot of torn patches, but put together and held by patches of love." Our sisterly relationship has flowered and grown over the years into a steadfast loving Godly bond.

I found when there is no love in a marriage, it begins to die and no amount of resuscitation can prevent its death. I knew I was trapped by my love for my children and my health. There was nothing normal about my marriage. Reality is a hard blow. I had no idea what normal healthy family parameters were supposed to be.

Black and blue

Life sure hasn't been what I dreamt,
I spent years beaten black and blue
With no thought of fate to tempt,
I have to myself remain true.

Oh, he swore to love me truly,
With cotton candy and desire
He wooed me carefully,
Now I am stuck in muck and mire.

Chastity was my salvation,
Innocence my middle name.
When I tempted fate's revelation,
I faced black and blue just the same.

Surely if I was only true,
Loving him forever,
He would see my worth,
And love me always and ever.

I wept bitter tears of redemption,
Settling my mind on angel wings,
I forgot my place and gave into temptation
Fighting back let me learn to sing!

He is now six feet under,
He's turning up daisies as I turn up hope,
I no longer linger in black and blue,
I do not hear the voice of *Thunder.*

Power driven by black and blue,
Lazy days envelop me
As I am true to myself,
I have healed, tears remain just a few.

I watch the stars above,
Sharing in the sun's intensity,
Staring at the past, I give it a shove,
Life is my whim, as I live comprehensively.

Chapter 23

Ah, the hallow halls of renewal,
Starting over, grabbing at pipe dreams,
Lightning strikes of anger,
Burning holes of despair,
Impaired, deceitful lies,
Stretching to the breaking,
Like straws in the wind,
Tossed by adversity,
Glued by hate,
Abnormal,
Rotten to the center of existence
Vanity, all is vanity,
Build on lies,
Covered with terror,
'The Man' has arisen!

1986-1987 Payette, Idaho

Idaho's desert air was a boon for my recovery from TB. I continued taking tetracycline for two years to eradicate its effects. The children liked their new school and were involved in the community youth league baseball program. My son was in heaven; he began to make new friends and was accepted at school. I was able to go to all the games and helped coach.

I took the children camping at every opportunity I could find. Idaho is a haven of campgrounds, fishing, and the beauty of this wonderfully natural state is ideal for families. Trout fishing became a favorite of my son and me. Occasionally, Noel would go fishing with us, but his meanness was getting worse. He always ruined the day. For more than three fourths of our marriage I can't remember one single day he made things happy and fun. I began living in state parks during the summer to get away from him. The children and I hiked, fished and lived very well in a small trailer or in a tent. We could bathe in the creek or lake; sometimes the campgrounds had bathing facilities. It was a wonderful time taking my children and teaching them the things I had learned growing up in the woods of Arkansas. They often took a friend along and we had a normal life as long as we weren't at home with Noel.

Noel insisted I buy the second trailer and leave it at the house. I didn't know his plans for it. He had his Boar's Den. He was furious when I remodeled and sold it. Why couldn't I have seen the symptoms of his evil? Hindsight is the window of failed opportunities misread and misunderstood; and the barbwire of guilt.

By the fall of 1986, Noel's violence toward me was increasing. He was trying to get me pregnant again. I was forty years old and just recovering from TB. A local doctor told him it would be a death sentence for me to become pregnant again and to make sure we used birth control.

That doctor's statement was a sign to Noel I was to become pregnant again. I realized he thought I would die if he impregnated me. The force of his determination swiped away my dignity and left my safety in question.

Noel wasn't about to relinquish his control. He didn't want a mutually satisfying relationship with me and didn't want to be a father. There was no equality of rightness in our marriage. He never exercised the proper responsibility for correct and manly authority with our children. His violence continued unabated, but he did understand the difference.

The Boise Veterans Administration Hospital doctors began covering up his abuse; there was not a way to counteract what he was doing to the children and me. I had no one to turn to. My pastor, Rev. James Hicks of the Fruitland, Idaho Assemblies of God Church began to encounter the real Noel. He tried to reason with Noel, but Noel used the pastor's reasoning with him to punish me further.

After forcibly removing my diaphragm, Noel held me down and raped me repeatedly. I became pregnant in December 1986. When Noel found out I was with child, he planted his feet in the middle of my back and kicked me out of our bed. He stated the baby was not his. He had raped me repeatedly for the past several months to make sure I got pregnant and now the baby wasn't his? His attacks continued all during the pregnancy making it one of horror instead of joy. His paternal denial of the baby was painful, but I shared his disclaimer with my doctor. I had two other children to consider.

Noel went to my family doctor demanding I get an abortion. I refused. I was not going to kill this baby even if I died trying to have this precious soul – I made arrangements for the children if I died. I began to walk, walk, and walk some more. I had not wanted another baby, but I prayed until love for this new baby flooded my soul. Noel decided we would adopt the baby out – it seemed he spent years fostering ideas of how to rid us of our children.

 He wanted to sell it in Mexico - I refused. All through the pregnancy, Noel tried to force me to abort the baby by his ghastly physical abuse. I only gained four pounds. For the last two and a half months of the pregnancy, I was dilated 2.5 cm. The doctor constantly worried about the health of the baby. Many people in my church prayed mightily for my safety and the growing baby.

During the pregnancy, Noel refused to buy or cut wood to keep the house warm for the children and me. Pastor James Hicks came and cut wood for us. He got pneumonia and almost died from helping us. He told Noel he was one of the sorriest men he ever knew and did not deserve his family or wife. He was the only man who tried to intervene for us or who stood up to Noel. Pastor James Hicks was a former boxer and a true man of God.

With a man as weak as Noel, having an unlimited ego and thirsting for control, there was not much lightness in our home. Noel was a toad, and no amount of kissing was going to turn him into a prince!

Pastor Hicks asked me to preach a revival for his church when I was six months pregnant and the church responded mightily. Fruitland Hiway Assembly of God was a wonderful church with lots of good people. The revival was uplifting and I saw God bless and do many wondrous things. I quit the Pentecostal Church of God in January 1989 and joined Hiway Assembly of God until I left it in the fall of 1990.

Because Pastor James Hicks believed in the children and me, I gained inner strength through him and his wife Phyllis' gentle loving ministry. Pastor Hicks, as well as the church people, was supportive of me all through the pregnancy. I began to see there were some good men in the world who were caring and kind. The children adored Pastor Hicks. He was a good man. He just didn't know, like me, the extent of Noel's evilness.

After a long and difficult pregnancy, my baby finally arrived after induced labor. I believe the prayers of my church assured my pregnancy was successful. Several of the church people were at the hospital praying while the baby was being born. Noel had bragged he was going to tell the doctor the baby wasn't his. I had told the doctor of his intent. Once the baby arrived, my doctor looked at Noel and said, "Mr. Snow, I understand you have something you want to say to me. Come on, if you have something to say, now is the time to speak up. You have just been given a beautiful baby girl?" Noel hang his head and didn't say a word. He could deny the baby was his as he did with the other two, but it didn't matter, I knew. Noel was a coward, all brag and no bottom!

The doctor insisted Noel attend in the delivery room as the baby was born. When she was born, Noel leaned over me sarcastically stating, "And I suppose you will claim this child is going to be your greatest blessing!" I smiled gently in his face above my baby's head, "Yes, Noel, this baby is from God, I will cherish her. I want her and she will bless me every day of my life." And she has.

When we were asked to fill out the hospital papers naming the baby for her birth certificate, Noel refused stating to the hospital official, "The baby's name is 'Nothing.' You do understand I am naming this baby 'Nothing'?" I waited until he left the hospital and called the hospital administrator to come to my room. I insisted *Nothing* would not be a name for this baby. I forced them to put the name I had chosen on the birth certificate. Noel pitched a fit, but my baby had a beautiful name.

She came with double pneumonia and was hospitalized for seven days. She almost didn't survive. I went to the hospital to nurse her night and day. Noel didn't make any effort to help care for her. Noel's abuse had almost cost my baby her life. She was my spitting image. She is beautiful, loving and my final joyful child.

Life riding sidesaddle can twist up time. Choices sometimes don't come naturally. We have to work at forming good habits. My hardest habit learned was trusting in God's faithfulness, but he proved himself to me in the darkness of the pain. I have never forget his goodness and mercy as they have followed me through life.

Chapter 24

Dancing shadows in the hallow halls of the church,
Those unseen evils that bedevil the saints of God,
Unseen shadow men, living as one,
Like shackling sins dancing in the flames of Hell!

Chained souls of the past dragging into the future,
Souls demeaned, chastised,
made partakers of hidden wrongs,
Cover-up, spittle of the damned.

Shadow men have followed
across the chasm of spiritual barriers,
Grasping, greedy men doing the dance of death,
Lost in the silhouette of mind games,
All done in the name of righteousness,
But was in the pattern of centuries old greed.

Spiritual incest, against the holy nature of God!
The young are thrown off the precipice's ramparts,
Sacrificed on the altar of malice,
The shadow man has come…

1988

A call came for me to preach a revival at Baker City,
Oregon, for Pastor Ira Buttram at Victory Tabernacle
Pentecostal Church of God. Buttram personally owned the
facilities. As the pastor, he'd heard about the revival I'd
preached for Hiway Assembly of God Church in Fruitland,
Idaho, and the great spiritual results. He was a man who
wanted to touch the magic of others' delight in God. He
scheduled a time for me to come to his church. I agreed to

go so I packed up the small travel trailer with the children and off I headed for six days of preaching God's word. I was excited. It would be nice to have a fun-filled week doing what I did best, preaching - and away from Noel!

The word had spread as I was the new Arkansas "hillbilly preacher" to the district. I was seeing good things happening in my gospel meetings.

On June 14, 1988, the revival opened with plenty of Pentecostal fervor and excitement. There was a giddy feeling reflected in the faces of the saints and the Spirit of God was mightily present. Word had preceded my coming and the church was filled to capacity each night. There was lots of gospel singing and fervent testimonies.

Wednesday saw five soul seekers come forward to acknowledge their acceptance of Jesus into their hearts. Everyone was looking forward to Thursday night with holy zeal. I was preaching my best; the children were being well-behaved and participating in the services as only children can. The baby won everyone's hearts.

That night three young girls came forward, whispering in my ear during the altar service that they were being hurt. I thought, "Hurt? What does that mean?" I asked them if they wanted to talk in the vestibule of the church. They nodded their heads, "Yes." I walked with them there and shut the door to the sanctuary so we could have some privacy.

I asked quietly, "What is happening to you and how are you being hurt?" To my surprise, all three began to cry stating, "We're scared and our lives might be in danger. We are being raped." I wondered what I had walked into. They refused to tell me anymore, but the next night I got them to talk.

As I was legally mandated, I called Health and Welfare to report what the girls had told me after the service. They asked me to get the girls to confide who was doing this crime and get a name. I went back the next night preaching with vim and vigor in this situation. It was draining, but I knew God was with me. I had to have courage and help these innocent children as no one had helped me, but I could make a difference for these three.

Again, the girls came up front asking to speak with me so I walked with them out to the foyer. I told them right up front I'd called Health and Welfare. I needed them to trust me. I asked them to tell me the truth about what was happening to them if they wanted help. They all three said. "Okay." I sat them down and asked, "Who wants to go first?"

The larger girl, said, "Grandpa is raping us." "Who is Grandpa and how long has this being going on?" I asked them. Each one of them indicated Grandpa had been hurting each of them for several years. They were still hesitant to trust me. I had prayer with each of them asking the grace of God to see us through this situation. Their fear was palpable.

They still refused to name or show me who Grandpa was. I was drained. Their fear led me to believe this went deeper than I first thought. I was committed to helping them find a way to name their perpetrator.

The next day, I sponsored the church kids going to the Sumpter Valley Railway to ride the train and go to the wonderful western museum there. We took our picnic lunch out to Phillips Lake. I did get permission from the pastor to have a *rap session* with all of the young people of the church while on this trip. I talked in a language they all could understand about sexual issues and wrong touching. I told them it wasn't God's will for anyone to touch their bodies in a wrong way whether it was with their permission or against their will at their young age. Their bodies were their own. I encouraged them to find the courage to speak with me about any wrong touching of them.

Out of this session, some adult women came to me privately, confiding someone in their lives had raped them.

It was a shocker to find as many had been abused as I had. I spent time at the church just having a talk session with all of the women, and they were all shocked to learn so many of their fellow women had also been raped. They were not alone. Nine-tenths of the group of women had been raped, battered and abused at some point in their lives. I realized these adults were living the same life as me. Some were living in present battering relationships. The Pastor's wife shared with me that her husband was battering her! Later, she confided to me that he had molested one of their children. I now knew why he didn't want me to pursue finding out who Grandpa was in the church.

Who was Grandpa and what could I do? It took me until Sunday to get a name out of the girls. I asked them to point out Grandpa to me through the small window in the foyer door. The man they pointed out to me was up on the platform leading the congregation in rousing Holy Ghost singing, Pentecostal style!

I was shocked, needless to say, because Joseph Daniel Baker was the head deacon of the church! Sexual abuse and domestic violence know no social/economic barriers and often leading men in the community are committing some form of sexual violence. They told me that they had been reporting his crime to every Pentecostal Church of God preacher coming through the door for the past year and a half. These young women had been begging for help from the violence committed against them. No one had helped them, but had engaged in a cover-up of this man's crime, telling the girls they were acting out sexually and enticing their Grandpa to rape them.

I now had a name to go with the rape charges, so I called Health and Welfare again, as well as the Baker Police Department. I wound up calling the State Police and the Sheriff's Department also.

Again, I told the girls I was a mandatory reporter and I would have to stand by my word to them and report their rape to authorities. I let them know I had already spoken to authorities at Health and Welfare.

I went to Pastor Ira Buttram's home and asked him to help me with the situation. He refused. His reasoning was, "Joe Baker pays more than $700 a month in tithes" and was his main support in the church. He certainly was not going to ruin a 'pot of gold' for a bunch of silly girls who were enticing their Grandpa to sin. I was stunned, angry, shamed and horrified at his response. Buttram was the Southern Idaho Pentecostal Church of God Presbyter and my immediate supervisor in the church. What bothered me even more was I had been going to Joe Baker's home to bathe the children and myself during the revival and every time I came to shower, he headed upstairs. Did he have a peephole in the floor of his upstairs to watch the children and me? I shivered in dread at what might have been going on!

I called the Drain, Oregon Headquarters of the Pentecostal Church of God and reported the crime. They didn't want to get involved. I relayed the Pastor's failure to report the crime to law enforcement and the names of every preacher who had preached revival at Baker City for more than eighteen months. The District had known about the crime, and about all the other preachers the girls had tried to get to help them. The church officials did nothing! I reported the crime to the National Headquarters of the Pentecostal Church of God in Joplin, Missouri. They refused to offer any help! Oregon State Trooper David Polentier of the Oregon State Police became involved and was a tremendous encouragement to me in trying to help the girls. He believed in their story and fought to get Joe Baker behind bars.

The church held a large potluck meal for me and the children on Sunday. I almost gagged at having to eat lunch with a rapist in our midst, but I ate and smiled often. I was totally stressed, but I was determined to do what I had been asked to do. I preached that night and spent the rest of the night on the phone with various agencies reporting the crimes and trying to get help. Drain Oregon Pentecostal Church of God headquarters denied any responsibility to help the girls in the Baker City Church.

I was exhausted having gotten little sleep in the past 72 hours. I was worried about our safety in driving the children home alone.

I had an eye doctor appointment on June 20 in Ontario, Oregon. I closed out the revival and headed toward home with my pickup and trailer. The children slept most of the way. They were unaware of what was happening, but the drive seemed endless to me. I was shocked because my church superiors were refusing to help stop a rapist!

I reached the doctor's office physically exhausted, in spiritual despair and disoriented by how the church was handling this situation. I went into the doctor's office, and as I entered the examination room and started to sit down, I told them, "I am going to be sick to my stomach and I am feeling funny." I passed out in the examination chair and was rushed to the hospital by the eye doctor. The hospital stabilized me, gave me something to eat and sent me home. I'd had a low blood sugar attack brought on by the stress of affairs in the Baker City Church. It was a moment of griping reality. I was all alone in this mess.

I spent long hours counseling Norma Hall, the mother of two of the girls and the aunt of the other young woman. I urged her to cooperate with law enforcement and to file charges against her father on behalf of the girls. Joe Baker was arrested during the early hours on Wednesday June 21, 1988. I spent much of the night encouraging Ms. Hall to follow through helping her family, which, like mine, was full of incest. I found out her niece's father had raped one of her older sisters. Due to the lack of help from the pastor, the Oregon Baker City Church was known amongst local

law enforcement circles as *The Church of Incest* and Mr.
Baker's wife as *'the Procuress.'*

On that Friday, June 23, 1988, I spoke with the Baker
City District Attorney and the Health and Welfare officer.
They believed Joe Baker was guilty of the crimes and the
police had a confession.

The city police screwed up the case even more. They
had a signed confession out of Joe Baker upon his arrest.
The police were delivering the signed confession to the
District Prosecuting Attorney across the street and into the
courthouse, but they dropped Joe Baker's full confession
"accidentally" in a city sewer drain. The Drain
Headquarters of the Pentecostal Church of God spouted
that this was the hand of God at work on Mr. Baker's
behalf. "Whoops," suddenly law enforcement didn't have
his written confession anymore so they couldn't file
charges against him for all the children he had assaulted. It
was a farcical situation except no one was laughing.

Saturday night, June 24, 1988, chaos broke out on our
street in Payette, Idaho. A black pickup fitting the
description of Joe Baker's sped through our neighborhood,
slamming up onto our driveway. Police swarmed our yard,
running in all directions chasing the suspect. They thought
it was Joe Baker coming after my family and me. I was
scared to death, huddling in the hallway with the children.
Noel went crazy, shouting and screaming curses at me for
getting involved, "How dare you do this! Now look what is
happening because of you, you stupid idiot, you have
brought this shit to our home." The police came inside our
home cautioning us to stay away from the windows. One
of the policemen slipped inside and stayed near the front
door just in case.

My children slipped around and peeked out the back
window of the kitchen whispering to me that they saw a
man in the woodpile. The police checked and didn't find

anyone, but the suspect had clothes lined himself and crawled up into a hole in the woodpile. He had pulled the wood in after himself, thus hiding effectively.

The children found the suspect's glasses the next day. The police finally caught up with the man. The driver was not Joe Baker, but someone else out of Oregon on the run from law enforcement. The man just happened to choose our driveway to dump his truck and run from the police. The man fled on foot as the police were closing in on him.

I called the officials at the Drain District Headquarters reporting to them what was happening with the Joe Baker case. I was told to not get involved or to cooperate in any way to help the girls. Noel ranted and raved at me, delighting in pointing out I was such a loser.

I asked for a church tribunal to be formed to see if I could get Ira Buttram kicked out of the Pentecostal Church of God in Fruitland, Idaho. A forum met, but came with made-up minds to keep Ira Buttram. I was ordered to keep my mouth shut or they would pursue legal recourse against me. I was stunned and furious. I was a woman and expendable to the hierarchy of the Pentecostal Church of God. I was to keep 'my place' and not make waves to help innocent girls. Joe Baker paid large amounts of money into the church coffers and I had very little to offer them except my talent as a minister.

1989

I am not a person to hide the truth. In good conscience, I could not keep quiet over the Pentecostal Church of God ordering a cover-up in the church about Joe Baker's sexual abuse. I kept fighting for the girls for the next six years. In public, Noel was the loudest proponent of getting Mr. Baker arrested and made to pay the price, but at home I was his number one loser. I learned religious perverts declare their innocence by demanding retribution for the same acts they are committing.

Noel was so indignant about Mr. Baker getting away with molesting so many of his family. He encouraged his murder.

On January 6, 1989, I resigned as a minister of the Pentecostal Church of God. Following are excerpts from that resignation letter:

Dear Members of the Board,
Drain, Oregon:

This is to notify you that on receipt of this letter that I am tendering my resignation from the Pentecostal Church of God effective on the above date. I cannot be a part of a church that has allowed sin to remain in its ranks. My conscience dictates that I must obey God's law first and the church's in this matter.

1. My resignation is in protest of this body allowing a rapist...to remain in the Baker City, Oregon PC of G.

2. I resign in protest of the boards handling of this matter...and ordering me to keep my mouth shut about this rapist.

3. I resign in protest that in allowing this type of sin to remain within the body, you have allowed Satan to cross the threshold and therefore, this whole church will suffer nationwide and in the future you will deal with God's wrath that you did not have the courage to do so now.

4. When there is no internal control such as is within the PC of G, you will begin to reap a whirlwind that you will not be able to contain the scandals that God will expose if you as Men of the Church are too weak to face now. I truly fear the wrath of God that is to come upon men and women who are refusing to stand on the word of God and condemn sin.

5. Incest, rape...will rise up to haunt you and Satan realizes that the church is too weak internally to control this

horrendous sin. Either you, as a body, will stand against these horrible sins or you will have opened a Pandora's Box, which will destroy from within. I, as a minister, refuse to barter with the devil on any issue of deviant sexual sins such as these...

6. I resign in protest against the pastor of the Baker City, Oregon PC of G. God is against this kind of sin being in the church. He, in essence, has fully condoned the sins committed against these innocent eleven sixteen and seventeen year old girls and so has the Board. May God have mercy on us all, if it becomes commonplace to accept rape, incest and think its fine in a marriage for a man to whip or slap around the wife. This mess, as you can fully see, has sickened my soul until I want to vomit thinking of the attitude of this board.

7. I feel I was plainly told to keep my mouth shut, ignore these things. You ought to be ashamed to bring this kind of mess to our attention. You have allowed my reputation to be destroyed in this area freely and yet were angry by my asking for outside help...I'm hurt to my soul but not a bit destroyed because when a door is shut, God opens others.

May God have mercy on all of us in these days...it has become easy to compromise rather than stand up and do face-to-face battle with the Devil -- compromise will not do! You have allowed yourselves to be held hostage by a few pastors threatening to withdraw from the church and others nationwide, now Satan.

Sincerely,

Joe Baker was arrested and charged with incest after six years for his rape of his daughter, Norma Hall and convicted in a Multnomah County, Oregon courtroom. The Oregon Supreme Court then threw out the case because they opined his daughter had been one day late in filing the charges. Oregon State Police Law Enforcement believed that Mr. Baker molested most of his 34 grandchildren and other family members.

Norma, his daughter, told me that she wanted to know where God was when she was being raped. I could only tell her God was holding her in his arms, begging Joe Baker not to do the sinful act.

She filed a lawsuit in Idaho against her father in civil court and won a settlement against him. Joe Baker fled Idaho to Missouri. He was arrested for what he did to the girls in Idaho, but they were too ensconced in the family cover-up and too scared; and in the end, refused to testify against the patriarch of their family.

His daughter had one wish to know if God still cared for her: let her father die of some horrible penile disease. He died of prostate cancer a few short years later. She felt God had heard her cries of desperation in her violation. She was able to move on with her life and, I believe, found some measure of peace for losing her 'knight in shining armor'.

The *Nampa Idaho-Press Tribune* reported Joe Baker was arrested in Warsaw, Missouri where he had fled trying to escape sex abuse charges brought against him in Idaho. He was charged with one count of first-degree sodomy, two counts of second-degree sodomy, one account of third-degree sodomy, one count of first-degree sexual abuse, six counts of second-degree sexual abuse, five counts of using a child in a display of sexually explicit conduct and seven counts of incest. He was jailed in lieu of $100,000 bail. The *Baker City Herald* reported Joe Baker was arrested in Baker City in Baker County on charges that allegedly took place from 1984-1990 when the female victim was age 12 to 16. Detective Kent Heady of the Canyon County Sheriff's Department and David Polentier of the Baker County Oregon State Police were instrumental in bringing

Mr. Baker in to face charges.

My friend's son, Charles Fenwick, had not escaped his grandfather's predatory actions which were to have grave implications later.

I would later learn that my son's molestation by Noel started after the Baker City case. Noel used the excuse if Joe Baker could get away with the rape of his family, so could he. Noel's heroes were evil men who participated in dastardly deeds. Noel was the Bluebeard of our souls - the man who stalked our nightmares tying a knot in our psyche and binding us in chains of silence. Our destinies were not attached to the stars, but in the flames of living Hell fed by Noel's perversions.

Noel spent days mocking me because I did not get Joe Baker in prison, but I know I did my very best to fight with what I had. Noel created a nightmare in my fighting for those children, but I did not understand why at the time.

I pushed my body into a state of exhaustion trying to take care of my children and help the Baker City, Oregon victims. The stress landed me in the hospital in May 1989 with double pneumonia. I was put on antibiotics and oxygen. During the second day of the hospitalization, I slipped away to God. The doctor told me I didn't fight or give any indication that I was going to die. I just died. I was floating above my body watching the doctors work on me, trying to revive me. They used the heart defibrillator trying to bring me back, nothing worked.

Suddenly I was drawn through a dark place and into sudden light. I was in the presence of Jesus. I was standing on a magnificent grassy hill with Jesus, looking toward the beauty of the Holy City of God. I could see back across the great dark divide between heaven and earth. There stood Noel holding my baby encircled in darkness. She was crying and screaming, "Mommy,

Mommy, come back, please." I could see the tears running down her two-and-a-half year old face. She was frantic, stretching her baby hands for me to take her. My husband had a dark countenance, smirking meanly, he was laughing, mocking, hugging her close to him and appeared to be happy I was gone.

Jesus took my hand, and led me forward, closer to God. There was light everywhere and the most beautiful city I had ever seen lay directly below me. "My child, you can choose to stay here. You can stay, or you can choose to go back to your daughter. If you choose to go back, you can go back, but you will never have another choice about dying. Next time, when you die, you will come here permanently. I looked with yearning toward the place I knew my grandparents were waiting with God for me. I looked back at my baby knowing she needed me, but I didn't understand why she had such desperation on her face. I thought at least she has her father, but the fear on her face drew me steadily to her.

I took Jesus' hand with regret and asked to return to my physical body. Just like that, I was back in my body!

The doctor later told me a bright light lit up the room at my re-entry. They were in the process of declaring my death when I came back. What I saw in heaven carries me on days I cannot find a hiding place to keep the pain inside. The doctor called me to his office wanting to know what I had seen. He said I had died without a struggle and he knew I had gone to heaven. He was impressed how God had given me back my life. He had many questions to ask about what I had seen, who, and where I had gone after dying.

For months, I mourned my return from Jesus. Noel was violently angry at my testimony of returning from death. He punished me in ways that are too horrific to put to paper. Finally, when I found out about what was happening with my children, I understood the look of terror on my baby's face, and the smirk on my husband's. I am thankful God gave me grace and allowed me to come back for my children. I do look with longing to return to God, knowing heaven is a wonderful place awaiting me if I am faithful to Him.

Noel continually mocked me about coming back from the dead long after my recovery. He would bring my story up in front of strangers, and then laugh hysterically about how I believed Jesus had returned me to life. He used this as 'proof' to his VA doctors that I was delusional. He resented my return as if I was tainted. His sexual abuse became almost more than I could survive. He reminded me only he had the power of life and death over me – not God. I had to wonder when he thought he had taken that power over me!

The intimacy of marriage is a scacred bond between two people. A harmonious loving relationship of natural matrimonial desires is wonderful. I had so desired to have a healthy sexual wholeness with the man I married. Instead, I faced the sickening facts I was married to a sexual fiend and pervert. Unfortunately, there are no words to express the depravity that happened in my children's lives because of my mistakes, blindness and ignorance. I spent twenty years in a blasphemous marriage. The sanity of that holy bond was corrupted by Noel's demonic nosedive into the gully of evil. Noel was a blister-blight on the landscape of my conscience and I had to learn to dig him out one day at a time.

It seemed my horror would know no end as I didn't know or suspect that Noel was victimizing my children. They were afraid and couldn't find the words or trust to be able to tell me of their father's duplicity. Children believe parents are all-knowing and all-seeing, and when they are failed, they have a righteous cause in feeling their intense betrayal. The perfidy and deceitful incestuous actions of their father and his treachery devastated me. It was, and still is, a soul stain that can't be wiped away. The tarnish of incest is a soul cancer that gnaws away at the very foundation of one's life. After twenty-four and one-half years, the mark of Noel's evil still haunts my nightmares.

Out of all of this, I have become an advocate for rape victims. I have sought soul redemption by offering counseling to many in my community who are in abusive situations. I have put my education and God-calling into action for the disenfranchised of society's sexually violated. I labor for those living in ignorance, preaching and trying to be an example for the communities where I live. There is no bliss in ignorance; there is only responsibility to make things right in the staggering aftermath of sinful choices.

As of June 2015, I have been in the ministry for fifty-two years – I have endured. I have come so far in so many different ways. I took the ashes of my terrible life and turned it around. I have created a new life for myself in all that I do, I love. I have taken the years of heartbreak and used all the terror, all the pain and rebuilt myself into whom I am today. The pilings and brokenness of the past are the building stones I use for the future. I have built a 'strong house' with God's help. I have never been alone in my journey; He has been through it all with me. I never lost the peace I felt on that heavenly hilltop with Jesus in 1989 or His assurance that I will return to Him one day. I think often of the song that Grandma Russell sang, "How Beautiful Heaven Must Be." It truly is a place to desire to abide and to know I will be home at last in eternal rest.

Hatefulness is like taking a wet Arkansas squirrel and slapping someone up along side of the head to get their attention! We need to care enough to stop and listen to our children when they tell us they have been hurt by someone in our lives. Children very seldom lie about abuse.

Chapter 25

The beribboned horse in the winner's circle,
Black horse of deceit,
Looking for the ultimate high,
Ridden hard and put away wet,
The bronco of desire,
Harboring the tree of hate,
Extended limbs of poison,
Dripping venom of the bizarre,
Unnatural, unborn depth,
Deprivation of the spirit,
Dead!

'The Man' sang a gleeful song, knowing he was the winner of all the prizes - the souls of the children. He had triumphed and trampled the woman's soul into nothing. He'd picked the fresh fruits of the children, plucked down from the place known as innocence. He had overcome the Shadow Man, and become in control of their life-long obsessive battle. He was 'The Hat Man.' He was full of badness and twisted by his choices, lifted by evil, contained in a body that plundered at will. Now, death must come to the wife, the core of his problems, and the crux of his despair. How he hated her! She was no longer a vessel of production. He would kill her; destroy what she loved the most, her children. He knew her love for the children far outweighed anything besides God in her heart. He could see it in her eyes since her claim of returning from death. Somehow, that experience had given her a place to run.

He silently chuckled at the pain in her eyes as he tore her pride, her soul and her sanity away. He would drive her to her own destruction - mad like a raving idiot. She was a fool! He controlled her. She just didn't realize that she could never win against him. His first wife had tried, even his mother had tried, but they were losers. He was driving this wife insane in hopes she would seek death rather than life. Why couldn't she just die? What kept her going? He mocked her God and her faith; yet, she held on and now he'd had the first blood of her children.

He often laughed in the nighttime as he heard her prayers wafting up to heaven. How he snickered, knowing he had overcome God. He was the god in the house now. The children were controlled, they were his in the flesh; even though he knew he had not 'fathered' them, he used their bodies as receptacles of his needs. The woman was worthless. She had aged, grown heavy in her body, and held no attraction for him. She had let the doctors take away her uterus; she had not obeyed him and his order to refuse the hysterectomy. That uterus had been his, his place to plant his seed. He mocked her each time he raped her, her fear fed his strength, and she died a bit more each time he humiliated her.

Piece by piece he was ripping God out of her, or so he thought.

He would burn and bury her soon. The place was prepared, soft and ready. His father, Satan, had given him the perfect plan.

He certainly wasn't offering a resurrection plan or any room for redemption for the bitch.

Chapter 26

Hatred danced a bizarre circle,
Encompassing the righteousness of my soul,
Lost in the blazing, scorching heat of hate,
Lifting, circling, and crushing the essence of me,
Until I was an empty shell of the past,
No future, damned and blamed,
The present crunched my bones to the marrow,
The muscles of my spirit were broken,
Sorrow was my name!
Yet I held on,
Despair my middle name.

1990-1991 Reign of Fear

Noel basked in the role of Devil's advocate and helper. His December 1, 1990 attack on me was the most violent yet. He threatened suicide all evening, raging and screaming at the children and me. He was threatening me, being violently abusive and raping me. I'd seen him in many stages of rage, but nothing like this. I feared for our lives. I did not know how to stop or avert his behavior. He alternatively screamed for me to die, to leave as he was keeping the children, and forced more damaging sex on me. I'd been experiencing heavy vaginal bleeding for several months. The doctors did not know what was wrong. My stomach began protruding in an odd manner.

I begged him quietly, "Please, Noel, I love you. You need to settle down or you are going to have a heart attack. You are acting like you've totally lost your mind. Do you need to go to the VA hospital? You are scaring me and the children." My timing with Noel never was right. I always opened my mouth at the wrong moment with the wrong words. It was going to get me killed. He made a run for his bedroom shouting he was going to get the shotgun and kill us all. I heard him pumping the shells into the shotgun. He screamed he was going to kill himself.

I grabbed my children and ran, knowing my chances of being shot in the back were immediate. I drove up to the local grocery store in Middleton and called the Sheriff's Office from the payphone. They responded and came to the grocery store. They took the children and me to one of the deputy's homes. It seemed like they interrogated us for hours. They took my house keys.

The Sheriff's officers surrounded our property. Law enforcement went to our neighbor, Ben Mill's house and set up a command post. They tried to get Noel to respond by telephone, but he didn't pick up. They asked me if I thought he had committed suicide. *I could only hope, couldn't I?* The officers believed he might have committed suicide. They used my keys to get inside the home. Noel pretended to be asleep. This reaction was from a man that would awaken at the drop of a pin or any small noise. There was no way these officers could have entered the home and him not have heard them. I do believe the Devil was helping him every step of the way as much as God was helping me. They removed Noel and took him to the Boise Veterans Hospital and put him on a mental hold

Noel was kept in the VA Hospital for several weeks. Dr. Eric Fisher and a clinical psychologist demanded I come in to meet with them. Dr. Eric Fisher demanded I bring my three children in to meet with him and the psychologist alone. I took the children in. Dr. Fisher refused to allow me in the room or discuss what the children told them. My son told me that he had told them everything. What that was I don't know, but later he said he told them "everything" about what Noel was doing to them and I had to know what that was. Then Dr. Fisher met with the children and Noel. Dr. Fisher told me if I tried to intervene in his seeing the children as a therapist, he would report me to the Prosecutor. The children were frightened to death of the situation.

I felt absolutely helpless and so afraid because the situation with Noel became worse. I was on the outside of a terrible situation with no hope of finding out what was happening to my children or helping them. The children didn't confide in me, but told the doctors their father was molesting them. The doctors broke the law in not reporting his abuse. The doctors failed in their fiduciary duty to tell me about the children's abuse. They did not report the abuse to law enforcement or to Protective Services.

Noel was allowed out on furlough for Christmas, but Noel wasn't in the Christmas spirit – he was not St. Nick returning home bearing gifts. The children walked around on eggshells afraid to talk. They hid as much as possible, helping me with the chores and were as silent as mice. I slid in and out of his personal space like a bitten cur dog. Our Christmas was a tense, deadly affair. The potential of death wrapped every present.

Finally, he made his move early the next morning, the day after Christmas. He ordered the children to stay in the house and keep quiet. I could see the fear on their faces as on mine - this was our final hour. He forced me into the pickup at gunpoint. He drove me down in the pasture at the back of our farm and violently assaulted me in the back of our truck under the camper shell. He tried to force me to fire the 12-gauge shotgun wanting my fingerprints on it. I refused. We had a small sinkhole, swampy area on the back of the property. When he raped me, he told me he'd dig in the center of the cattails and bury me there. I was bleeding very heavily, was weak, and his threats immobilized me. My body felt laden and the blood sloshing through my body was sluggish as silt. I distanced myself during his assault. He seemed to hold all the cards with me as prisoner because I was financially dependent on him. Where could I run? Whom could I trust? I was too sick to work and support the children. I had no money in the bank or hidden away. He blamed his crimes and his attitude on me. I was weak-minded. I'd never found the words to speak in self-defense to Noel or my parents.

After his visit at Christmas and the field attack, Noel stated he was going to force me to become pregnant again in spite of my severe bleeding. It didn't matter how heavy the bleeding, he assaulted me hoping to impregnate me again. We certainly didn't need a fourth child.

Noel returned to the hospital after Christmas. He was allowed another furlough after a few weeks. His behavior was repeated. I had been ordered by Dr. Fisher to come in weekly for a marriage counseling session with Noel. It was a "beat up the wife" session trying to convince me I was the crazy one. In one session, Noel was sent from the room and Dr. Fisher told me I wasn't cooperating and that he was thinking of taking my children away from me and letting Noel have them when we divorced. I knew something was wrong and it wasn't me, but what it was, I couldn't figure it out.

I was so scared; my stomach and guts were in knots. I couldn't sleep; fear ruled my waking and sleeping. My children were silent shadows and I couldn't get them to talk to me and share their fears. I begged them to tell me what was happening to them. They told me that Dr. Fisher had told them it was between Noel and them. I was not to be told, but the children thought the doctors surely had told me their father was raping them, but they hadn't. In hindsight, I can appreciate my children's anger and how it must have appeared to them.

In late February, Noel was still in the hospital and Dr. Barbara Battalino came on board at the Veterans Hospital in Boise, Idaho as another psychiatrist. She was a Veteran also. Noel begin attending in-house daily group therapy sessions with the other hospitalized patients on his floor conducted by Dr. Barbara Battalino, Dr. Eric Fisher, Dr. Larry Dewey and a woman clinical psychologist. Toward the end of Noel's hospitalization around March 1, his VA doctors insisted I come down for a visit.

I was told to go to Noel's room and visit with him; this was the very first time I had ever been allowed to go to his room in our twenty year marriage. When he was in the hospital, I had always waited in the waiting room until he was brought out of the ward. I thought this was certainly strange. When I got into his room, he shut and locked the door. He pushed me into a metal locker in the room and violently raped me. He dragged me out into the open room he shared with another patient who was out of room at the time, and continued his anal rape. I kept begging him to stop. I was in terrible pain and afraid someone would walk in on us; he laughed stating no one was going to bother us as this was his time. I said, "The doctors have keys and can get in".

"Nope," he snorted, "You are all mine now." He forced me to strip naked, scattering my clothes about the room. Oh, God the humiliation of it all! I was shaking so badly that I could hardly stand up. He shoved me into the bathroom where the violence got worse. I was brutalized vaginally and anally and too terrified for my life to even squeak. I begged him not to do this as I was his wife and deserved to be respected, but to no avail. In fact, I think that stirred his brutality to a higher level. I knew if I resisted him here and he came home, my punishment would be greater! He said his doctors had given their permission for him to have sex with me in his room. He made no offer of using the bed; it was all about humiliating me. He was laughing like an idiot. I still believe to this day there were cameras in that room for someone to watch what was happening to me. I was cornered and had no place to run.

When I went back into the dayroom with him, Dr. Barbara Battalino came to me, smirking, and stated, "Now this little visit will settle Mr. Snow down considerably, don't you think?" *Wink, Wink!* She was gloating and I was so humiliated and sickened I wanted to vomit.

Noel bragged while he was in the hospital that he'd had sex with a woman named Julie who had AIDS. Because of this, the children and I had to be tested for several years. Noel also bragged that he had sex with Dr. Battalino. In fact, he stated he liked this new doctor (Battalino) as she believed group sex was great. Julie *was* on the same ward with Noel and acted provocatively around him in front of me. He gloated, nodding to Julie saying, "She wants me and I don't care if you don't." I thought his talk was all from his mental illness. I couldn't even believe that any doctor would allow such debauched activities. He swore it was happening; he then asked what *psychotic* meant. He said that Dr. Battalino was telling him all his thinking was psychotic. I believe she was manipulating the Veterans with their illnesses to cover-up her illegal sexual actions. It was a nightmare! It was the end for me in believing any of the Boise VA doctors could help Noel's condition or secure the safety of the children and me. I was up against a medical giant and had no hope of winning.

Dr. Battalino worked from February 1991 through October 1991 in the VA's Psychiatric in-patient and out-patient units where she provided treatment to patients who, were, in most cases, combat veterans. Noel was one of her patients. In October of 1992, Vietnam veteran, Edward Arthur, filed a civil lawsuit against Battalino and the United States for sexual harassment and abuse against him. He was receiving out-patient psychiatric care through the VA Boise hospital. In addition to receiving therapy from the psychologist, Mr. Arthur consulted with Dr. Battalino concerning his medication. He claimed medical malpratice and intentional and negligent infliction of emotional distress against both defendants. He claimed that the doctor had sexually abused him and harassed him in her office at the VA on June 27, 1991 and that she attempted to initiate an ongoing sexual relationship with him thereafter. Dr. Battalino's position was that she acted within the course and scope of her employment with the VA. Even after dismissal from the hospital, she embarked upon a course of professional misconduct and harassment calculated to dissuade Mr. Arthur from pursuing legal remedies against defendants Battalino and the United States. (*Edward Arthur v. Battalino and United States No. 93-35967*). He won January 4, 1995. Dr. Barbara Battalino was charged by Attorney General, Janet Reno. Charges against Battalino were pursued and she was fined $3,500 and she served six months of home detention. The press did little coverage of this debacle.

Noel told the VA doctors I was mentally ill. I was imagining all the things he was doing. He manipulated the doctors with his sob story. I couldn't understand with Noel's long mental history why the VA doctors in Boise hadn't helped the children and me. I knew the Boise VA doctor had access to his federal VA records from Little Rock from 1986 backwards all the way to the 1940s.

When Noel was dismissed from the VA Hospital, he came back into our home by order of the Prosecutor. I begged the VA doctors to keep Noel longer so I could recuperate! The Prosecutor threatened to charge me with 'elder abuse' after his hospitalization if I didn't let him come back home. The Prosecutor was aiding and abetting Noel's rule of ruination. Noel was an angry blazing monster, breathing the fires of the indignant, offended husband. He sat and gloated at my powerlessness. He watched me at night with a loaded gun to my head. I wasn't allowed to sleep, but had to listen to his crazed ranting. He repeatedly went over his murder plans. He spewed hate at me while the children were in school.

The VA doctors lied to the Prosecutor. I couldn't believe I hadn't found help. I was desperate – in a no man's land, without a boat to paddle out of the troubles in my home. I was a walking talking zombie and what was happening was surreal. I had never known such desperation that I was living in now. I had desperately sought help, but received none. The ogre's lair had been invaded from outside. The litany of my supposed sins was building into a pile of dung expounded on by Noel.

The VA doctors ordered Noel and me to come in for weekly counseling sessions at the Mental Hygiene Clinic after his hospitalization – and I was to participate in their 'counseling'

Evidently, each time Noel came home from the VA hospital in early 1991, he had been taking the guns out of the locked utility closet and hiding them around the property. The VA doctor and law enforcement had me lock them up after his arrest. The officers ignored the fact I was being battered and raped. When I told them he was a paranoid schizophrenic, they had a legitimate excuse not to put him in jail but hospitalized him. The children and I were left on our own with a heartless monster – in 1991 there was no protection available for us from anywhere in the Idaho Law Enforcement corral.

The violence was escalating. He was calling his family for support and reinforcement of his growing paranoia when I went to church. When I came home from services, I'd find an open Bible on the dining table with a pen pointing to a scripture about a whorish woman, Proverbs 6:26. With hate-filled eyes, he would demand, "You read this now," and shove me to the table. His hate was a living and breathing entity, like a hot fire directed against my soul – I didn't have an extinguisher to put out the belligerent fire in his belly. The violent rape escalated after the children left for school. The days seemed endless with me remodeling the houses and bearing his animosity.

I had secretly made an appointment with Nampa, Idaho psychiatrist Dr. Charles B. Green in February of 1991. I took a bit of money from the bank account each time I bought groceries and hid it so I could pay him. I laid out my childhood abuse, my marital rape and my ill health. I shared with him that my husband was telling the VA doctors I was crazy. I let him know, "If I am insane, prove it to me today. If you find I am mentally incompetent, send me to the Idaho Blackfoot State Mental Hospital. Please see that my children are safe." He put me through all kinds of tests and stated, "You have no psychiatric issues. You are sane. You are just very ill and not able to defend yourself. Your first priority is to have this hysterectomy before the bleeding kills you. You have a lot of decisions to make in the next few weeks."

 Dr. Green sent a letter about his findings to my lawyer, Glenn Lee, of Fruitland, Idaho because I was facing the hysterectomy. My attorney agreed with Dr. Green. I must get the legal issues addressed before the surgery and get my health restored. My lawyer, Glenn Lee, helped me prepare a will and placed the psych report in the file. Mr. Lee promised if I died during the procedure, he would fight and take my children away from Noel. Glenn was a wonderful man.

I knew something was terribly wrong in my home and began to suspect Noel was hurting my children. I had no proof, just a fearful gut feeling of terror. I couldn't get the children to talk. I told them no one was supposed to be touching them in their privates and if that was happening, I needed to know. Silence!

I went to Noel's VA doctors in Boise on March 21, 1991, and reported I believed Noel was raping my children, but I had no proof. Dr. Dewey laughed at me. The Federal VA doctors were again refusing to help me, but that day, Dr. Larry Dewey, one of Noel's psychiatrists noted my accusations in the file where I had reported I believed my children were being raped. In fact, Dr. Dewey told me that if I could get one of the rapes on tape or a confession from Noel, he would see that Noel was charged and arrested. Me! I was supposed to somehow magically find a tape recorder which I could turn on while being attacked and brutalized and "catch my husband in the act" and Noel not find it out in his room! Ridiculous!

Later, when I brought a lawsuit, they cleansed the file of all my letters begging for help, but could not erase the March 21, 1991, statement. See lawsuit settlement statement at back of book.

Noel left the day before my surgery for a six-week vacation to Arkansas. I had saved $750 to help pay my part of the surgery. Noel found the money and bought a plane ticket to Arkansas. He objected to my having the hysterectomy as I was taking away his "God-given right" to have a place to plant his seed. He made me feel like a garden stripped of all its nutrients. He was fixated on my uterus and if it was removed, I no longer was acceptable for sex. I lost value as a woman, but now he threatened to discard me like an old shoe. He considered me useless – he argued, shook, kicked and browbeat me trying to force me to keep my uterus – to no avail. I had to have it done quickly. The odds of survival were not in my favor. On April 17, 1991, I faced the surgery alone.

The doctors found a large fibroid tumor in my uterus and a cyst on each ovary. The left ovary cyst had burst. I was full of infection and was placed on several rounds of antibiotics. The tumor was so large the doctor stated it appeared I was more than four months pregnant. Dr. Immanuel Benjamin got very angry during the surgery, thinking I was using a hysterectomy to end a pregnancy. During the surgery, the mass was so huge he cut a main artery trying to remove it. I gave permission for other doctors and nurses to observe, as he wanted to do my surgery as a teaching surgery. He stated, "If I hadn't had all those doctors and nurses there to help, you would have bled to death during the procedure." I lost half of my body blood. Noel was not there to sign for blood transfusions as my next legal kin. Two years later, I developed pernicious anemia from the blood loss. I went home twenty-two pounds lighter.

I could not get out of bed by myself because of the large incision and pain, but I was released to go home. The children were alone and needed adult supervision, as they were only four, thirteen and fourteen. They couldn't lift me out of bed to use the bathroom. I could not use a bedpan and did not have a bedside commode. So, the children would all sit on a chair next to the bed so I could pull myself out of bed. They propped me up along the wall to the bathroom. The children were scared because if something happened to me, they would be all alone. I fought to recover to help them.

I assisted them in planning what to cook and to eat. They fed me the best they could. It was hard on us, but we managed. How I wanted to flee while Noel was in Arkansas, but I didn't have any place to run, no money, and was recuperating from major surgery. I knew I couldn't hold a job and provide for my children.

After my surgery checkup, Noel returned from Arkansas late May, 1991. He was in a rage because I'd had the surgery and began immediately to rape me. He told me I was nothing but an empty hole - of no use to him – a dud. I began to plan and prepare, knowing I was going to leave. I was in a bad shape physically, but I made a garden that summer and canned, crawling on my knees to do what I had to do. I believe my dream to be free drove me forward at one of the lowest points of my life to do the physically impossible. Noel slapped me around, demanding I work harder.

I told him, "I don't know how I can work more or harder as I am doing everything I can to provide food for you." He didn't realize I was planning for the children and me after I got away.

Noel would scream at me to hurry up, hoe the garden and cook him a meal. The neighbors could hear his abuse. The children stayed out of his way as much as they could. We dug earthworms and sold them for extra cash. I was hiding back a bit of money. The abuse from Noel intensified and I believe he could see in my eyes, I was going to get away. He was losing his grip on his punching bag.

Before my surgery in April, I began refusing to go into the VA counseling sessions with Noel. The Dr. Fisher called me, demanding I come in with Noel. I told him I was done with participating, but I would drive Noel in for his session. It was during one of the times that summer that Noel began acting crazy in the car as we returned home after a session. My baby was in the back in a car seat. He grabbed the wheel of our car trying to force the car into the oncoming traffic. He told me he was going to kill me for turning him in to the Sheriff's Office and humiliating him by having him arrested. I told him he was acting crazy and he needed help. He talked in strange voices calling me and the baby vicious names. She was terrified, screaming and begging 'Papa' to stop hurting Mama. He yanked her hair and grabbed me, shaking me like a rag.

I started praying and asking Jesus to help me, to stop the madness. Noel grabbed the wheel of the car even harder, trying to force me to let go of it. I hung on, praying. All of a sudden, he slapped me, but I managed to pull the car over to the side of the highway. He had this deranged look in his eyes. His eyes looked like live fire. He began praying against me in the name of Satan. He acknowledged Satan as his father. I was never so afraid in my life. He told me I had better never pray against him to Jesus again or I was dead. I kept praying, and paid for it when I got home.

In the late spring, his violence escalated to an unprecedented level so far in our marriage - I doubted my survival. I began cleaning around the old barn, tearing down fences, and building a garden area. I gathered large piles of lumber for burning. He forced me to go out to the barnyard late one night after the children were asleep, held a gun on me, and made me dig. I dug until I was exhausted and then continued to dig by the light of the bonfire.

His sociopathic nature took a dangerous turn. He read the Pope County newspaper and become obsessed with the Ronald Gene Simmons case. Mr. Simmons was his new hero and Noel's lunacy revved into high gear. He dreamed, lived and ate what the Pope County, Arkansas newspapers reported about all the murder tragedy and incest from Dover, Arkansas. Ronald Simmons had impregnated several of his daughters over a several year period. He murdered his entire family on Christmas Day. He had buried them around his place on Bloomfield Road near Dover, then went to Russellville, Arkansas and murdered several more people. He received the death penalty for his crimes. He was Noel's hero. Noel used any means necessary, including violence, to attempt to control my thoughts, my feelings, and all the actions of me and the children. He exploited all of us. I just couldn't put a finger on what was happening to the children – I pleaded with them to tell me if they were being touched in any manner, they lied. Incest is a crime of secrets and the exploiter is a master of manipulation and keeping his sins from others.

I knew my time had come and he was going to fulfill his fantasy of being like convicted murderer Ronald Gene Simmons. Noel insisted I read the newspaper accounts repeatedly. He would recite the case as I read it aloud.

Noel was spellbound by Simmons impregnating his daughters and then murdering his entire family on

December 22, 1987. Simmons was put to death on June 25, 1990, in Arkansas by lethal injection for murdering sixteen people. Noel clued me in how he had figured out to fool the police. He thumped his chest and bragged he would do a better job at getting rid of the children and me than Simmons had done. I often asked, as the public has asked for many years about Simmons crime spree, how did my children and me escape the public notice of what Noel was doing to us? How did we manage to survive?

That night as I dug, I was sure this was my final resting place. Noel explained very carefully how he was going to wait until the children were gone to school and then kill me and put me in the grave. He impatiently explained how he had rolls of plastic ready to spread out to kill me on and there would be no blood splatter in my death. He was going to put a twenty-two bullet between my eyes. He told me there was plenty of lumber in piles I had torn out; he would burn the wood on top of my grave to hide the digging. He bragged he was getting the neighbors used to the idea of him burning lumber at night. He said he would have willing vessels when I was dead. The vessels would be my children! He explained to me how he would kill the children if they didn't cooperate, one at a time, pretending to the neighbors they had been sent to live with various relatives. He planned to bury them the same way as he was planning to bury me, very deep. The neighbors, by then, would not think anything about him burning the lumber at night. He would tell them I had gone on a trip to Arkansas and no one would care about my disappearing.

He would be a grieving man whose wife had run away and deserted her children and wonderful husband. He bragged he was much smarter than Simmons and wouldn't be caught as that fool had been.

I was frozen with fear, numb and scared I was going to die and be shoved in a hole. I was afraid of the dark. I felt like all the air rushed from my lungs. My body blazed in pain and my mind skittered here and there, seeking a way out of this situation. Where could I run? I could not leave the children behind, as he would murder them. Fear oozed from my pores and my mind felt like Swiss cheese. I understood fear, as I had lived with fear all my life, wetting my pants when I was cornered. My love for my children was like lead boots that kept me from running. If I had run, he would have shot me in the back. He kept pushing me back into the grave, telling me to dig faster.

Finally, he ordered me out of the hole. Then he demanded I fill it up. I felt such relief; I was going to live, at least for a while. "This is just a practice exercise in what I can do and will do if you don't do exactly like I say from this day on," he angrily told me. I knew my choices meant death for the children and me. I had to convince him he ruled me. I knew him to be brutal. He forced me to go to the house and raped me. "I own you, bitch, and there ain't nothing you can do to prevent me doing this. You turned me in to the Sheriff's Office and to the VA. I am eventually going to kill you, but you are going to suffer until I choose the time you are going to die." The coldness of his words left little doubt of his hate. His actions for the past several months had slaughtered any love in me. I lived in horror, but the trepidation didn't secure my forgiveness. I was resolute in my despair. He would not own me or my children. One inch at a time was bringing me to the edges of the despair he had created. You can kick a dog only so many times before it turns on you and bites. I focused on his toad-like face. I was resolute in my exhaustion!

I hunkered down behind the hall door each night armed with two knives. How could I defend the children and myself with two knives against the guns he had? I became so sleep-deprived, it was only gravity that bound me to the earth.

Wisdom is more valuable than foolishness, just as light is better than darkness. We have lived without light so long as victims of domestic violence – find the light – live in it. Be wise and seek help, be safe, enjoy living and grow old with great joy because you have found the freedom road.

Chapter 28

Gloating murders
Swollen minds,
Rotting senses,
Hell and turmoil,
Partners in crimes,
For whom does the death bell toll?

Noel became even more obsessed with murder when a Canyon County woman killed her husband. She caught her husband raping their nine year old daughter. She shot him to death. She was sentenced to six years probation for murder. Richard Harris, the Prosecuting Attorney, gave her hell. Noel fixated on me either killing him or him killing me. Mind grisliness could only describe what I was living. I was Noel's prisoner. I couldn't trust anyone. I had told the Canyon County Sheriff's Department in December, 2000, but to no avail. When they did not investigate why the children and I were terrified; the old distrust of law enforcement surfaced from my childhood. I remembered Aaron's teachings. Law enforcement was not my friend.

I was hiding all Noel's evil from the children, or so I thought. I did everything Noel demanded. I placated him with whatever sexual demands he made. It was never enough. It did not stop his torture of me. He described day after day how he would cut up our children in pieces if I tried to get help again. They would simply disappear and I would never find them. I walked carefully to escape death.

The children were too afraid to talk to anyone at school because he made it clear he was a killer. I tried to appear as normal as possible so the children would not realize the severe danger they were in.

He would order me to whip the children. I whipped myself and had them cry as if they were being beaten. I had them put towels in their clothing where nothing would harm them. It was mind draining. I hardly slept at night fearing our murder. I kept a five-gallon bucket in my bedroom so the children and I could use it rather than the bathroom by his bedroom. All I could think about was I had to live for the children.

My son's bed was in the living room. I did not know my husband was abusing him when I slept from exhaustion. No one was allowed into his room unless he called our name, but he would come out and order me to the bedroom in front of the children, telling me, "You either come now or I will rape you right here." I walked as he ordered.

I would turn the television up loud so the children could not hear me crying from his rape and beatings. I would cry and beg him to stop hurting me, afraid if I did not beg, he would kill me. He liked having me beg; it turned him on to even greater heights sexually. He brought up the December 1, 1990, police raid frequently, reacting violently.

He forced me to lick his behind. I had to tell him he was 'The Man,' and he owned me. "Your father showed me how I was to treat you the day you took me home to meet him. I saw what a 'treasure' I had gotten in the marriage bargain. I am going to make sure you pay me back for me taking you in, especially since I know your mother, dad and brother had you before me," he mocked. He didn't know about all the uncles who had abused me. I feared if he had, I would have died.

I replied, begging, "I am nothing, you own me, just don't hurt the children. I will do anything you say, but leave the children alone." He would manipulate me with his fingers and if I didn't reach an orgasm, his violence would escalate. I faked many orgasms. Fear is not a good stimulator. He kept raving about how women were nothing but pussies. "Women are always out having sex with someone else rather than the man who owns them," he would scream. He would list his mother and first wife often during sex and tell about his father's abuse. He said the 'old man' had taught him evil things. I believed him.

Fear was a living, breathing entity in my soul. I had nothing left inside me, no ground to stand on - it felt as if my spirit had gone. I almost lost hope in God; was he hearing my pleas for help?

The next few days, Noel kept talking abusive things to me in front of the children, and when I walked close to him, he would grab my arm, forcing me to hurry to his room. He seemed to keep an erection all the time. I became a walking dead woman. He would force me go to the grocery store and leave one of the children with him, telling me if I screwed up, (pointing his finger to his head like a gun) that I would regret it. I obeyed very carefully. I knew all our lives were on the line. How was I to escape? I had tried to get help in December, 1990. I kept focusing on that refusal, knowing that Prosecutor had given me a death sentence. I endured with mind-numbing fear, knowing at any moment the children and I would be murdered.

He began 'spouting-off' about Joe Baker from Baker City, Oregon, and how the Pentecostal Church of God wouldn't help those children. He said, "You weren't even woman enough to stop him and look how the church wouldn't believe you. No one will believe you if you try to tell them what I am doing to you. I own you now and you will do what I say until I decide to put you out of your misery. I want you to suffer. You will pray to die before I am through."

I planted one foot in front of the other those long months, praying for deliverance and to find hope to cling to.

Around September 8, 1991, my youngest came to me and told me "Papa is hurting my hole." I asked my baby where and she pointed directly to her vagina. I checked her and she was bleeding! I sucked in my breath. Nausea

overwhelmed me. He had raped my baby! I cried out,
"Oh, God, give me life, and help me know what to do."

Noel was at the hallway, beating on the door and
demanding to know what I was doing with the door locked.
He screamed in rage. I made up some excuse. I gathered
my three children together behind the locked door. The
children slept. I stood guard over them.

Around midnight, on September 17, 1991, Noel
grabbed my hair awakening me and demanding I go to his
room or he would rape me in bed with my baby. He gave
me a shove down the hallway. He then planted his foot in
the middle of my back as I entered his bedroom, knocking
me flat on his bed. He ripped my clothes from my body
and raped me anally and then vaginally. The pain was
unbearable; my soul dignity was shredded.

He demanded I cook him breakfast so I picked up my
tattered clothing and did as he commanded. I made biscuits
and put them on a lower heat. My heart beat faster than a
drum with sweating fear. I was afraid he would decide to
kill us this morning. I ran to the barn, milking the goats as
fast as I could. I fed all the calves, hogs and baby goats.
While I was out doing the chores at the barn and the two
older children were still asleep, Noel was raping my baby.
I ran back to the house, took out the biscuits and made him
eggs and bacon. I got the two children up, shushing them
quietly, and helped them get dressed. Now if I could only
get them on the school bus quickly! He was ranting and
yelling, being his usual horrible self. The children ate in
silence. My food roiled in my stomach.

The baby was asleep, sobbing softly, I wondered why.
I hurried back to the barn to finish the chores. When I
came in, I caught Noel with my baby's panties off and he
was pulling her legs back and forth in a weird fashion
looking at her vagina. I grabbed her, dressed her and took
her with me to finish the chores. The older two children left
for school on the bus. My little one was a shadow hiding

with me the best she could that morning – she was mute, fear glistened in her eyes. I knew something was terribly wrong.

Noel had a medical appointment with his psychiatrist, Dr. Eric Fisher, that morning at 10 a.m. in Boise at the Mental Hygiene Clinic. Dr. Fisher was not an ethical psychiatrist nor was he a man to be trusted. The VA doctor demeaned me for several months in front of Noel. The doctor's mocking me was encouraging Noel's growing paranoia. The sessions had become 'beat up the wife' sessions insinuating I was unstable.

I was finished, fed up, desperate and I decided I was not going to participate in their games another second. I stopped sitting in on Noel's counseling sessions after seeing Dr. Charles B. Greene on March 27.

After the children got off to school, I took my baby with me to finish up the chores and before we left for Boise, Noel raped me again. He locked our baby in the hallway of the other bedrooms. I knew today was the day I would die if I did not stand up for my children and myself. I shook badly from his brutal attack. I could hardly think, much less drive. I do not remember the drive into Boise for the medical appointment; I knew there no more being the coward in thinking Noel would ever change. I had to get away. I could no longer walk cat-footed quiet or in denial. Reality is a terrible thing to face.

I came up with a workable plan. I took my little one with me and knew if God was with me, the plan would work. I was determined I would get the help I needed to escape. Noel was watching my actions like a hawk. He was diligent about one of the children being with him at all times at home. If I did something foolish, we were all dead. Today was my last chance of getting help. I got Noel to the VA Hospital for his ten o'clock mental hygiene appointment with his doctor. I believe Noel's violence escalated because he sensed I was slipping from his control.

I'd seen the light of his unmasked evil.

While Noel was in his session with the psychiatrist, I slipped away and went to the State Capital Building. I kept asking for the Attorney General's Office, telling anyone and everyone I needed help or I was going to die. They told me the Attorney General, Larry Echohawk wasn't in. I knew this was my one last chance to get away and if I failed, Noel was going to murder me that night. There was a fanatical light in his eyes as he raped me that morning - something different - the hate more intense. My heart beat so hard in fear I could barely continue standing in the Capital Building. I had a sickening fear so bone-deep and I could barely hold onto my youngest one's hand.

I was standing on the second floor, terrified of what I was going to do, weeping silently and in desperation. A man came up to me and asked me if I needed help. I broke down sobbing loudly, too incoherent to speak. I fell onto the floor in a heap holding my baby to my chest. I must have looked like a deranged woman, yet he stopped and quietly spoke with me. He took me by the elbow, assisting me to stand, telling me that he had a quiet place where I could tell him what was troubling me. He led me to an empty office.

I told him how the Canyon County Sheriff's Office had refused to help me in December, 1990. They told me I needed to quit persecuting that 'poor old man.' The Attorney General investigator believed me and told me he would make sure I got help. He helped me with a plan. I was to go home, pack my medications, get the other two kids and be ready to flee when he called me signaling he had legal help in place to start the ball rolling against Noel. He told me he would report the rape and abuse. He urged me to listen when he called my home, not to answer back, but say "yes," and then pretend the call was a wrong number.

When I got back to the VA compound, Noel was

running around and around looking for me, demanding to know where I had been. He slapped the baby trying to make her tell him where we had been. Thankfully, she was too scared to say anything. She understood what I had done was a secret and it was about her papa hurting us. She was deathly afraid by this time, but God gave us both grace and deliverance in our hour of need.

Noel grabbed hold of me and shook me until it felt like my teeth rattled in my head. Noel slapped me around several times; drawing the attention of passing VA patients who yelled they were calling the police. Noel shoved me into the car, screaming he was going to kill me, forcing me to drive us home. He'd raped me twice that morning. I endured more attacks after we got home. He locked me in his room so I couldn't get out. I could hear my little one screaming. I was beating on the door, screaming, "Noel, what are you doing to the baby, leave her alone. Oh, God, help us not to die this day. Let me save my babies." The Red Bird fluttered all around me trying to help to me.

He unlocked the door and roared back into his room, shouting obscenities at me. He shoved me onto the bed, told me if I valued my life, I wouldn't move. He raped me again, and said, "Now I have mingled the youngest one's blood with yours. Tonight I am going to have you and the two little whores in the bed together and there ain't anything you can do about it. Do you understand, bitch, you are going to die and I am going to have your daughters any time I want?" His revelation hit me like a ton of soul-crumbling bricks. There was no mortar left in our marriage. His admission was a tandem truck rolling over in my life. The scales and delusions were torn from my eyes.

I floated in my mind up onto the rooftop and watched what he was doing to my body. The Red Bird moaned in sympathy. Oh, God how would my babies survive if I died? "Make the pain stop", I moaned! He ripped harder and strained to push his fingers into my guts through my vagina opening.

I begged for my life. I knew I had to live. I screamed for my life unmindful of any pride left in my heart, just the will to survive. I screeched in shock; my screams fed his ego and lust for control even more. I asked for God's forgiveness for my sin in marrying him. He laughed and cursed me loudly without forethought about the evil he was doing to my body and mind.

> *Oh, God of heaven above do not abandon me now,*
> *In my terror, offer me survival,*
> *Let my Red Bird fly with me once again,*
> *Cover me with your blood, O, Christ,*
> *Nestle me in your bosom,*
> *Feathered friend so bright,*
> *Keep me in the light,*
> *It is death I stare in the face,*
> *Keep me filled with life,*
> *Golden voice, please sing to me of Jesus pure,*
> *Shelter me in your wings,*
> *Keep me earthbound for the need of my children,*
> *Courage, I beg give to me,*
> *Hold me tight, feathered friend,*
> *Guide me to the path of escape,*
> *Because in you, I am depending!*

The terrorizing assault continued and the tearing pain was unspeakable. Then he forced several fingers up my rectum telling me he was going to kill me. His fingers dug at me like a dog wanting to bury a bone. I could feel my flesh ripping with each tug of his fingers still ripping inside my vagina and intestinal walls. He told me when he was through with me, "You will dig the hole back out by the barn. It's time I permanently put you out of your misery." The pain was so bad; I prayed for my death, yet begged for my life.

"You are going to pay for all you have done to me, you bitch. " He talked in my mother's voice, his mother and dad's voice, my dad's voice, his voice and two other people's voices, one of them - Joe Baker. My tears dripped down my face in agony. His face was twisted in evil, a reflection of his heart. His punishment was merciless and lasting forever. He informed me he was going to slit my throat and then kill the baby. His eyes were glazed over, and snot was hanging out of his nose. He was pumping in and out of me, grunting and saying, "I am going to kill you. You took my God-given place away to make babies. You weren't supposed to have the hysterectomy. I had a right to make babies in your belly. You are dead. I am going to fix you where you won't ever be able to have sex again. You are dead…dead!"

The pain was agonizing, yet he kept forcing his fist into my vaginal area and rectum. I believed I was going to die, in fact, at that moment, death would have ended my mind panic. I could hear my baby screaming from the back of the house for me to help her. My mind kept trying to process his threats. He meant to fix me where no other man would want me? He wanted me dead! He kept mumbling, "You have sinned. You took away my place to plant my seed. The Bible says it is a sin to spill my seed into a whore's belly. I am not going to spill my seed on the ground. I am going to have a tight ass to use. You are nothing but a hole. You are nothing. You are a whore and whores die; 'The Man' told me so. I have to do what 'The Man' told me to do." Again he talked in Joe Baker's voice, my mother's voice, his mother's voice and his father's voice. I believe he talked in Ronald Gene Simmons' voice, but I had never heard his voice so whose it was, I didn't know. It was a male voice of vileness. It was eerie listening to him ranting in so many voices. I thought I was already in hell.

He put a pillow over my face, telling me, "You are going to die, bitch. You are just like my mother and a whore just like my first wife." He forced me to have an orgasm and the nauseating feelings of this pushed me to the edge of losing my sanity. The Red Bird wrapped its wings around my face, protecting me from seeing Noel at that moment.

The psychological and physical damage of that day left me unable to explain the effect of his final rape for more than two years without debilitating panic attacks. I worked intensely in therapy even though it was horrifying and draining, but I've maintained my sanity. Noel described my baby's body parts, comparing them to mine as he raped me bragging how he'd had her first blood. I wept until there were no more tears inside and his punishment continued. The physical and mental damage are permanent. Oh, if only I had been able to testify in court what he confessed to and what he did to me. It took more than fifteen years for the panic attacks to become manageable.

I managed to get up and out of the bed, but he chased me into the hallway beating his chest roaring, "I want you to kill me. You are going to kill me like that Nampa bitch did her Mexican husband who she caught raping her daughter. Kill me, bitch, kill me! You don't have guts enough to kill me. I want you to kill me." He began shoving and pushing me, trying make me go pick up the gun. "I mean for you to get the gun and shoot me. I want to die. You are going to kill me, bitch. I have raped your kids, as they ain't mine anyway. Mother told me they weren't. I want to die; kill me, kill me. You don't have the guts to kill 'The Man' who has raped your precious children. You just think you are smarter than me, but I have had your bastards." My terror at his confession wiped the last visage of hope from my mind. The question of his guilt was redundant with his bragging admission. He wasn't delusional, but laughing about raping our children.

His depraved words wiped the slate of marriage vows away.

I twisted away from him, trying to reach my baby. He grabbed me in the hallway to my bedroom, trying to throttle me with his hands. I was begging for my life and for my children. He tried to crush me in a bear hug, squeezing and squeezing until the cartilages broke between my ribs. I screamed in pain. I thought he would crush my spine. He was laughing loudly, screaming, "You are a dead bitch. Dead, dead, dead!" The echoes of his threats filled the house like echoes of demons on the rise. My baby was screaming, and then all was silent. I begged again, "Please let me go." He finally gave out and couldn't break my back as he threatened. I lay on the floor gasping for breath. My present day constant pain never lets me forget the evil I'd been sleeping with.

I got up off of the floor defiant. Stumbling, I made it to the living room and then collapsed in a green office chair. I was suffering total disassociation. I was lost, somewhere in my mind, on the rooftop, yet talking to him. "Noel, I have been a faithful wife. I have given you three wonderful children whom you have denied. Now you tell me you have raped our children, and all of your older grown children and many more?"

"Yes, I have been enjoying them for years. I like a tight ass," he yelled. "Why can't you have guts to kill me like the woman from Nampa who killed her husband she caught raping her child. I need to die. Kill me, and you will be rid of me, but I will have won, because then you will lose your bastard children." His slap rang my ears, but I refused to give him what he desired most – relief from his hatred of me.

"You are too big of a coward to kill yourself and I won't do it for you," I sobbed.

He shoved me out of the chair, kicking me in the back. I slowly climbed back into the chair, stubbornly ready to die, but I wasn't going to kill him.

He kept chanting, "Kill me, bitch, kill me!"
I prayed, "Father, give me strength to not do evil to this desperate man. Keep evil from my thoughts and mind, and please have mercy on this wicked man".

He fist slammed against my head, but I wouldn't kill him. Even in his blind rage, he hit me above the hairline.

My head stung as he rained blow after blow along each side, but I wasn't going to let him win if I could hold out. God's courage came flooding into my soul. Noel would never win, never again.

"I have been faithful as a wife, Noel, enduring your abuse and violence. You are going to be surprised at my strength, when you least expect it. I thought you were mentally ill, but no man, husband or father will touch my children."

He bellowed in rage!

His eyes filled with insanity, exploding and demolishing our lives for always.

"Dear sweet Jesus, spare my children, give me courage to save them and myself," I cried in desperation. I wondered if the Red Bird could help my children. They had no one but me. I'd had the Red Bird since childhood to give me a place of escape, but the children hadn't met my Red Bird.

My heart was thudding like a hard-pulling freight train, and my breathing wasn't doing too well either. I was in the throes of an asthma attack, gasping for breath.

"Oh, God, intervene, help me!"

He meant to kill me this time. He was operating under an evil influence, persuaded by his paranoia to kill me if he could. I could see it in his eyes. All the years of my childhood and marital abuse joined me in that one final moment of terror. I was going to die.

The Red Bird hovered close, fluttering in desperation to try to deflect Noel's blows.

It seemed my horror would know no end. He was admitting he had raped our children! My heart shattered; my mind skittered away. All the love I'd tried to keep alive for my husband was blown into a million pieces. My monster had escaped from the closet.

My children were had been victimized by their own father - my husband! The man I had stood by through thick and thin, made excuses for, cared for and worked to make sure we prospered – a rapist! My precious children hadn't been able to find the words or the trust to tell me how they were being hurt. My husband confessed to the ultimate betrayal - their father was a heinous madman! He had terrorized me for twenty years, a living breathing dragon taken to my breast, my life and his name was destruction. There was no worse betrayal than Noel's incestuous actions. My brain seemed to bounce in my head, round and around it went trying to grasp the ugliness Noel had just blurted out. It was and is still a deep everlasting pain that can't ever be wiped away. The stain of incest is a spiritual cancer which has gnawed at the very foundation of my life.

The phone rang. I was prepared to answer it first. I twisted out of his grasp lunging for life, gasping for air but determined to win. I beat Noel to the phone and answered it, gasping, I stuttered, "Hello". The Attorney General's investigator asked me, "Is your husband in the house and can he see you on the phone?"

"Yes," I answered.

He replied, "Do you have everything ready."

"Yes," I replied.

"Then run, and when you get safe, call this number."

It was the number to reach Sheriff Deputy Bob Miles. I committed it to memory on the spot because I knew my life depended on that number. I disconnected. Noel shoved me against dining room wall, his face rumpled in rage.

"Who was that on the phone?" demanded Noel as he tried to grab the receiver. His eyes looked demon wild.

"Another one of your men you have been whoring around with?"

"Just a wrong number, and no, they didn't say who they were," I cautiously replied, ready to run.

He knocked me to the floor. I was sure he would kill me now, but I stumbled to my feet and for some reason or other, he stayed his fist. I felt like I would never get my breath back because the fear churned through my stomach, panic was screaming for me to run, but I couldn't. I had to protect my baby and the other children would be home from school soon.

He suddenly turned away from punishing me. He ran in a rage through the kitchen and out to the barn screaming at me that I was dead. I managed to get up and sit in the chair. Sweating fear ran down my face. In spite of being bone tired, I had to stay alert; I couldn't slack off for a minute. My body pain was so bad I could feel the darkness closing in.

Hearing Noel's confession during his last assault released a powerful freeing flood. Hate ran rampant in my heart, loosening his power grip, lifting his evil mantel and soul corruption in our lives. I was free of his control; his violence and admission finally opened my blinded eyes. He used any leverage possible through twenty years of marriage to bind me in our marriage: guilt, abuse, violence, battering me to the point of death, but I was a determined mother now. I was fleeing with my children.

I floated in my mind. I lost sight of the Red Bird, blinded by fear and tears. My baby climbed onto my lap whispering, "Mama, I love you. Papa 'hurted' you like he 'hurted' me, didn't he? It will be okay, Mama. Jesus is going to help us." I wept bitter tears as I held her close. I had failed my children; the evil of my childhood had come home to my house. How was I going to survive this nightmare? Oh, God I never wanted my children living my nightmare! I waited for my children to get home, cuddling my little one in my arms. She sobbed quietly and I knew Noel had raped her while I was locked in the bedroom.

"Oh, God what a wasted life I have lived! Give me grace, forgive me my sins and help me to escape this hell. Save my children." I floated to the rooftop to watch myself losing it.

Noel's violent attack proved he certainly wasn't my 'white knight champion' in the lover department – never had been. I had created an illusion which had never been real. Noel became a skulking monster in our home. He never inspired faithfulness – he was unfaithful; he never gave me praise when I excelled. Nothing was ever good enough for him.

It took me more than two and a half years of intense therapy before I could find the words to describe the gut-wrenching sickness of being married to Noel Snow and the horrific violence I endured. What he did to my body and mind loosed the demonic force which lived in him. Words fail me in trying to put to paper all the abuse I endured. How could a husband and father be this corrupt and damage his wife and children?

How could I have given my body, soul and mind as one with him in marriage? His shouting and praising God was a spiritual cover – all a lie. I suffered disassociation for many years after his crimes. Having to deal with the out-of-the-body experience of watching yourself is disconcerting. I couldn't talk about the injuries to my mind without suffering a panic attack in my counselor's office or anywhere I had to remember the violence. Screaming silence is a destructive soul affliction. The pounding of my heart, the dragon of fear grabbed me when I would least expect it. How could I deal with the last rape where he compared my baby's body to mine and bragged of what he had done to her? There aren't enough buckets to catch all the tears I have shed trying to heal myself. Self-forgiveness has been very difficult to achieve. The night terrors and body memories were two of the hardest things in my life to conquer.

I managed to get up and get my purse packed as the Attorney General's Investigator instructed me as soon as Noel had gone to the barn. I could see Noel watching the back door over the haystack out close to the grave I had dug and filled back in. I knew he had access to various weapons. Was he just waiting for the two older children to get home to kill us all?

My son came home from school. I stood in the front door motioning him to come to me at once. I quickly told him about the State Investigator believing me and that he was turning in Noel to the proper authorities and getting us help. I told him we have to leave now or Noel was going to kill us. My son said, "Mama, we can make it; I will help all I can." He was only fifteen. I hated the fear on my son's face.

"I have my purse packed and I want you to take your little sister to the car. When I get to the back door, son, I want you to run out the front. We can't take anything with us because we have to run now. I am sorry, but your father mustn't see anything on us except my purse. He is very suspicious of me." I instructed him to start the car once he saw his father run for the back door because I was coming out the front.

My son grabbed my purse and the baby. I know he was scared to death as he was white and shaking like a leaf, but he was determined to help me all he could. He was very plucky and trusted in my word. We were finally escaping the monster! He was a good son and didn't deserve to be in this situation. I had to protect him. He gave me the greatest gift - of his trust at that moment - I would get us away despite my panic.

I stood at the back door and shook my breasts at Noel, grinning as if I wanted him to come for more sex; in reality

I didn't know whether he would shoot me or come running. He bellowed like a bull; rage mottled his ugly face and he made a run for the back door. I turned and fled out the front door, though I was shaking so badly I almost didn't make it to the car. My son moved over quickly as I got into the car and locked all the doors. The motor was running; my baby was in the back car seat.

By this time, Noel had made it through the house and out the front door. He was pounding on the car, trying to break out a window, screaming, "Get out of the car, bitch. You are going to die." Thankfully, Noel didn't have the time to grab one of the guns he had taken from the house and hidden in the sheds.

My son screamed, "Go, Mama, go! He's gonna' kill us!" I managed to get the car out of the driveway and rushed to the high school to get my oldest daughter who was at an after school activity. I was so afraid Noel would follow us in the pickup, I drove like a maniac. We fled to the Crossroads Assembly of God Church at Wilder, Idaho, where our pastor, Rev. Dan St. Clair, hid us. The pastor interviewed the children our first night in the church and they told him of their father's abuse. My baby had taken a doll; it was covered with Band-aids and in ink marked the "sores" where Papa had hurt it like he did her.

My redemption would not come easy! I began to doubt myself; self-guilt was a load dragging me to the pits of a personal hell. Something rose up in me that last day; such anger even above and beyond what I had felt at fifteen when I tried to kill Betty. My sense of self-preservation gave me the strength not to commit murder, but I finally felt God's strength surge through me. The pain of Noel's rape revelation drove me into the darkness of PTSD. It took me two years to be able to begin to discuss his last attack. The pain was like a ball of fire; if I tried to get to close, the burnt mind flesh drove me to suicidal thoughts.

The Sheriff's Department finally removed Noel from

our home after I got a Protection Order which took days. I had custody of the children. After being removed from our home, Noel fled to the Salvation Army Homeless Shelter, no one knew where he might be. After I found the courage and went in desperation to the Idaho Attorney General's, the investigator's insistence forced Canyon County involvement in the case. Richard Harris fought convening a grand jury for the abuse of the children.

When Noel was arrested, people couldn't look me in the eye; many would turn and walk across the street to avoid contact with the children and me. I was ostracized by many of the teachers where I taught school. I became a pariah, the wife of a rapist!

Chapter 29

Where do you hide from the monster?
Is there a cave deep enough?
A road wide enough to take you away?
Is there a well deep enough to climb down into?
How is the mind, the soul and body insured safety?
No, no, no, there is no safety in which to hide!
The law is not always just or merciful,
The Devil must laugh like a jokester!
Justice is supposed to be blind,
However, when the blindfold is lost,
Vengeance would be an eye for any eye,
When the scales are out of balance,
All are losers,
Surely, God gives solace,
Benevolences is found,
Hope in the heart,
It is trust that must not be misplaced!

September/October 1991

I came out of hiding in Payette, Idaho, and went to court. When I returned home, I discovered Noel had beaten and sexually assaulted my nanny goats. He didn't have me or the children to use so his bestiality fetish kicked in full-force. My goats were in bad shape. A friend helped me move all my goats to a safer place until things settled down and we dried up their udders. I sold the goats with the ruined utters and continued to nurse the rest of them back to health. I was grateful for at least one brave friend. She later confided in me that Noel had attempted to assault her one day when she came to visit and I wasn't home. He grabbed her and tried to force her into the house, but she managed to get away in her vehicle. She was too afraid to tell me or law enforcement because she was thought he would come after her if he got out of jail.

The legal atmosphere in 1991 for rape victims was like an icescape of frozen tundra. If you were a woman with children, no money, and being discouraged by the Prosecuting Attorney's Office not to press charges, you were in a no-man's land of nothing. With the Prosecuting Attorney threatening to arrest me, I needed guidance for my children and me. I knocked on lawyers' doors throughout the Treasure Valley. I called, explained, cajoled, begged; it was useless. There wasn't one charitable heart! I must have appeared mad with the PTSD, desperate and afraid for my life! I had to find help! I was down to my last effort when I found a young Hispanic attorney, Sergio Guiterrez in Caldwell, Idaho. He agreed to take my case for the change in my pocket. If he hadn't taken me as a client, I don't know what I would have done that night.

Well-intentioned people began stopping by telling me if it were them, they would just kill Noel. I was told by many God-fearing people that surely I had sinned, that I needed to repent and be saved. I held on to God by a thread. I found trying to live after rape was traumatically difficult, especially if I believed in the law. Murder would have been too quick, too easy for Noel. Surviving the pressure drove me into a zombie-like state.

One night, a man came knocking on my door after midnight. He explained, very convincingly and sincerely, that he had a big metal barrel prepared and he would gladly kill my husband for me. All I had to do was just say the word. He described how he would cut him up, put him in a barrel filled with acid, and dump him over the bridge into the Snake River just below Boise. I declined his help.

The next man came offering to kill Noel slowly, painfully, and grind him up, burning him in a desert location. These midnight visits terrified me. My new lawyer and I both knew that if I were to indicate acceptance of these offers, I would be immediately arrested for accessory to murder. We both felt these men were sent by Richard Harris to try to entrap me and that both men were probably wearing a wire. I was walking a tightrope to prevent my children being removed and put into foster care. In my heart, I wanted Noel to die a painful, slow death, but I wasn't a fool. I thanked them politely; scared to death maybe they were making the same offer to Noel about the children and me. Fear was a living dragon in my breast; my brain felt like a rock-hard lump of pain. Thank God, I had a will in place. If something happened to me, the children would be safe with a lawyer friend in Arkansas. God was indeed taking care of me.

I had no money to feed the children so my lawyer had me hold a huge garage sale, cleaning out my house, my garage, and the storage sheds. I had to sell everything. I had to sell the children's toys – anything they liked, it was gone. All they got to keep was their clothing, bedding, towels and a few personal items. I cleaned out Noel's closet and counted 189-200 shirts in all colors, coats, dress suits, vests, ties, 79-100 pairs of blue jeans and dress slacks, and 72 pairs of shoes and boots. He was a clothes horse and an Imelda Marcos in the making! Yet he often told the VA doctors I was depriving him of clothing. He had almost a hundred undershirts and as many briefs. I stacked his clothing where people could sort through it and people came from all over the county to help us out by buying something. but I sold several thousand dollars' worth of things during that one garage sale and was able to pay debts, cover Noel's hot checks and catch up on the utility bills which were past due.

The guns my husband owned were put up for sale at that time. My lawyer and I figured they might have been tampered with. I sold them with the condition that they all must be taken to a gunsmith and thoroughly checked for tampering. Each man who bought one of the guns either dropped back by or called me letting me know the gun that they had bought had indeed been altered in some way. My pastor bought the 270 Ruger rifle with a scope and 22-pistol. If I had shot any of the guns, they would have exploded in my face. We slept on the floor bare of furniture for a time. It felt like we were in the middle of an atomic blast with no storm shelter.

Just a few days after my huge garage sale, a law enforcement officer from another county who had heard about the gun situation came to see me. Knowing I was without a means of protecting myself, he brought me a brand new single-shot 20 gauge shotgun and traded it for a little bit of cash and some nanny goats. He said the gun was his contribution to helping the children and me. He stated he had been contacted by a friend from a fellow agency and told I was in extreme danger and needed a gun. He advised me to kill my husband if he broke into the house. I knew I could do it now and was prepared to do so. I almost wet my panties with fear at the thought, but that monster was never coming back to my home or touching my children again.

My lawyer decided I must tell my story publicly to every person I met. I went on television to get public opinion on my side while I was in hiding before help became available from law enforcement and the Prosecutor's Office. I systematically began to tell what happened to anyone that would listen. I was not in the greatest mental shape to take on this Herculean task, but for the sake of my children, I buried my mind panic and did as the attorney suggested. I campaigned for the new sheriff, George Nourse, and new Prosecutor, David Young, at every other house in Canyon County and told what Richard Harris and Gary Putman had refused to do – arrest Noel.

David Young won by sixteen votes. I got a phone call at midnight from one of the defeated Prosecutor's Office personnel telling me I was a dead woman and I replied, "I have you on tape." The lawyer had me put the tape in a secure place. I am sure that tape saved my life. My lawyer emphasized I was not safe unless I got public opinion behind me in forcing Noel's arrest. I was naive and thought if I told the truth, I would be believed and given help. I got none for weeks.

I know it was horrifying for my children because I exposed their trauma, but my attorney didn't believe we would be safe without this course of action. I was stressed, suffering severe PTSD, yet trying to hold us together in spite of the panic attacks and the anger of my older two children. At times I couldn't breathe, my mind screaming in agony at the body memories of Noel's assaults.

Someone called Health and Welfare and told them I was suicidal or had already committed suicide. They invaded my home like locusts, scaring my son to death. I was at my lawyer's office and had to rush home to prevent the removal of my children. I left my attorney on the phone dealing with Health and Welfare as I drove like mad. I believe Noel's sisters made the call. They were determined to finally destroy me, especially now that Noel was revealed at his evil worst.

I discovered my phone was tapped and we didn't know by whom. My attorney would call; I would have to go to a pay phone somewhere and call him back as we knew the phone was tapped after the Health and Welfare invasion. One of the Health and Welfare people mentioned something to my son that only my lawyer and I knew and were discussing on the phone before I went into his office. I was living in a nightmare of fear – I could smell my fear – I sweated fear into my sheets at night. I had to abandon my marriage, my home, myself, and step into the world of fear of the unknown. The unknown is the worst fear of the battered spouse. Nothing in my life had given me resilience for Noel's ultimate betrayal. Noel's admission and revelation of his duplicity against our children created an emotional earthquake of gigantic repercussions, shifting my psyche into the pit of Hell, creating a soul avalanche that couldn't be stopped. His bragging started a mountainous roll tumbling down the hillsides of our lives, gathering speed and destroying everything in its path.

There were several attempts by Noel to harm us. I know it was hell for the children. I got a Civil Protection Order against Noel, but it didn't deter him a bit. The Order had to be served through his attorney, as we couldn't find him. Law enforcement didn't respond with the Order in place until Sheriff George Nourse took office. I notified the school and gave them a copy of the Protection Order. I lived in fear that he would attempt to kidnap the children or have someone do it for him. My heart failed me every time the children left for school. I prayed for their safety and God's mercy for them during the day.

I and the children had escaped in our little Ford station wagon. After I was able to return home, I started driving the pickup, but it drove funny. I took it to a mechanic. The brakes had been tampered with, and the wheels were on the verge of falling off the vehicle. Noel had tampered with the brakes as he had tampered with all of the guns. He had loosened lug nuts on each wheel and one of the wheels actually fell off into the mechanic's hands! The man told me if I had driven another few feet or at high speed, the children and I could have been in a bad wreck.

Noel came back that fall and poisoned my young broiler chickens. After butchering them and during cooking process, a hideous smell came from the skillet. We couldn't eat them, so I had very little food for the children except my garden canning. I applied at a local

food bank and got food for the children. I also got food
stamps and Aid for Dependent Children for about three
months. Pride has no place when your children are at risk.
I put my pride in my back pocket and faced the truth – we
were hungry. The children got free school lunches. Many
times, I had nothing for supper, but I pretended I had
already eaten giving them food first. I ate their leftovers, if
there were any.

I went to the bank to empty my bank safety deposit
box and the bank refused to let me into the box. The box
was in my name only, but because Noel had committed a
crime, I was not able to get my records. I had to fight the
bank for a several hours to get possession of my legal
papers. On the advice of my attorney, Glenn Lee, I had put
the titles to the vehicles, birth certificates, marriage license,
extra keys, property deed, along with bank records and tax
records there. My lawyer finally persuaded the bank
officers to let me into the box and get all the records
necessary to show legal proof where needed. Noel was at
the bank by opening time the next morning. Even though
he was not a signer on the account, the bank let him open
the box. That was unethical if not downright illegal!
There were many illegal things done by various
entities which added to all the pain and turmoil of the
crimes. God gave me many times of grace during this
ghastly period. I determined I would never give in to evil
again in my life. I have fought for many victims, aiding
their attorneys and offering free counseling.
In the spring of 1992, the bank repossessed my station
wagon. I had not missed a payment and paid for half of it
at purchase. The bank used Noel's criminal charges as an
excuse to repossess my station wagon. They put the write-
off amount on my credit record. I fought and got it
removed and my credit restored. The IRS came after me,
but when they found out what Noel had done, wrote me a

letter absolving me of any liability for the write-off of the car debt. I never failed in paying a debt. Fortunately, I was able to keep my credit, even with all the debts. Tom Scott, a local car dealer in Caldwell, Idaho, helped me over the years each time I needed a vehicle. He gave me a line of credit so I could pay off the vehicles which helped me keep good credit. There were many good people who stepped forward to provide help.

I was forced to assume all marital debts because of Noel's crimes. He raided our bank account and I chased a nightmare of hot checks. I was able, with the grace of God, to satisfy all creditors. Though it took a few years, no creditor suffered financially from his crimes. Many of my creditors, because of Noel's crimes, gave discounts to help close out the debts. I was thankful to be honest and a living example for my children.

Governor Cecil Andrus, as well as Congressman Richard Stallings helped me behind the scenes. What a godsend these two men were! They believed in me and helped me fight to get my husband arrested and charged.

Evelyn Bow was a child advocate/lobbyist in the state of Idaho. Governor Andrus sent her to take me by the hand and help us out. She would call me daily and say, "Girl, are you going to give up? Now pick yourself up and do what you have to do." She was member of the Church of the Brethren, feisty, and knew how to fight. Her belief in me gave me strength to stand up and fight. She joined in helping my attorney and taught me how to grow a backbone and come out a winner.

The children were plunged into a nightmarish state of affairs – blown apart emotional, spiritually and physically. I am sure they didn't know what, who or how to even trust me, though I set in motion escape for all of us. I began to change slowly, but surely. It took a few years before I wasn't the crying, whimpering, fearful mother they had known since birth. I slowly gained an emotional grip on becoming a strong, different, a take charge kind of person whether I wanted to or not. I got the concept of freedom and what it could mean to me. The fear and abuse I had lived with for more than forty-four years gave me the strength to grow up. I had been brainwashed into submission all of my life. If someone said jump, I asked how high!

It is extremely difficult to overcome brainwashing, fear, and the lack of control which grips a person in a prison of violence. It is almost unbreakable – and for many- they never manage to escape. I believed I had deserved the rape, the abuse and the pain and living in drudgery. I had been conditioned to accept such actions as reasonable under my parents' control and then passed along to my husband's control – even if I did choose him. When Noel screamed at me that I couldn't protect my children and not kill him – it was if the lifetime scales slid from my mind. I grew a backbone! Yes, it took a long time for me to find the strength to keep the steel in my spine, but I kept making baby steps until I did it.

I knew only I could prevent Noel from ever touching any of us again. I vowed to make life a living hell for him anyway I could – and I did. I hated him with a passion he had never stirred in my soul through my love for him. When my baby told me what Papa was doing to her, something black and lethal took a hold in my mind. Horror, disgust, and self-loathing overcame me at my failure in not knowing the monster had abused them. My first thought was to murder him, but then I realized the children would have no one to care for them if I killed him and was sent to prison.. I decided I would find the guts somewhere to get him arrested. Eventually, I did!

When the Canyon County Sheriff's Office couldn't find Noel to arrest him, Deputy Bob Miles had me to go all of the places I thought Noel might be and tell them if they saw Noel; he should go to the Veteran's hospital. The deputy wanted me to act as if I was worried about Noel and his welfare, though in my heart I wanted him to drop dead on the spot. Law Enforcement felt if they could get him into the VA hospital they could keep track of him. He showed up at the hospital before midnight – so one of the places I visited knew where he was.

I found him a second time after the Grand Jury gave grounds for charges. I went to the Boise VA Hospital and talked with a secretary and asked her for help with his address. She came to Middleton at midnight and gave me his address. My lawyer gave the address to the Sheriff's Office. The Canyon County Sheriff, Gary Putman had pretended his deputies couldn't find Noel to arrest him. Noel was arrested and charged with two counts of Lewd and Lascivious Conduct with a Minor and Sexual Abuse of a Minor in Canyon County. He made bail. Prosecutor Richard Harris was of the mindset that my daughters enticed their father to have sex with them. My daughters were four and fourteen. They were innocent children. My oldest daughter had never dated. When it was time for Noel's arraignment, he couldn't be found. I found Noel for the third time living in an apartment less than ten miles from our farm.

From the beginning of my youngest daughter's disclosure, Payette County Prosecutor, Bruce Birch, refused to press charges against Noel for more than 200 counts of sexual abuse for each of the children. We had just moved to Canyon County about a month before I learned Noel was molesting the children. Birch didn't want the expense of the prosecution even though there was medical evidence provided along with the children's statements. The Idaho Attorney General's Office refused prosecution stating that there were two counties to do so. At the time, it was almost impossible to get anything done to a man who had raped his children in Idaho. Payette

County Sheriff, Bob Borowsky, tried to get charges brought and did a thorough investigation, but Birch refused to do anything to help the children. We had just moved to Middleton in the fall of 1990. The prosecutors fought over who would bring charges and pay for the trial.

After Noel bonded out of jail, he came back to the house several times, trying to break in. The children and I lay under the dining table in abject fear on one particular night, and the Sheriff refused to respond to our call for help. I thought for sure Noel would get in the house and we would all be murdered. Noel was at our side living room window of our home. It was almost pried out of the window frame. It only opened by turning a handle. I was shaking so badly I had to lie down on my back and brace the gun between my knees. My son was going to pull the trigger for me because I did not have the strength to do both. I didn't know it at the time, but the 6mm Japanese rifle wouldn't have protected me. It wouldn't even fire! We would have been dead if Noel had gotten in.

In early 1992, Richard Stallings helped me under a 1941 military law to get most of Noel's VA compensation so I could support the children. We had lived on nothing and suffered shortages in most things; now we were able to have money to live on again. I was able to buy beds and furniture. Thank God! I gave Mr. Stallings signed permission to get into my husband's VA records and that is when we found out the doctors had tried to cleanse them. Mr. Stallings had checked the medical records and was appalled that Richard Harris made no effort to subpoena them. Canyon County Prosecutor, Richard Harris refused to subpoena Noel's VA files. Positive proof of Noel's rape was in the records and a jury would have given him prison time. The Sheriff, Gary Putman, of Canyon County did not arrest my husband.

Former Governor Cecil Andrus, Evelyn Bow and I believed there were pay-offs by Noel's wealthy brother and sister. It was feared the Prosecutor would put a hit out on me because I was fighting to get Noel arrested. There was a Canyon County rumor that Richard Harris or someone ordered the death of at least three witnesses in various cases.

My lawyer found a note in Noel's courthouse file apparently left by accident. The note stated, "Wife acting up. Must be controlled." Also in the file was a letter from an older former church member who was best friends with Noel's older sister attesting to what a wonderful man Noel was. Also included in that file is a letter from his 3rd oldest daughter by his first wife, Clara, claiming *I* had possibly molested her baby! She would bring her baby out for me to take care of for several days at a time to give her a break from mommy duties or for her and husband to go somewhere. Yet, she accused Noel of molesting her when she was young, talking about her breasts all of the time and touching her as she developed as a teenager, but she would not testify against him. The note pointed to hanky-panky in the case.

My lawyer, Sergio Guiterrez, felt I was in extreme danger and he needed to know where I was at all times. I know I acted weird as my PTSD and fear were in control, but fear was a catalyst that drove me forward, no matter the obstacles.

I lived in desperation believing there was no help available. Noel could have moved back into the house and law enforcement wouldn't have prevented him from coming in. My standing up and fighting put me in danger from my husband or persons unknown. Evelyn Bow attended all meetings I had with the Prosecutor at the Governor's request as a witness with me in the presence of Richard Harris. Harris told me to keep my mouth shut to the news media or suffer the consequences after my TV appearance. Evelyn Bow asked Harris if he was threatening my life, and he told her, "Take this any way you want to, I am going to get her one way or another." He wanted me to be guilty of the abuse along with my husband. He refused to even listen to what abuse I had suffered for twenty years.

I told the Prosecutor I refused to be quiet. I went on television giving a statement to rally public opinion in the case. Public opinion was a powerful weapon in the hands of a helpless woman.

My pastor, Rev. Dan St. Clair, asked to testify at the trial, but Richard Harris, the County Prosecutor, refused to let him give testimony. My next-door neighbor, Ben Mills, also wanted to be called to testify as he had observed the abuse I was enduring. He told the Prosecutor's Office he knew my husband was dangerous and hurting all of us. His efforts were rebuffed.

This was one of the most freaky and dangerous times in my life. One night, I was awakened with the sound of my bedroom window screen being cut and ripped. I woke up shaking in fear. All of a sudden, Noel stood beside my bed. I could see him, smell him and knew he was there with a knife in his hand. All of the windows were locked. I started praying to God, begging for mercy and protection. All of a sudden, Noel disappeared. Then I could hear him outside of the house telling me what he was going to do. I jumped up, grabbed the 20-gauge shotgun the deputy had brought me.

I ran outside screaming like a wild woman, "You sorry man, I am going to kill you." He was at the gate to the driveway. When he saw me come around the corner of the house, he started pounding down the highway. He jumped into a car by our neighbor's farm and sped away. I was still screaming like a banshee trying to get close enough so I could kill him. I was brandishing my shotgun with only one bullet in it, but I was going to shoot him! As the car sped away, I vomited in reaction to the fear and stress. The Sheriff's Office refused to respond to my call. Thank God

I didn't become a murderer.

A counselor trained in pictorial forensics had me bring in the pictures of Noel. She explained she believed he had seven different personalities. She was a Catholic and had no trouble believing Noel was demon-possessed. I knew the last time he raped me, he talked in seven different voices and I thought I was going to die. Looking into his eyes, I knew the look of evil with death as his goal.

In the weeks after the children and I escaped, my attorney fought to get CARES forensic rape exams. Canyon County did not want to pay the expense to get the proof. The results of the Idaho CARES exams showed that all three of the children had been raped. The exam also stated that my oldest daughter was pregnant. I asked that she not be informed of that fact and I demanded medically-induced abortion pills for her. I could not bear for her to carry a child of incest at fourteen years old and ruin her life. An Oregon doctor had certified the baby's rape, but Payette County refused to file charges on her behalf. Yet Noel, even after testimony and the CARES exam, was given a seven-and-a-half-year sentence and *PROBATION!* My oldest daughter wrote this letter to the judge the day of Noel's sentencing:

10-5-92

Your Honor,

It is hard to express what that man did to me. The reason I call him that man is that he doesn't deserve the honor of being called father. He has been touching me wrong for so long I don't even know what a good touch is supposed to be like from a father. He has put my family and me through living hell. Your honor, please put my nightmares of his hands on me to rest. He deserves to be put away for the maximum sentence for the rape of me and my sister! Thanks, (signed by my oldest daughter.)

Noel served only thirty-seven days in jail for the damage he had done to our children and me, but that was the legal atmosphere at this time in our country. I felt betrayed by the legal system I worked within – at that time I felt I should have murdered him instead of going the legal route. His was the first conviction obtained by a wife who fought and won in Idaho. I might have been worthless, but my children meant everything to me.

> *Pain of evil,*
> *Denial,*
> *Brokenness,*
> *Helpless shadows,*
> *Hatred versus love,*
> *Upheaval,*
> *A moat of despair,*
> *Water,*
> *Drowning in tears,*
> *Rejection,*
> *Repeated,*
> *Voiceless,*
> *Destroyer - the evil,*
> *Lingering on!*

My oldest daughter was in love with her father. During the years of therapy, she never recovered. When the therapist confronted me with about her being in love with Noel, I thought my heart would shatter. My precious daughter was forced into a world of darkness not of her making in an incestuous situation of evil. I believe she suffered from the Stockholm Syndrome, but after his death, she decided I was the "bad one."

She defends her father even though he raped her for

many years. She hated him until his death and then, out of guilt for her testimony, began to claim he was innocent. This is normal behavior for a rape survivor. It is common for a guilt complex to develop and stay with an older child for many years. She became very abusive to my youngest daughter and me.

Children of rape often identify with their rapist. If it is a father, the child comes to believed any touch is love, and any attention, even though bad, is better than being ignored. Even after several years of therapy, she reverted to scenarios where he couldn't have raped her, she was his special princess, daddy's little girl, and how much he loved her. She lives in total denial of the horrible man he was. She turned her back on my youngest and me, clinging to the memory of a monster. I couldn't allow the farce to continue.

She is the product of her father's crimes. As a child, she did not have the knowledge to give consent to participate willingly in his sexual assaults, but in the end, he convinced her she wanted to become his lover, even though she was his daughter. Noel created a sick triangle. I could not encourage her being "in love" with her father as it was a sin. She engaged in a sick after-death love relationship. However, as an adult, her decisions had serious consequences. She will always be my beloved daughter and beautiful princess, but I will never again live in denial or any kind of abusive relationship. In 2006, I decided it was healthier to walk away from my older daughter. It has been several good years without the constant drama of my oldest daughter's anger. Good years, but painful ones because I still love her more than my own life.

My oldest daughter's therapist recommended I leave Idaho as she felt my oldest daughter was planning matricide, so I left. It was the hardest decision of my life to set her free and take my freedom from the drama she created by her hate and denial. It was better to leave than to have her become a criminal. She had such potential to be whomever she decided she could be. She drank heavily all through college, and hating me was her pastime. I understood I was alive and an easy target for her anger. She had more than one personality and one didn't remember what the other one did. I couldn't fix her, though I tried for many years to help her. Her rage was too much for my aching heart. It wasn't healthy for me to stay in her life. I paid a heavy price for the sin of marrying Noel Snow. The cost was my older children.

Shortly before I left Idaho, my oldest daughter came to me a few weeks after her marriage demanding her "inheritance." I was so shocked I could only stare in disbelief. I had given her years of therapy, paid all of the bills, but she had not tried to help herself. She believed I had money somewhere when I had nothing!

I made a life-altering choice at that point to avoid control, power, and manipulation in my life. I had walked away from my family as a young adult and from my abusive marriage and now the anger and bitterness of my daughter.

I do know if you have been victimized, you are not at fault. It is possible to heal, but you must fight for yourself and your family. Know you are an important person worthy of being loved in a healthy manner.

Tap dance, eat cotton candy, laugh riding roller coaster and enjoy the world opening up in front of you. Life is to good to let circumstances control you. You are just what you decide you can be. Be all you can!

Chapter 30

A Christ Child is born,
His love does us adorn,
Come, Angels on high, blow your horn,
His love we have worn,
It is the season of hope,
Of grace and with the gift of wisdom,
Come, dear Savior, deliver us from evil,
Give us our daily bread,
Fill us with warmth and joy.
Give the angels a place to sing in our hearts,
In addition, let your light shine brightly in the heavens.

Christmas at Valley View High School 1991

My life was in shambles. Barely escaping Noel, there
was no money, three hungry children and hot checks rolling
in. Frankly, I was scared to death, living in a fog, dazed -
an angry rape survivor! Some days the pressure of the fear
kept me frozen inside. There would not be any Christmas
for my children; presents were out of the question, but God
had other plans for us.

I needed a job to support my children. I had not held a
job since 1980 and my resume was outdated. What job
could I handle with PTSD? Shortly before Christmas,
Principal Allen Lake from the Middleton School District
called me up and offered me a substitute teacher job! He
helped me fill out the paperwork for a background check,
knowing I was stretched to the breaking point with my
ongoing ordeal. He had faith in me and taught me I was
worthwhile as a human being. His faith gave me hope that
maybe, just maybe, I could survive.

One of my students stopped by my classroom at lunchtime wanting to know what I was doing for Christmas. I replied, "Nothing." The Student Body President and two other students then asked me why I looked so sad. He stated, "You have the saddest face and eyes of any teacher we've had. We want to know why you are crying with no tears." I told them I couldn't discuss my personal issues with them.

The three students persisted. Finally, their kindness and caring broke me. Unprofessional, yes, but I started sobbing. It was as if a dam broke inside me after months of overwhelming fear. I told them I couldn't provide Christmas for my children. I explained I was in a situation and couldn't legally divulge anything, but my children wouldn't have Christmas.

My son had been begging for a leather jacket for Christmas so he could be like the other students in his high school class. I wept at night because I knew there would be no leather jacket for him at Christmas, no gifts at all for any of them. I felt like a horrible parent. My anxiety was skyrocketing.

It was time for the school Christmas break. I went home, leaving the school with a heavy heart and full of despair. What was I going to do for my children's Christmas? My oldest daughter was at school for cheerleading practice and I had to pick up my youngest daughter from daycare. I wept all the way from Valley View to Middleton knowing there was no way that I could provide any kind of Christmas. How was I going to look at my children and tell them we weren't having presents this year? We'd had enough hurt, but there was going to be the absence of anything under our tree. I could see the need in their eyes to believe in Christmas. I kept telling my children God is going to provide. I had no idea where anything from Christmas would come from – I was counting on God and his Angels and *HE* sent me many!

As I pulled into the driveway and stepped inside my home, I stopped in shocked surprise. What was all of this stuff in front of me? My living room was full from one end to the other, stacked with boxes, clothing and food about four feet high! My son was standing there as if bemused. He was trembling so hard, I thought perhaps there had been a death.

I said, "What in the world is all of this, son?" He cried, "Mom, your students just left. They waited for you to get here, but they had to get on home. They came with several pick-up and car loads of all of this and presented it to me."

"Can you believe this, Mom?"

I sat down in amazement with tears running down my face! My baby clung to me in fear. She thought something bad was happening because we were crying.

My son suddenly started weeping harder. I looked up, and there he stood with a leather jacket in his hands, tears streaming down his face, hugging that precious jacket to his chest! It was almost like the one he had been dreaming of owning, a soft fawn leather jacket, beautiful in his eyes. God had heard my tears and prayers. I was left staring in shock. God still knew me and had not forgotten my precious children during this season of His Son's birth! My wonderful son got his precious jacket for school! Oh, how proud he was when he returned to school in January! There were clothes, shoes, coats, socks, anything that children could desire for Christmas. There was even clothing for me! We had food to last us for a year. My students' kindness and generosity restored my faith that the evil of Noel would surely fade in time.

When my oldest daughter got home, we all sat and wept at the beautiful Christmas God provided for us. I will never forget the thoughtfulness of the student body of 1991 at Valley View High School in Caldwell, Idaho. I was so thankful for the hard work they put in to making Christmas our very best ever. They heard me with their hearts and what a surprise and loving care they provided. They were my angels. My baby had dolls and toys she would never have been blessed with except for their caring. More gifts arrived, left on our doorstep in secret. I pray God will remember those thoughtful hearts in that community for eternity.

I will never forget! Neither will God!

Chapter 31

The law is not always just or merciful,
The Devil must laugh like a jokester!
Justice is supposed to be blind,
However, when the blindfold is lost,
Vengeance would be an eye for an eye,
When the scales are out of balance,
All are losers,
Surely, God gives solace,
Benevolence is found,
Hope in the heart,
It is trust that must not be misplaced!

The legal atmosphere in 1991 for rape victims was like an icescape of frozen tundra. If you were a woman with children, no money and being pressured by the Prosecuting Attorney's Office not to press charges, you were in a no-man's land of nothing. With the Prosecuting Attorney threatening to arrest me, I needed guidance for my children and me.

Well-intentioned people would stop by telling me if it was them, they would just kill Noel. Staying alive after rape is traumatically difficult, especially if I believed in the law. Murder would have been too quick, too easy for Noel. Surviving the pressure drove me into a zombie-like state. Twice, men come knocking on my door after midnight. One man explained, very convincingly and sincerely, that he would gladly kill my husband for me. All I had to do was just say the word. He described how he would cut him up, put him in a barrel filled with acid, and dump him over the bridge into the Snake River just below Boise.

The next man came offering to kill Noel slowly, painfully, and grind him up, burning him in a desert location. These midnight visits terrified me. I called my attorney. He and I both knew that if I were to indicate acceptance of these offers, I would be immediately arrested as an accessory to murder. We felt these men were sent by Richard Harris to try to entrap me and both men were wearing a wire. I was walking a tightrope to prevent my children from being removed and put into foster care. In my heart, I wanted Noel to die a painful, slow death, but I wasn't a fool. I thanked them politely; scared to death maybe they were making the same offer to Noel about the children and me. Fear was a living dragon in my breast; my brain felt like a rock-hard lump of pain. Thank God, I had a will in place if something happened to me. The children would be safe with a lawyer friend of mine in Arkansas. God was indeed taking care of me.

Noel's brother who was a millionaire and was footing all of Noel's legal bills. I had nothing and no one to turn to except God, but his grace was sufficient.

I was still contemplating suicide. The nights were hellish. God must have gotten tired of having to constantly keep His angels guarding me and keeping me alive. Many nights after I got back home from teaching school, the mental agony was so bad I sat in the bathtub with the shower curtain closed holding a shotgun in my mouth, believing that the children would be better off without me.

Thank God for Rev. Dan St. Clair who was willing to sacrifice his sleep to listen to my pain. I promised him I wouldn't pull the trigger without listening to him each time the pain overwhelmed me. He never let me down as my pastor, and was always there praying with me and begging me to put the gun down. His wife stood by him in helping me. When the Assembly of God began putting pressure on him to stand by Noel, I left the Wilder church rather than put these two wonderful people in the middle of my trouble. Brother Dan St. Clair later resigned from the church and from the Assemblies of God, because he was an honorable man, refusing to cover up Noel's rape.

I have chosen to stop and smell life's roses! I savor each day as if it is golden. Each morning's sunrise is glorious. I am so blessed.

Hitch a ride on the midnight train to somewhere, ride the rails to heaven and back. You can see more than the good, the bad, and the ugly. Wash clean as snow, know that God loves you.

Chapter 32

Jackals living in my nightmares,
Devil shadows from Hell,
Ripping the flesh from my bones,
The terror of finding out the horrors,
Exposure of the father's sins,
Betrayal of marriage vows,
Sorrow of the pain,
The hollow eyes of the children,
Grasping at life,
Hanging by the edge,
The screams of the children,
Haunting nights, longer days,
Blinding, grinding edges of the psyche,
Slipping reality and harsh self-punishment,
Brutal self-doubt of soul anguish,
Mirror reflection of what Hell must be,
Nowhere to run, nowhere to hide,
Societal judgment, pain, pain,
My silent screams, raw sewage of the soul,
How will the children survive?
How will I?

I got all of us into therapy with some wonderful professionals. In the process of getting Noel arrested, charged and convicted, I knew the only way my family could survive was to have mental, emotional and spiritual help. Thankfully, I found Wanda Newton and Carol Collins, in Caldwell, ,Idaho, to help us. Both were towers of strength in a time of troubling turmoil for the children and me.

My youngest struggled to survive emotionally. I held her on my lap week after week during the therapy sessions.

She would pull out my hair in terror, dig the flesh from my scalp during therapy and beat my body with her baby fist. I couldn't let her see my tears. I learned to cry inside, bleeding to death emotionally. It was the only way she could find peace. The therapist and I decided it was the 'monkey syndrome' or a reversion back to animalistic behavior of survival that caused her instinctively to reach out to me when angry and in pain. Wanda understood her four-year-old lips and hesitant speech.

Noel insisted she was retarded. I demanded and won a forensic mental exam for her. She wasn't retarded; in fact, she was highly intelligent. She suffered Aphasia, losing the power of understandable speech which was the result of her rape trauma. She was in speech therapy at school for several years and I worked with her extensively. My baby daughter was emphatic that it was her father who had raped her, not only to Wanda, but during the CARES medical examination. She was only four years old, but she knew the difference between truth and lies. My husband and his family told the Prosecutor I was insane and had molested the children.

My baby would draw on her legs, ugly, grotesque things that seemed to flow out of her pain. I asked her why she was drawing on herself and she explained if she could make her body ugly enough, Papa wouldn't come back and want to hurt her again. She would rock for hours, endlessly screaming in pain, emotionally fragile, beating her body, pounding with an intensity that almost drove me mad. I held her in my arms for hours, days, weeks and months, giving her a safe harbor to cling to. Oh, God, there is no way to explain the devastation that rape causes or the pain I saw in my children's tortured faces! The therapy was unleashing the children's memories and emotions

If my youngest went to sleep, she would scream most of the night. I was teaching with very little sleep; my health was shot. I would be holding my baby, comforting

her, and down the hallway, my oldest daughter would be
screaming, "Please, Papa, don't hurt me anymore, stop!" I
would go give her comfort in her sleep and then I would
hear my son screaming with nightmares. As soon as I
would get them calmed, my baby would start screaming
again. It was a never-ending nightmarish cycle from Hell.

I came up with an idea that gave my baby some
control. I hung up a pillowcase filled with old soft sweaters
and we called it our "mad bag". When her pain caused her
to feel out of control, I would take her to the mad bag and
tell her it was Papa and to beat the bag as if it was him. It
was a ritual she performed often, and after more than three
years, she was able to stop drawing on her body. It took
much longer to stop the body beating.

Therapy was a frightening time for her and sickening
for me. The therapist explained I must keep the faith that
she would be able to reach my child and help her, but her
nightmares were horrific and breaking my heart.

One afternoon, I was lying on the bed holding my
baby, trying to give her peace so she could take a nap. I
was praying softly asking Jesus to help us. She had told the
therapist Papa hurt her with his extra finger. It came to me
suddenly to ask if she would like to look at Mama and see
if I had an extra finger anywhere on my body.

She sat straight up in the bed, looking very scared, but
also very interested at checking my body out. I told her,
"Now Mama is going to put her hands over her head and
you can undo my housecoat and look me over. I want you
to make sure you look everywhere on Mama to see if you
can find an "extra finger" so you will know if it was me or
Papa hurting you. She cautiously undid my housecoat and
looked me over. She slowly pulled my panties down and
then she bent down, sat on her knees and carefully looked
at my genitals. The look on her baby face was one of pure
wonder as she gazed on my nakedness. She started
jumping up and down, hanging onto my knees screaming,

"Mama, you don't have an extra finger between your legs. Papa pushed his extra finger in me and it 'hurted' so bad."

She flew up into my arms, sobbing her little heart out in relief. I cried with her because we had found the key to unlock her horror and help set her free. The therapist was ecstatic with the breakthrough.

In therapy, we began to learn that Noel sometimes wore a wig along with several of my dresses. He even went as far as to wear my panties and pantyhose. He would talk in my voice and tell her it was Mama. My baby knew in reality it wasn't me, but she was still afraid it might have been. Thank God for His inspiration!

I had her pick out the dresses he had worn and we took them to the therapist's office and let her cut them up and throw them in the trash.

During the baby's therapy, she wanted to write Noel an accountability letter and the therapist and I thought it would be a great victory for her. I worked and found Noel's address in Arkansas where he had gone illegally.

I gathered dried old 'horse puckey' and then I let roses die and mold. I took a shoebox full of the 'horse puckey' and the moldy roses to the therapist. With our help, my little one wrote a letter telling Noel that he had no right to rape her, that he was evil, and she hated him. She and the therapist put the letter in the shoebox, wrapped it tightly, and took it to the post office and mailed it to Noel in Dover, Arkansas.

My baby counted the days until we thought he had gotten the 'gift'. She giggled and worked with the therapist on how Noel must have felt when he got her letter telling him he was no longer her Papa. She laughed and laughed how he must have looked finding the horse puckey and those nasty roses! It was an empowering moment for her. I believe this gave her the courage to begin healing.

Ms. Newton was instrumental in my little one's recovery. Through her guidance, and extra mothering, my little one grew during the years of therapy. Ms. Newton has a place of honor in our hearts forever for her expertise and hard work.

Unfortunately, my oldest daughter did not try to help herself or be honest in therapy about her abuse. I paid for her therapy for four years. I could only do my best, but it wasn't enough for her and it was too late.

My oldest daughter was and is a talented, beautiful young woman. She was a varsity cheerleader for four years. One of my teacher friends was the cheerleading coach. We talked about my daughter's need to have a sport in which she could excel. She tried out and won a spot on the team. It was a wonderful moment for her. She was good at what she did and I was so proud of her. She was my joy, but I lost her to her anger for what Noel had done. She now deifies Noel as a 'God-like man', rather than the rapist he was.

She entered the Idaho Dairy Princess Contest and won it! She was the Meridian Dairy Princess for the year – what a joy for her. She led the parade all through the town. She was beautiful.

She worked as a llama farm pooper-scooper all through high school to earn her spending money. Then she began acting out and developed two personalities. One was good and the other was bad, so bad I didn't know if I could survive it. I lost a precious part of my flesh when she turned her love for me into hate because I had 'taken her father away from her.' I had no choice. He was a criminal and not allowed to be near her as his rape would have continued or he would have killed her. He was fixated on impregnating her as Ronald Gene Simmons had in the Dover, Arkansas murder case. I wasn't going to let his evil continue one moment longer than necessary to get us away from him without our dying.

My son chose to smash and burn his father's heart pills as a way to release some of his anger – it was very revealing that Noel lived without his heart pills in his possession. Anything I thought would help my children recover, no matter how painful it might be, I let them do, as I was determined for us to survive. I kept my pain hidden away almost too long.

My son was a good young man. He worked in the farm fields each summer pulling tassels off seed corn to earn spending money. He saved it to buy a car. I bought him a bicycle so he could have a means of transportation. I had no means to pay for car insurance or a car for him. I took him to the truck pick-up place where many other students met for a ride to the various farms. They were paid at the end of the summer. It was godsend for my son. He was hurting so badly and tormented by what had happened to him, he couldn't talk to me about his abuse. He went to therapy for three years, but chose not to engage in healing.

My son turned to sports to deal with much of his angst. He lived and breathed basketball, but he was fragile. He was more than six feet tall and only weighed 125 pounds. He felt so unworthy, yet had a brilliant mind. I made sure the coach of the school where I taught put him on the basketball team each year. I was determined he would have his dream.

He can't see me as it reminds him of the trauma of his abuse. When I left Idaho, he gave me a hug telling me how much he will always love me. He was my best friend, and part of me died when he walked away to survive in his own way. I thought I wouldn't survive losing my two older children. The pain has almost broken my fragile spirit, and I have cried a million tears, but at least I saved their lives. Their freedom was worth all the torment.

I wanted charges brought against Noel for raping me. At that time, wives weren't getting justice for marital rape. The Prosecutor, Richard Harris, refused to let me see a doctor for more than a year or have a vaginal exam or medical treatment for the damage Noel had done to me. He told me if I had a rape examination, he would put me in jail for tampering with the case. He laughed scornfully, "A man has a right to have sex with his wife; so what if he got rough with you!" If it not had been for Dr. Charles B. Green's psychological test and report, I would have been jailed on a rapist's word as somehow being an accessory for his criminal violence.

I had my own private funeral for Noel, which was extremely therapeutic. My therapist went with me out to a very nasty swamp. I burned Noel's photos - ashes to ashes, evil to evil - and then did the prayer ritual for a funeral service. I consigned him to Hell and threw his photo ashes into the nasty swamp. It was a cathartic moment for me.

Sit on a swing, let your life flow through the air of hope. You can find yourself sitting in the birds-eye-view of the past and move into the future. Grab a hold of peace, determine to live it. Blow like thistle down across your life choices and gain a new vision of all the tomorrows. They are yours.

Chapter 33

The sway of the justice dance is done alone,
'The Man' could only shuffle,
Whimpering in the casting of Justice's shadow,
The world now knew his secrets,
No more two-stepping into avoidance or denial,
Caught in the trap of his own making,
Let him now dance to God's tune which will play,
Play on through eternity,
Judgment in Holy Hands,
'The Man' will stand in that court of justice one day,
At last his sentence will be just,
No more dancing, no more lies,
All will be known,
That will be the final dance!

Finally, Noel's court hearing arrived - on August 10, 1992. How ironic, it was our 21st wedding anniversary! Noel made this statement to the court:

"I am not under the influence of any drugs or alcohol at the time of executing this agreement and I fully understand all of my rights and the consequences of my acts and I believe that it would be in my best interest to enter a plea of guilty to the charge mentioned above and do hereby authorize my attorney to enter a plea of guilty to the said offense and ask the Court to proceed to Judgment and sentence after the entry of the plea..."

On August 24, 1992, I got a Letter of Notice from the Prosecuting attorney's Office, which read as follows:

Dear Kathyrn:
"As you are aware, the defendant in the above-

referenced case entered a plea of guilty to the charge of
sexual abuse in Canyon County District Court."

October 5, 1992, Noel opted to take a plea bargain
conviction for our oldest daughter in front of a judge, thus
avoiding a jury trial. Legally, we were free of him.
Charges against him for the little one's sexual abuse were
dropped as part of his plea bargain. The conviction was a
travesty, but one of the first convictions in the State of
Idaho with a wife fighting to save her children. I was
awarded full custody of the children. Noel had made us
believe he had the power of life and death in our lives. My
youngest daughter helped catch him and thus, she, of all the
three children, was the victor over him.

Bob Miles, a Canyon County Sheriff Officer wrote this
to my youngest that, *"I feel bad when people hurt children.*
I know you are a courageous girl for being able to tell
about the secret touching. It was the right thing to do. I
know you are very happy and are growing to be stronger
each day. I want you to know I care about you, your
mother, your brother and your sister in helping make all of
you safe."

Mr. Miles was a caring law officer, always there if I
needed to talk, interested in how the children were doing,
and offering encouragement. I was very angry with him
during a lot of the case because I thought he was lying to
the Prosecutor and to me. After we had a long talk, we
figured out that the Prosecutor was lying to the both of us.
I learned to talk to him directly and not let the Prosecutor
know we had spoken. It was a long, hard, twisted ordeal of
getting my husband arrested, charged and convicted. If
only we had figured this fact out earlier in the case. I
appreciate everything Mr. Miles did to encourage me to go
back to college, to stay in church, and to raise my children
the best I could. He was rock in a storm that almost
swallowed me whole.

Canyon County Detective, Kent Heady, was instrumental in helping my youngest daughter in her recovery process. He worked in therapy with her letting her know he cared about her. He played the part of her Papa and let her talk to him as the 'bad guy'. He and his wife were bricks with their support and being there for us. He stayed in touch with my youngest, encouraging her and making sure that she knew he was one of the 'good guys'!

One fact I learned after the trial was that Noel had taken, and miserably failed, a polygraph test. The Prosecutor failed to notify me or my attorney of his test and failed to enter it into the court proceedings.

According to Noel's parole officer, Dennis Bodily, he was one of the worst pedophiles he ever supervised. He thanked me for fighting for my children. He wasn't the only person in the Treasure Valley horrified by the suspended sentence. He shared Noel's pre-sentencing court-ordered psychological exam which showed Noel as a sociopath. He couldn't understand how Noel got off with such a light sentence after all he had done to the children and me. Noel should have been locked in a mental ward of a prison instead of being free to rape countless others.

Judge Gerald Weston ordered probation for Noel and released him into the custody of his brother. Noel was to go to a nursing home and live there until he died. That was setting the fox loose in the henhouse. Noel never complied with the court order. Nothing was done about his parole violation by the Idaho Parole Board or law enforcement. He was unsafe to be around whether it be a woman, a child or an animal - male or female. It didn't matter to Noel, he would abuse and violate anything he could get near.

Noel filed for a divorce in California in 1993 and for custody of the children. My lawyer told me that he just might get custody of the children as his brother had lots of money. I had nothing left. My Idaho attorney hired an attorney out of San Francisco to represent me in Stockton, California in the divorce proceeding. She let me pay her in installments. The divorce decree was signed on my birthday in 1994.

Happy Birthday to me! This was the best birthday present ever! I won the right to have the property settlement decided in the Idaho court. I was awarded all of the property. His criminal conviction denied him all rights to the children. Thank God! He was ordered to pay child support. He never paid one dime of support so I was able to appropriate most of his VA compensation for the care of the children until each child graduated high school.

He married Eva Smart in 1998 in Pope County, Arkansas after illegally returning to Arkansas. His new wife babysat eight of her grandchildren, thus giving Noel a brand new crop of children to molest. It is rumored that Noel molested two of Eva's grandchildren and nothing was done about it. I personally faxed copies of Noel's conviction and the Judge's orders to her family and to the Pope County Sheriff, Jay Winters. Noel was never to be around children under eighteen. Sheriff Jay Winters refused to do anything about him. Mr. Winters informed me that I should leave the 'poor old man' alone. I found out later that Noel and Winters were distant relations. Noel never registered as a sex offender in Arkansas, even though he was a high-level sex offender.

My biggest fantasy was that I might tie Noel to the gatepost of our small farm in Middleton, Idaho. I would place a pair of large fish hook grabs into his testicles, tie heavy fishing line to a slow-moving tractor, and drive off very slowly. My fantasy gave me a measure of comfort and power over the man who tortured me for twenty long years. Surely, my hurting mind cried, I should have been allowed to participate in his punishment. I knew Noel would one day have to face his Final Judgment.

I filed a lawsuit in Federal Court in 1992 against the Boise Veterans Federal VA Hospital and the doctors who had cared for Noel. I refused to be intimidated any longer. It was an uphill battle. I took on a giant and won! It was the first Federal VA lawsuit against a doctor's failure to report sexual abuse of a wife and children. I won the case and settled out of court for an undisclosed amount. I refused to settle without a letter of admission of guilt. What I got in writing was the most valuable piece of paper in our healing process:

Quoting from the July 4, 1994 Federal VA Settlement document:

"This claim arises as a result of the care and treatment by the Department of Veterans Affairs Medical Center, Boise, Idaho, beginning in 1986. The veteran's wife and children complained of abuse in the home by the veteran, but the matter was not reported to the child protective services. Subsequently, the veteran was accused of and pleaded guilty to sexual misconduct with the children. The failure to report was a direct and proximate cause of the subsequent abuse suffered by the mother and the children."

My children were my life; rape was never to be part of their life. The devastation left in the wake of Noel's sexual abuse took a lasting toll on my fragile health. I killed my emotions, murdering parts of me so I wouldn't feel the twisting horror. I am sure I looked the same, felt the same, smelled the same, but the woman my children knew as mother had retreated behind a wall of insurmountable pain. I was irreparably different. The two older children never accepted the changes. I am still in recovery approaching old age, but I am a walking, talking, breathing survivor by the grace of God.

I have had more than twenty years to study my marriage to Noel. I've researched it from every imaginable angle. I left no stone unturned; blamed myself in a thousand different ways for my children's abuse. I've had to live with the resulting 100 % physical disabilities. I crumbled under the crushing shame of Noel's crimes, but I've rubbed him from any segment of my life by getting rid of all his possessions, and pictures – especially those with the children. The sickening smell of him embedded in my memory has been the most difficult to eradicate. I lived with hate, pain and anger; now I live without the nightmares. I stand with God!

Lock the door a thief is coming! He slyly enters our world, steals the innocence of the children. Lying around the corner, in wait, chasing terror like frozen frost! Believe your child! Hug them tight, help them fight for what is right. The thief cannot give back innocence. It is lost forever – a pit that is dug!

Chapter 34

The road was rocky and long, pitted with mistakes,
Washed slick with tears,
Painfully paved with so many regrets,
Deceit filled every crevice of memories,
There was freedom in the knowing,
That I danced alone, paving memory's lane,
With love, daring, and choosing,
What freedom!

1994-1997

In the fall of 1994, after getting my divorce and settling the VA lawsuit, I resigned my substitute-teaching/aide job with the Middleton School District. I returned to college, eventually earning my degree in Secondary Education, Speech, Drama, and Communication. I held teaching endorsements in each of those fields along with Business Education and Natural Science. I had come full circle, finally free to choose whom I was becoming. It was a hard two and a half years of studying and raising my children. I was remodeling houses, working at anything I could find so that I could remain in college and get my degree. I created ways to function with incredible pain and build a new career finishing out my life's dream of teaching.

I was blessed by Pat Sayers from the Middleton Food Bank. She supplied me with groceries weekly so I could feed my family as I returned to college. Pride had no place in building our future.

Idaho Rehabilitation certified me as disabled and paid my transportation costs to and from college. Many encouraged me to fight for and win a life. I am grateful for all of those who stood beside me with their encouragement to succeed, Patsy Kretsch, Dale and LaVonne Kyle, Pastor Lura Kinder-Miesen, Rev. Daniel St. Clair, Sheriff George Nourse, Detective Bob Miles, Detective Kent Heady and Allen Lake, principal of the Middleton Middle School.

My children were my inspiration giving me the courage to go back to school and earn my diploma. It was a proud day in December 1997 when I was awarded my college degree. What a blessing my education has been! The pride I felt as I got my diploma can't be explained. I discontinued my college education when I married Noel, but the degree now was mine! My Communication Professors at Boise State University were absolutely wonderful in helping me succeed, especially Dr. Marvin Cox, Marty Most, Dr. Mary Rolfing, Dr. Sue Wade, Dr. Pat Bieter and Dr. Ben Parker.
I suffered bad panic attacks in the classroom, but my professors agreed I could leave any time it was necessary in order to gain control of myself.

Many of my professors encouraged me to write about my rape and abuse and do research studies that allowed me to write about issues I needed to understand. What a blessing! Many of my fellow students were helpful to me as a returning older student. I found the world was a wide open place with so many, kind, helpful people willing and ready to reach out to encourage me.

Chapter 35

The cloud of doom no longer lingered,
Shuttled behind the mountain of regret,
I learned to look beyond the clouded horizon,
I looked in the face of God,
Found His loving kindness, walk in His light,
Nor did the shame of the past grasp me in its headlock,
I am free,
dancing to the music that only the angels can hear!

1998-2000

In 2000, after earning the money, I went to court and dropped my maiden name from my birth certificate. I declared my independence from Aaron and Betty Russell becoming my own person. Aaron humiliated me by claiming I wasn't his daughter so I got rid of the stigma of his name along with Noel's name. I love the person I have become. I was able to walk out of the courtroom with pride of self.

The years of the incest and rape sloughed-off in the courtroom when the judge asked me if I was sure I wanted to become a new person! It was wonderfully freeing and gave me the courage to reclaim the many years Noel had stolen from me.

The little things make such a difference in our psyche and give us our courage back. I am no longer a cowardly lion. It is important as a survivor of violence to accept the right to feel joy.

On December 15, 2000, I had surgery to repair the internal damage Noel inflicted on me September 17, 1991. When I woke up from the surgery, the surgeon explained there was barely enough good tissue to sew me back together. I would never work again and had a five pound lifting limit imposed. I spent the next five years fighting to recover and live. The scar tissue is still holding me together. The pressure of the guts against the incision is incredibly painful. I have a difficult time walking or standing, but I refused to give in – life will end with me still fighting. For ten years, I couldn't sit or stand without terrifying pain. The doctors finally found a permanent stitch had torn loose. The stitch was as if I was sitting on an inch-long cable that ran through the internal surgery incision. They snipped the stitch as it was acting like a saw in the incision. Thankfully, now, I live without that degree of excruciating pain.

It has been a long, painful recovery. My youngest daughter stood by me, and at thirteen, became my caretaker. She made sure I was bathed, fed, and the home kept spotless. She graduated high school with high honors and from college with high honors. She took on a large responsibility. She demanded I live each day with the fiercest determination that only a child can demand. She never seemed angry because I was so ill. She was always there if I needed her. I am very independent so I did my best to not be a burden to her. I credit her grit for my life.

Besides the grace of a wonderful Heavenly Father, I acknowledge Hannah, our beloved cat, with a great deal of my recovery. The cat would cry and demand I get out of bed to let her in and out of the house. She would sit by my bed, or lay on my pillow, keeping me company and begging me to stay awake and care for her while my daughter was at school. The cat was persistent. If I didn't respond to her meowing, she would nip my fingers to get my attention. She would run to the door, demanding to be let out, or fed. If it was my mealtime, she would squall until I crept out of bed to eat what my daughter left by my bedside.

I started walking just a few feet at a time. Our beloved

dog, Hudson, took over for me outside. He would walk slowly and patiently nudge me to walk by his side with my hand on his head. It took me months to build up to a mile a day, but Hudson was right there pushing me forward. The neighbors thought I would die, as I was in such a bad shape. I refused to give up. After school, my daughter would help, walking with me and encouraging me to live. I could only look in her beloved face and pray that God give me life - and he did! Her faith in me keeps me living today.

The doctors gave me only a 50% chance of recovery and survival, but thank God, I have seen my daughter graduate high school and college. She has been the truest, rarest gift from God filling my life with gumption.

Time chains of woven peace braided into a rope of joy cannot be easily broken. Strength comes in fighting together to stop the evil of abuse in any form.

The windows of freedom are found by personal choices to walk in the beauty of wholeness. It is believing that the window is truly opened that is hard for the victimized to accept. May the light of day and God's love be your guide.

Chapter 36

Fear is a great motivator of survival,
Praying each moment for one more day,
One more hour,
Pain surreal,
Mind over matter,
One step at a time,
Slow as the ticking hand of the clock,
Determination and grit,
Hanging on for the future,
Granted life,
Appreciating hope,
I am standing, battered, but alive.

2001

I'd been legally free of Noel for eleven years, but not free of his threats, stalking and demented behavior causing me mind-boggling fear! It was hard living with the boogeyman loose. I would look up, and there would be a car in my driveway. I rarely got a single night's sleep without being fearful. I was haunted by the thought that if I closed my eyes for too long, Noel would kill me and the children. One night he tried to run my baby and me down while we were walking along the highway. The phone would constantly ring, sometimes sixty to seventy times a day. The frightening breathing would begin and the grating sounds, grunts, and sighs with the freak evidently being sexually aroused by the calls. He was obsessed with us, but the frightening phone calls by the destructive wretch were draining until Canyon County Sheriff George Nourse facilitated my disappearance from all records. I sold the farm in Middleton and moved to Greenleaf, Idaho, but the torment didn't stop. We couldn't figure out how he was getting our unlisted phone number because I changed it frequently.

At last, one of the VA officers, Bob Secrist, in Boise figured out how Noel was finding us. He called me and told me how Noel was getting my phone number each time I moved - this time to New Plymouth, Idaho. I had to report our new mailing address to the VA for the children's insurance and to continue receiving the VA benefits checks. Noel would find our new number by searching our medical records and payments through the California VA system. Against the Court Order, he was living in a rooming house where children were present. Immediately, my number was removed from all payment records. My permanent Protection Order helped get my car tags expunged from Idaho State records (Law enforcement could still verify, but no one else). His torment of us was exposed by the abrupt halt of the terrifying phone calls.

I was certified 100% disabled by Social Security in 2001. The surgery, the backlash of Post Traumatic Stress Disorder caused by my injuries, along with several other health factors, accounted for my total disability.

Noel never paid any of his court-ordered responsibility for the medical care of the children. In 2001, he was living in Arkansas so I filed a lawsuit against Noel in the court system there. The lawsuit was to collect back medical payments for the children's care, which he had been ordered to pay from his rape conviction. I paid out $60,000 for all of the children's therapy, hospital bills and doctor bills after insurance paid. He never paid anything. I hired an Arkansas lawyer, Bunny Bullock, to help me recoup half of the medical expenses. She filed a court claim against Noel as he had been ordered to pay half of the bills as part of his criminal conviction.

He was served with the lawsuit in December near Atkins, Arkansas, where he lived with his new wife, Eva Smart. When Noel was served with the papers for the lawsuit in December, he had a small stroke. I believe the fear that his new wife was going to find out he was a sex offender caused the stroke. I don't believe she was aware of his conviction. I notified her children, but they said they were going to keep Noel in their family as he drew so much VA compensation. Money was more important to them than the safety of their children. If he did molest two of her grandchildren and nothing was done to stop him, Eva and her family will have to face judgment from God for keeping Noel around the children.

God must have a sense of humor even when we are hurting. It pays to keep a smile! I prayed often Noel would know he was dying and have time to repent or acknowledge his evilness. I was always a dreamer of good even as a child! The Devil laughed his last in my life that day and then cringed for the man he supported through his earthly life was coming to Hell!

In February, 2002, a Pope County judge ruled he would hear the case. When that happened, I knew I would get an Order for him to pay me the $30,000 as his part of the medical bills. The money would be a godsend to me financially. "At last," I thought, "I have him cornered like the rat that he is and he will have to pay." I wanted him to take responsibility – and yes, to pay publicly for his private crimes!

When Noel was served with notification the judge was going to hear the case, he had a massive heart attack. He lingered in St. Mary's Hospital in Russellville for two and a half days before dying on February 24, 2002. God answered my prayers asking to know Noel had time to face his sins before dying. It was worth the $30,000 I lost to know he was dead

My attorney, Bunny Bullock, called me and asked,

"Are you sitting down, Cae?"

"Yes," I replied. "What's going on?"

"Well, I have some good news for you.

I replied, "You do? "

"Yes," she replied, "You've finally killed the bastard!"

"Wha---t?" I questioned in a panic, "What are you talking about?"

"Your ex-husband is dead! Let me read his obituary in The Courier to you!" She exclaimed.

S   he proceeded to read me the obituary in the local newspaper. It was Noel! He was dead! Hallelujah! He had escaped court justice, but he was in the hands of a just God. God did not forget the little children and me. I laughed and danced with joy. I cried because I was still under the gun financially, but the freedom knowing Noel Snow couldn't hurt me or my children ever again far outweighed the financial loss.

I hesitated in telling the children their father was dead. Inside, I felt jubilant that we were free of the man who had made us all suffer greatly. Not once after his conviction, did he ask about the welfare of the children. He never asked our forgiveness for the open wounds created by his evil. His death was my day of victory! It was a resurrection moment! The Centaur rode no more!

Chapter 37

If you dance with the Devil,
Be prepared to be burned by the music!
If you drink with the Devil,
you will sup with him for eternity,
When in debt to evilness, there is a payday,
It is not fair, nor is payday one that you can skip,
Death is the final great equalizer,
Freeing those who are damaged,
God doesn't forget the weak, and the young,
Never dance with the Devil,
He is a partner that never lets go!

How can I describe an ugly terrifying creature, lacking humanity - a ghoul - Noel?

I was left with a bag full of guilt. Once again, I assumed responsibility for sins that weren't mine.

I began a journey to differentiate between humiliation, culpability and *freedom* - time to discover the value of myself or if I could survive without abuse in my life. I lived in a corner for much of my life as surely as if I had been locked behind bars. I finally moved out of the dungeon. It has been so freeing to own a new perspective rising out of the ashes of violence.

Mam and Pap railed I was a bad seed – this certainly wasn't self-esteem building – then marriage to Noel reinforced their treatment – I was bad and worthless. I became a perfectionist. I had a rigid set of guidelines I adhered to for survival. It has been a long road in releasing this former belief system of bondage and violence. I always met new people with the expectation of rejection, but rejected them before they could reject me. I lived in the parameters of extreme stupefying rigidity. My expectations of God kept me walking upright – how *He* survived my

rigid religious expectations of myself is a wonder. I know
that my religious rigidity offended people, but at the time
my soul survival needed a sturdy framework to be set in
stone. Unfortunately, for many years, I saw the world
through Aaron's and Noel's eyes. I thank God for hanging
in there with me until I could find the difference – looking
out through the eyes of my heart, the world is good!

The isolation and despair I lived with in my marriage
were reality – spurred on by my foolishness and Noel's
control. His humiliation-based view of the world, my life,
my marriage and my future were cycles of unshakeable
bondage.

My self-value was buried under an avalanche of
dysfunctions, fears, behaviors, mistakes, rejections,
imperfections, self-loathing, powerlessness, and feelings of
sin. I couldn't obtain perfection, so I walked in silence.
This life failure, the unrealistic expectations of my parents,
husband and myself reinforced that I wasn't good enough.
Shame for the sins committed against my body kept me
chained as indubitably as handcuffs in the marriage
relationship.

Forced guilt and shame are the backbone of doubt.
Aaron, Betty and Noel were regular beasts in creating both.
Guilt was like acid eroding my heart in not knowing how to
protect my own children, Ruth and Ezra Joel. Oh, God, the
misery eating at my soul is hard to bear; there aren't words
to let others know how to escape the trap I fell into. I
fought hard to have a value system that honored God, but to
fail Him in protecting my children was a poisonous asp in
my soul. *I made a sickening mistake when I married Noel.
My attitude and behavior were wrong, I looked for love in
the wrong place, wrong people, and my ignorance was
destructive.* I walked in shadows blinded by my past. I
lived with shame-based ideas, the fear of abandonment and
rejection. Now I faced the reality of my marriage – a sham,
deceitful and putrid. Daily, I fight against self-destructive

behaviors to give myself permission to live a full life of enriching joy. I have not given myself the right to enter into another relationship.

It is extremely difficult for a victim to accept self-forgiveness. I've come to understand that I can, and must, forgive myself of the sin-guilt burden-bearer I was for Noel and my parents. I am a person of value, blameless, worthy of being forgiven as I've not sinned, but have been sinned against. It has been a long, hard-fought battle. I've accepted that the enlightenment of the shame of my childhood wounds influenced my tragic mistake in marrying Noel. Therapy taught me the intrinsic value of *owning* a healthy-based belief system.

I have accepted my mistakes and failures and used them as   to provide invaluable learning experiences. Only I can change my behaviors and attitudes and take charge of my life from here on out.

In the meadows of life I walk, hand in hand with God my father. I am glad I am His daughter! I want to thank Him for being the best Father in the world – mine!

Chapter 38

Generational in the giving,
Abuse so blind,
Taking the innocent, using and abusing,
Lost children of a generation,
Vulnerable, spiritual destruction,
Heaved aside, denial, protection of insidious lies,
Professional users, spiritual manipulative perverts,
Hiding under a God-covering,
Sins which God forbids,
No atonement, sacrificial lambs,
The children, the innocent, the wronged,
On the altars of self-gratification!

On March 2, 2004, a late night news bulletin flashed across my TV screen. I blinked, and then blinked again thinking I heard the announcer wrong. I reached for my phone, dialing Boise Channel Two News. "I just saw a news bulletin on your news report. Could you please confirm the name and the story you just ran?"

"Yes," they confirmed that former associate ex-pastor, Charles Fenwick, had just been arrested and jailed in Boise pending extradition back to Oregon on charges of a sexual relationship with and abuse of a 14 year-old girl. The young victim did not deserve being used and abused by Mr. Fenwick. She was a child and deserved the preservation of her innocence.

I was astounded and heartbroken, but not surprised that the sins of the grandfather, Joseph Daniel Baker, were generational as well as the sins of the Pentecostal Church of God and their continued cover-up of sexual sins.

"Thank you for your confirmation of the news

story," I stated and hung up the phone. I sat in stunned silence because Charles Fenwick was the grandson of Joe Baker from Baker City, Oregon, and the son of my friend Norma. I had to sit quietly to absorb this tragic news. Mr. Fenwick had been a victim of Joseph Daniel Baker as a youngster and now, at thirty-six, he'd victimized a young woman. Incest is a sin that must be faced with education and ongoing legal changes in order to eradicate it.

Even though it was past midnight, I dialed information, asking for the Veneta County District Attorney and the Sheriff's Department. I left a succinct message on both of their phones requesting they call me immediately. I told them the reason for the call. I received a call early the next morning from both entities. I told them I had a file on Charles "Chuck" Fenwick's grandfather and what the grandfather had done to his grandchildren in Baker City, Oregon. I also informed them I had written a counseling book about Pentecostals and Sexual Abuse. I emailed them a copy of the book and advised them to read it before questioning Mr. Fenwick. I also copied and faxed the file I had of the Pentecostal Church of God's response to the Baker City debacle from 1987-1989 and why I resigned the church. I answered many questions following these initial contacts. It was time the Pentecostal Church of God was held accountable for their continued cover-up of sexual abuse in their church.

Mr. Fenwick was arrested in Boise as he was packing his van in preparation to flee to an undisclosed location supplied by the Pentecostal Church of God. Mr. Fenwick was transported back to jail in Eugene, Oregon, by detectives. As he was transported, he was questioned based on what the officials gleaned from my book and copies of the Baker City, Oregon, information. Fenwick stated his grandfather *taught him all he knew.* It was a telling comment, as he didn't know about the information I'd supplied or the information and insight from my book. In court, he denied all allegations.

The Drain Headquarters of the Pentecostal Church of God began another cover-up of sexual abuse for Charles Fenwick, as they had done in 1987 for Fenwick's grandfather, Joseph Baker, in Baker City, Oregon. Church officials accused the young victim of enticing Mr. Fenwick into sinning.

The young victim was able to provide her prom dress to the police and Mr. Fenwick's DNA was found on it.

During the lengthy Veneta, Oregon, investigation, National Headquarters for the Pentecostal Church of God began destroying paperwork from the Baker City, Oregon, case, plus other complaints against Fenwick. A man from the national home office began feeding me information about National Bishop Phil Redding's cover-up. Mr. Redding's secretary started saving the trash and providing this godly man with the information, which he forwarded on to me. I gave all documents to law officials, and the victim's attorney. The Bishop of the national church, Philip Redding, was forced to resign his position. It is rumored that he heads up a ministerial training facility near Vilonia, Arkansas.

The Veneta Pentecostal Church of God congregation was ordered out of their church and forced to hand over to the Drain District Headquarters, a $1.4 million dollar church, with the excuse they weren't paying their bills. Unfortunately, the Drain District Office destroyed the congregation, moved an outside pastor from another town into the people's church and they fell by the wayside. Members had worked years to build and pay for the church facilities, but chose to stand against Charles Fenwick. Rev. Ron Crandall became very ill with a blood clot in his lungs and resigned as the pastor, thus paving the way for a District takeover of the church. As reported in *The Register-Guard* by Jeff Wright and the congregation's attorney, Tom Alderman stated:

"They have taken away from those who are entitled to its possession and delivered possession to others. If the district and national denomination officials don't rectify it, they're ratifying an atrocity."

The local Pentecostal Church of God members and I spent endless hours fighting publicly. Jim Nelson, an Albany, Oregon, attorney, fought for the congregation who were bullied out of their years of labor. Pastor Ron Crandall became a pariah – losing his way for a long time because of the pressure of the National Pentecostal Church of God.

The victim was nineteen at the time of Fenwick's conviction and she bravely stood in court telling him, "You have taken everything from me, but you can't take my faith in God away."

Charles Fenwick pled guilty to three counts of third-degree sodomy and one count of third-degree rape. He was given five years in prison. Fenwick has served his prison term and his wife has welcomed him back into her home.

According to *The Register-Guard*, Lane County Sheriff's Detective Michael Lamb stated, *"The Pentecostal Church of God officials had known of the abuse and did nothing to help the young woman when she reported the abuse at Bible camp. She returned to her church and told Pastor Ron Crandall about the abuse and he reported the abuse to law enforcement the next day."* He, his associate Pastor, Larry

Williams, and Deacon Jim Williams were three voices crying out in the wilderness in the Pentecostal Church of God against sexual exploitation.

The young woman filed a $10 million lawsuit against the Pentecostal Church of God and settled out of court for an undisclosed amount. According to *The Register-Guard,* and because of the abuse and exploitation, the teenager suffered permanent emotional and psychological injury requiring long-term counseling and medication. She deserved the compensation the court awarded her from the National Pentecostal Church of God. **She** is a young woman of extraordinary strength, valor, and faith in her Heavenly Father.

Many lives were ruined by the thoughtless actions of Chuck Fenwick's choice to rape and abuse a child. It was thought that Fenwick had victims in as many as four states and the Pentecostal Church of God continued to cover up his sins.

I appreciated the work of all the law enforcement officials involved in Lane County and their tireless efforts in stopping Fenwick from harming any more victims.

There was a shake-up at the Pentecostal Church of God Headquarters because I refused to be quiet. I sent letters to every state bishop in 1988-89 presenting the evidence of Joe Baker's crimes and the failures of the local pastor, Ira Buttram. In, 2004, every state bishop was notified and urged to remove the officials who had participated in the cover-up of the abuse of this young girl. Someone must stand up for right. I refuse to see children harmed. The community, the victims and church congregations must hold the mother church, regardless of the denomination, accountable, as one day we will meet God. I am one woman, but I hope and pray my voice will make a difference for the children who cannot help themselves.

Epilogue

There is life,
That life is good,
There is hope,
Peace and joy!
The dance is not complete -
Until the shadows are wiped away.
Laughter is the greatest erasure,
Peace is the door of closure,
And life does go on,
Dancing brings the world in a full circle.
I am glad that I can dance!

In retrospect, September 17, 1991, to the present day has been a test of human endurance. The madness drove me to plan murder and revenge against Noel Snow, but in a split second, I chose to walk away from a failed marriage full of violence. It never pays to look back. I have chosen a future filled with hope, healing, and freedom.

The day I escaped almost cost us our lives, but the pain of leaving Aaron and Betty in 1965 paled in comparison to my escape from Noel. I had not escaped my parents as I had thought. I had married both my parents when I fell in love with Noel Snow. I am free. The blackening years have left a permanent soul stain. My path of deliverance from evil has been a rough one healing from anger, hate, bitterness, isolation and painful anxiety attacks.

The recovery journey has taken more than twenty years. I continue the fight for justice. The sins of my ex-husband, his and my family and his abuse are theirs alone.

I medically retired in 2001 from a position as a college instructor in a medium security prison. I loved teaching, but my body couldn't be put back together after surgery in December, 2000. Years of physical and sexual abuse had taken its toll.

I have tried to be a living example of hope. I learned that the law is at times kind, unrealistic and unjust. It even commits crimes against the victim by letting the perpetrators go free.

Dealing with anxiety attacks prompted me to write this prayer. It has sustained me and kept me sane as a survivor.

Anxiety Prayer

Dear God, when despair grips me
Forget me not.
When breathless terrors come,
Forget me not.
If I can't see, feel, or hear,
Though bands tighten my chest,
I am confident in you.
When dread shakes me,
You are here.
When I cannot speak of you,
Sit with me.
Anxiety is not caused by lack of faith,
You are you.
With hopelessness, I am overwhelmed,
You know me.
Hold my hand in the grip of discouragement,
Show me gentleness.
When I have no faith, be my center,
Cherish me, I am important.
When fear separates reality,
Give objectivity, a neutral place of safety.
When control is lost in panic,
Be in control of me.
When my place of hope is disconnected, center me.
In detachment, forget me not,
Be with me in moments of isolation.
Apprehension lives in preoccupation,
Be solid earth beneath my feet of fright.
Guard my vulnerability as my special task force,
I know you know me.
While I deal with being perturbed,
Be my constant promise.
When the living terrors arrive, forget me not.
When I can't see, feel, or hear,
Forget me not, thwart calamity,
Foster my honor, I am yours.

Noel's death was the incentive to unhitch from the runaway train in our lives. For the first time in my life, I am free of abuse, but not the guilt nor the feeling of shame in my situation. Noel's depravity lingers on. Time does bring healing and relief from living in the smack-daube middle of Hell. I am determined Noel will not win from the grave. I am thankful the grave is holding his remains.

In June, 2007, I visited the Johnson County Adam's cemetery where Noel is buried. The next day was Decoration Day. Memorializing the dead is a Southern tradition of gathering at the cemetery, tending the graves and 'dinner on the ground'. I took a sack of doggie doo-doo and spread it on Noel's tombstone. I wanted his family to know we had won. He is buried in the ground - no longer a threat - we are the victors. The lightness of freedom drew me into its arms.

I began to dance on Noel's grave with great abandon and joy. "I am alive, I am alive, and I survived. You didn't win. God is just and has given me life. You didn't beat me. You didn't win the sick game you played with my mind for many years. You didn't break me, nor did you own me. I survived your games. I am free, free indeed!"

All of a sudden I could hear Grandma Russell singing, *"Amazing Grace, how sweet the sound that saved a wretch like me, I once was lost, but now am found, was blind but now I see!"* The wind seemed to sizzle with electricity at the sound of Grandma's voice. I thought at first I was hallucinating!

I looked up, laughing in joy at my freedom and there stood Grandpa and Grandma, arm in arm, smiling as I danced. Circling around their heads was my Red Bird. The beautiful bird landed on Grandma's shoulder, then came to rest in her cupped hands - fluffing its feathers and giving me a happy birdie look.

I felt a gentle breeze surround me and knew it was the breath of God sheltering me for the moment. God has remembered me all through the tormenting years. In the long nights of silence and horrific pain, God held me.

I was home at last! Free, Free! Ah, how sweet is the taste of freedom!

I looked at my wonderful grandparents, who smiled and waved to me, and then they were gone. The Red Bird fluttered, dipped, and landed on my shoulder - then into my hands, rubbing his beautiful head against my chest. He lifted away from me, up into the blue sky, circling one last time, and then up into the heavens he flew. The notes of *Amazing Grace* seemed to flow from his mouth! His job was finally done! My lifelong friend sent by the Holy Spirit returned to God.

Noel stole my peace, but he didn't destroy my spirit, though he did try. I lost all the mother things I had tried to give my precious children because of his crimes, but we all have survived, each in our own way, and we have moved forward.

I believe I have found the answers to Betty's rejection and hate. I believe she had a pregnancy addiction. I feel when she was pregnant with Samson, the excitement and the encouragement of Aaron's gladness of proving his manhood in her pregnancy caused her to want Samson. I think that Aaron's approval waned after this. Her deep psychological problems and being a rape victim herself twisted her. She was in love with the feeling of being pregnant with Samson, the approval of Aaron and those in the logging camps around her, but after his birth and her attachment to him, she was never again able to recapture that feeling so she rejected each newborn baby in our family. She was pathologically lonely, isolated, feeling the outside world was threatening and foreboding, and had no friends. There was no other outlet in her life to motivate or teach her child-rearing. She had never had an example of a functioning family. She liked the feeling of admiration of others at being pregnant, but as soon as the baby was born, she rejected it as it was too much for her mental capacity to handle the responsibility of that child. In her rejection of us all, she lost her opportunity to have been loved. She and Aaron were pathologically dependent on each other and the havoc they wreaked on our lives cost each of us children tremendously.

There was no choice in avoiding failure. Fear of failure has been a motivating force behind my modest success in life. I have picked up life's pieces, gluing my life together with prayer. Rivers of tears have washed my soul clean of the pain from the distant glistening shore. At odd times, I can see the raft of love that I have built. There is life after all!

Through much affliction, I have won redemption. I have found absolution. My soul is cleansed. I enjoy working as a community chaplain and counselor for the abused as there are so many who need healing and guidance into the survivor's light of life. Living is acknowledging the good and bad of our lives and making the best of what we are left with. We must stand back to back to fight the insidious sin of incest until finally the world is free of its stain. Redemption is possible!

Redemption
A quiet, white world of silence arrives,
Not a sound is heard, lost.
Life, peeking through the snow-covered landscape,
Giving the darkness an ugly clarity,
The slate is wiped clean.
Crystallized silence given us during our night of rest,
And an arriving morning of splendor offered.
Life renewal,
An awakening of inner recognition of our need.
Offering to us the chance to listen with our heart to God;
The soundless soul beauty of hushed, breathless silence,
Moonlit paths of prayer to heaven;
Empty steps left in the snow-covered landscape of our past.
All things made new, wiped clean.
In the breathless gift of snow,
The ugly covered in purity,
Lighting the woodland with silence;
Shining paths of prayer as angels hover near us,
They listen in awe of our "gift", prayer and praise.
Restoration of our souls, snow-covered; no blemishes.
Fresh steps in the snow renews our hearts,
In God's forgiveness, fresh steps offer life.
The melting of the past, welded in winter,
Renewed in hope of the past drifting into spring,
Washed clean in the snowdrifts of heavenly joy,
Abiding in peace,
Redemption has surely come, drifting down,
One unique shaped flake at a time.
We are human,
Standing in the white landscape,
Seeing where no steps have gone before.
We walk the new path; choices in life,
Marking the clean, the pure, and the peace,
And redemption's clear path.

The following are excerpts from *The ABCs of Understanding Sex Abuse* coming soon:

My last marital rape occurred in September, 1991. It took me more than two years to be able to say aloud to my therapist, "He raped me." The trauma of that rape ripped my mind, soul and body apart. My known world was shredded and one of my last memories of the event was my mind sitting on the roof of the house looking down into the bedroom, watching. My spirit fled because it could not stand the horror of what he was doing to my body. My reality as a person died. I murdered my emotions to survive and to hold on to what was left of my broken self.

After many years, I embarked on my own healing journey of recovery and restoration. I remember asking my therapist if there was something in print that could explain what I was experiencing. But, unfortunately there was nothing to read that would adequately explain the pain or offer hope that would help in the healing journey in 1991.

I needed help to heal. I strongly affirmed to myself and to my therapist that when I had healed, I would develop a way for other victims to obtain the knowledge they needed. I want others to be able to visualize their own pain, to see a pictorial description of the feelings of the aftermath of rape, to understand what is happening to them in their moments of blind panic attacks, depression, loss of self-esteem and distorted pain. I want others not to feel as lost and torn apart from sexual abuse and domestic violence as I did. In order to find the future in recovery and restoration, there must be an understanding of the personal destruction in one's life in order to provide cathartic explanation for the pain

Whether the abuse is physical, mental, sexual, or any form of domestic violence, or self-hatred, lack of self-esteem or lack of love for one's self, whether male or female, we work toward the goal of Restoration of Hope (Self-image, Spiritual maturity, Self-confidence), Health (Mental and Emotional) and Wholeness (Physical) in the pattern of the Triune Trinity; God, Jesus and the Holy Spirit.

Sexual Abuse Dynamics

Rape, incest and a variety of other sexual crimes are happening against women, men and children, both male and female. Rape is a crime and has nothing to do with the sexual gratification of the perpetrator. It is a crime of anger, deviance, power, control and manipulation which stalks innocent victims. There are more than 15 million women who are rape victims working toward becoming survivors. This statistic does not include boys or men of rape. This number includes only about 10% of cases being reported to law enforcement.

"Rape is an unmitigated act of violence committed out of extreme anger and the satisfaction of forcing fear, control and power on someone else. It is a way to force the anger of the perpetrator on the body of another." Cae Cordell

Rape is the forcing of a person to have sexual intercourse against his/her will. Rape is the use of any form of sexual penetration, stimulation, and aggression to cause harm. Rape is the act of sex with any part of the body or of the mind. (Ellis, Hazelwood, and Burgess, 1993).

In Violence against Women, Social Psychology of Rape: "Rape is defined as all forced sex. This coercion may manifest itself psychologically, economically or physically. At the opposite end of the spectrum are those who do not acknowledge that rape exists. What falls between the two extremes is a myriad of opinions which include bits and pieces of each extreme and modifications of them." In 1983, The New York City Advisory Task Force on Rape presented some of these facts:

1) Rape is a crime of violence.

2) Women do not provoke rape nor do they want to be raped.

3) Rape does not occur for sex, but rather for domination and humiliation.

4) There are women who have been raped more than once; they did not provoke the rape incident on either or any occasion.

5) Police and government studies indicate that the way a woman is dressed or the way she behaves does not cause the rape.

6) Rapists use physical violence, threats and weapons. "Victims are often too scared to venture into the unknown without support. The legal system fails victims, by letting the batterer or rapist out on bail to batter and rape again and again – often leading to death for the victim." (Cordell, 2010)

7) Victims of domestic violence often become so brainwashed by verbal abuse that they believe they cannot survive without their batterer. (Cordell, 2010)

8) Rapists can be of all races, but non-white rapists are more likely to be prosecuted than white rapists. (Cordell, 2006)

9) Rapists come from all walks of life and socio-economic backgrounds.

10) Rape is often committed by friends, relatives or acquaintances, people the victim already knows. This

is especially true of the younger child victim or date rape victim.

11) Rape is when someone does not consent to sex.

12) Rapists violate a victim's civil rights.

13) If a woman is fortunate enough to have had some training in self-defense, she will know when it is safe to fight back.

14) All rape victims deserve support and care from their families, the community, educators and local churches after surviving the incident.

The Invasion of the God House

The Judeo-Christian biblical creation story will be used in the literary explanation focusing on the issues of the effects of abuse in *Understanding the ABC's of Sexual Abuse.* The creation story gives a *feeling* way to shed light on the myths that have become comfortable and acceptable as facts in our present society. The Biblical Creationist account gives a *feeling* way to express what sexual abuse or domestic violence does to the victim and why the common ideas exist toward victims of rape. This biblical story provides a background explanation for present reasoning involved in attempting to understand the patriarchal power and influence that have held sway far too long in most of our spoken and unspoken legal ramifications for victims.

In the beginning, God created man and woman to be special, wonderful beings without knowledge of wrongdoing, Genesis 1:27. They were the perfection of God's image. This early biblical account is a wonderful recording of how humankind was afforded a comfortable creation imagery to begin their story of life. God *chose* to create these human beings to share in a personal fellowship with him where they could walk with Him in the "cool of the day" in the Garden of Eden, Genesis 2:7, a utopia.

This early Garden of Perfection was a private set-aside place of natural beauty and innocence, Genesis 2:15. It is a place where God provided a sanctuary for both men and women to be absolutely safe from harm and only He could come into their sanctuary. They had no recognition of their impending sexuality. They were as one with nature and their Creator. It is this set-apart safe place that is referenced in this section and the undeniable causes of how that environment faced the pollution that has entered into religious tenets and societal beliefs by patriarchal decrees.

The recognition of the need for a sanctuary to be a hiding place or a safe place began early in church history and was added to as the centuries rolled forward. If a man who had committed a crime, or a person who had a crime committed against him, could make it to the inside doors of the sanctuary of the church, they were free of reproach or judgment by those involved or holding them accountable. It is the belief of the author that this concept grew out of what God meant to be an established place only with Him in each person's private, inner soul-sanctuary, not a place for lawlessness.

Those in authority began expanding the true meaning behind the sanctuary concept until a myth became an acceptable practice. The religious leaders left behind the secure, safe places of the innocent one's rights and started protecting the perpetrators of crime. In those days, it was often sons, brothers, fathers, friends, or the person in power who were committing abusive crimes so they wanted to be sure to have a safe place to hide away from their cowardly acts against nature.

With the creation or beginning of man and woman, God created a special place, a sanctuary, for His communing with them each day in privacy. This was a place of holiness where only God was allowed to be alone with His creations and to spend time with them in the pureness of this daily visitation. They were free of fear and talked freely with God about their caretaking responsibilities when He visited them each day.

The day when recognition of wrongdoing arrived for the first man and woman and their acceptance of wrongdoing brought about a crash course in the art of survival in a world gone wrong, Genesis 3:8-13. It was the beginning of their simple acceptance of pure myth, which they knew wasn't what they had been told by God, to explain away facts that brought downfall to their Eden and it became easy to ignore the rules they were to abide by in the Garden. So have myths been perpetuated and continued, until our present day, by ignorance and acceptance without proof of facts.

Then the snake entered the picture and captured the imagination of the first man and woman. When this happened, myth was easier to accept than facts by simple word changes. What a creature! He was able to breach the place of sanctuary, come near enough to speak with them, and lie with tantalizing, mind-boggling ease, Genesis 3:1-3. In Satan's doing so, he chose to violate the law of nature God had put into place with mankind, this private, alone, safe place.

The first man and woman recognized they had personally allowed this holy place to be violated by their unwise decisions and choices. This newfound knowledge and wrongdoing recognition caused them to hide in fear from their Creator, God, their Father, in the falling evening darkness, Genesis 3:7 and to cover their nakedness. Their unwise choices forced both of them to play the blame-game equally with each other in accepting the false words of the Tempter. They had enjoyed the tempting visit from the snake. Satan must have been beautiful, plus he could speak their language. They had exercised their first deadly free-will choice and thus began the myth of the evil nature of woman and the fall of man caused by the woman's willful wiles. Because of woman's allure, so the story goes, man was tempted and fell, Genesis 3:12.

Isn't it fact that neither had recognized their sexuality until this point? How was one guiltier than the other? Patriarchal and societal myths encourage control, anger, and violence to be directed toward women by men. Violence and abuse have been accepted as a man's factual right to rape and plunder the weaker sex.

Myths, by twisted happenstance and responsibility, pure and simple, have entrapped women for millenniums in social bondage. Countless women, for centuries, have been punished because of male domination and perception of "Eve's fall from grace".

God's heart was hurt by both Adam and Eve's choices. Their fall from grace placed both of them outside of the garden (Genesis 3:11-24) which was no longer a sanctuary for them or Him. The blame of their choices was placed directly on both of them, but God was compassionate in their fall. He chose to place in them an inner, personal, soul sanctuary with the same focus as the garden where they walked with Him alone each day in personal fellowship. He told them again they would have to make their own choices about whom they would let in that special place inside of them. This was a special sanctuary, a set-aside Holy of Holies, within all mankind. The human race was given the choice of free will and self-ownership.

Now God had to be invited to visit with man or woman and with free will choices made about that God-invitation. He granted humanity the right to privacy and the right to choose who was to be close to them. This holy free will choice can only be equated to the right to choose the first personal sexual relationship. Any other approach is by force and is rape (Deuteronomy 22: 13-27) (Leviticus 18:1-30). Adam and Eve lost all garden rights of God innocence they had once enjoyed in the garden by their choices. They were in control and now must choose who they would become involved with by invitation to enter their personal sanctuary. They could recognize right or wrong by choice.

When this right is ignored and forcible intrusion occurs, this is a God House invasion of privacy, forced on a victim against her will in the inner sanctuary causing forever damage. This rape violation is against the nature of humankind provided by the Creator. This occurrence is lasting in nature and the innocence is ripped away and cannot ever be given back to the victim in their lifetime. It is an act against an innocent's will that causes a separation of the established placement of the body, mind, and soul.

It is this God House invasion that cannot be put back together again. This is why victims cry and believe God

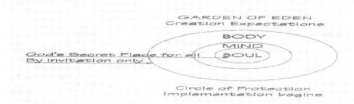

has abandoned them and they wander alone in a void of darkness that truly does exist for them always.

The Body, the Mind and the Spirit
(Rape victims are both male and female, but for convenience, all references will be to the female gender)

This is the core of the inner person, a center place, the place of the soul or spiritual concept being of self. It is a connecting place to the inner being of the body, protected by the mind within the body, that only God is to be allowed to go into and visit because of the absolute trust placed in His goodness, thus, making it safe to invite Him to visit often with one in this secret place. The spirit and mind exist within the parameters of the body. Figure 1

Our body was formed and created in the likeness of God in the Garden of Eden so that we might be a reflection of His creation by how we live, act, and understand the three-part oneness of self. As depicted in Figure 1, these creation expectations were part of God's secret place where each of us were free to invite Him to visit with us when we are alone and private. This inner sanctuary was to be entered by Him at our invitation only. It is in this inner sanctuary where God placed the soul to be encircled by the mind, encasing them with the beautiful human form that reflected God's image in the placement of body as the protector of this special inner sanctuary. This implementation and special placement began at creation. It was a Divine circle of protection given from the best of God to us. This triune circle of protection is a gift to each human.

When the act of rape occurs, this placement is disrupted and becomes askew. It causes an interruption of the internalization of self which is a natural process intended to be in place in a person as a psychological safe haven. This disruption (attack) upsets the natural balance of each victim and the natural defenses of self-protection are lost in this displacement.

When rape occurs, this natural balance and self-defense mechanism is interrupted; the mental and spiritual processes are thrown into shock from the occurring trauma. The shock and trauma become internalized as self-pain. Often, this unnatural interruption is never addressed due to the shame, societal non-acceptance, denial of the crime and the expectation of silence and self-blame felt by the victim. The victim may believe she did something to cause this crime to happen to her. Societal beliefs have thrown a shadow of shame over divulging the crime of rape and have made it a matter of personal shame for the victim to report the crime. These myths and the blame should not be allowed to occur for the victim's mental stability. When rape trauma occurs, the victim of sexual abuse or domestic violence is forced to bottle up the trauma inside of her emotional parameter. It becomes an unnatural stress eating away at the victim's peace and self-esteem until it usually results in Post-Traumatic Stress Disorder which has many side-effects. When the trauma effect is ignored, a flare-up will eventually occur. This eruption can be cataclysmic to the victim and those around her.

If the rape trauma, body memories and mental stress of the occurrence are not given immediate attention through therapy and are forced to be buried by the victim, the eventual delayed trauma destroys many normal sexual relationships or marriages and sometimes the victim is destroyed by drugs, suicide, alcohol and other destructive behaviors. The trauma interferes with good parenting skills; victimization attracts domestic partners who are abusive. The abuse trauma may prevent many children from functioning at their full potential and often destroys families. It hurts many of the personal relationships of the victim because recovery and restoration is not sought. It leaves millions of victims in a lifetime struggle for emotional balance, seeking to leave behind their stunted emotional growth. The rape trauma syndrome (PTSD) is a fact. The devastating effects are far-reaching in the lives of millions of survivors. It is a crime of hurricane force in the lives of victims and leaves such devastation behind we have yet to understand the deep emotional damage carried by victims. There must be community, educational, and spiritual healthy support.

A community-trained, certified abuse response trauma team is needed to act in assisting victims within twenty-four hours of the reported crime to help victims, friends, and families through the legal system, to be with the victim through the examination, the investigation, and all court hearings. The shame of rape can be removed so the internalized displacement of the natural process of self regains balance without shame and guilt. Rape is an unnatural occurrence.

The community trauma team needs trained sexual abuse medical examiners, psychologists, certified recovered rape survivors and trained ministerial or clergy personnel that will work with empathy to stand with the victim. Expert law enforcement emergency response teams should offer the first line of defense for victims by their prompt investigation and handling of the attack. When all of the above is part of a normal expectation and reaction to the crime of rape, more victims would feel free to immediately report their attacks to law enforcement officials. This support would establish legal guidelines and produce more convictions in the courtroom so that sexual predators would receive stiffer penalties for this most personal of crimes and would be removed from society, thus preventing serial rapes. This support would reinforce and ensure the victims' rights and we would experience an enormous drop in rape crimes.

After the attack has been reported, the victim should seek help through facilitated restoration and recovery programs so that guilt is eased. (Seek personal counseling with some trained in rape and abuse issues, such as psychiatrists, medical doctors, or victims programs that can be found through hospitals, law enforcement referrals, prosecuting attorney victim coordinators, and ministers).

Victims go through de-personalizing physical exams; evidence gathering can be mishandled; cases are never filed because victims know the societal consequence they will face and often refuse to work with law enforcement; blame games are played; exams are delayed and the collecting of semen specimens for DNA testing is neglected; many cases are routinely plea-bargained. There is a lack of psychological training in dealing with victim trauma and inept police questioning can make the victim feel re-victimized from the rape attack. This kind of mishandling can shame the victim into not reporting the rape. **This shame must be removed from the crime scene of rape**. The victim is totally affected by this traumatizing experience and will need priority help. At the heart of stopping sexual abuse crimes or domestic violence is prioritizing: victim first.

What rape victims need is empathy from well-trained personnel that immediately alleviates any fear of repercussions or reprisals from the perpetrator, the court, or from examining officials. Victims can utilize help to get them through the next several months of court, therapy, recovery and restoration to a healthy life if their immediate pain and trauma issues are addressed with assurance and gentleness. Dealing with the victims' perceptions will make the difference in stopping the perpetrators of abuse and gaining a conviction.

Rape isn't about sex; it is about violence perpetrated against another person out of rage. It is almost the same word:

RAPE - RAGE

Figure 2

When Rape Occurs, What Happens?

When rape occurs, as seen in Figure 2, there is an unwanted invasion into the natural protection of the inner self-process plan that God implemented for humankind.

As you can see in the rape frontal drawing above in

Figure 2, when the invasion of rape occurs, the natural placement of Figure 1 is disrupted and the natural balance of nature is turned inside out. The spirit or soul is drawn to the outside of the life circle; the mind is thrown outside of the body and soul in self-defense which is unnatural; thus, creating trauma for the victim because of abuse misplacement. In the research of this material, this happened to every victim interviewed and Post Traumatic Stress Disorder is the end result. This abuse displacement must be addressed through a recovery and restoration service offered in counseling, group support, a twelve step program and/or medication.

The sexual abuse and domestic violence trauma is invasive by the nature of the crime. Acculturation (absorbing societal culture from birth) pressures stigmatized victims to hide in shame when the normal response should be one of anger with justification-revenge thoughts. Victims must be empowered to share in the prosecutorial process with a guaranteed Victim's Bill of Rights (which is included in *The ABCs of Understanding Sex Abuse*) and testify against their attackers and abusers. Victim empowerment will facilitate change in our sexual abuse and rape laws in this country.

The victim should not be ashamed. Perpetrators used manipulation, control, and power to instill fear into their victims. The guilt the victim assimilates stifles the recovery process. The guilt load haunts the lives of survivors. Unless there is a legal, educational and spiritual realization of the stigma of rape and removing the ignorance in the
the victims will continue to grow around the world; and the perpetrators will harm countless numbers because their victims are shamed and frightened into silence due to the secretive nature of rape crimes. A response trauma team can prevent the present neglect, misunderstanding, and the re-victimization from occurring.

Figure 3

In Figure 3, the rape occurrence is seen in a side view illustrating what happens as rape invades the inner sanctuary of the victim.

The victim is thrown into a disruption cycle and the circle begins splitting apart in this God House invasion. The disruption is permanent and may become life-threatening for the victim if assistance isn't given. The victim's emotional, mental, and spiritual health is separated by the intrusion of the sexual abuse or domestic violence. This split of the holistic abilities of the person must be quickly addressed because of the trauma at the impact of a rape occurrence.

The Forever Damage

The emotional, spiritual and physical violation disruption is beyond the normal person's perception and understanding. This leaves victims extremely emotionally weak and vulnerable with scars that will be with her forever. There is little victim recovery education in place or trained personnel available to treat these hurting victims of violence with compassion and caring. Recovery and restoration hope for victims is the goal of this training program and twelve-step program.

Somehow, as educational, community and religious leaders, we must reach beyond the letter of the law with education and training to serve victims with comfort and assistance in their healing journey. The forever damage that occurs to the victims of sexual violence leaves them permanently damaged with their life focuses askew. Extreme care must be exercised within the areas of human concepts that deal with the lifetime suffering they are going through. The victim needs an atmosphere of focused internalized healing forgiveness that recognizes the emotional and physical pain as real and leads into self-forgiveness. The victim needs this alternative healing to recover to the degree to become fully functional again.

There must be recognition of the rapist's sin act against the rape victim. This is not addressed in most Judeo-Christian religious teaching nor is the victim's need for justification-revenge considered in victim treatment processing. Our society has fostered within religion circles and through offender expectations the idea that the victim is the one required to forgive. This is an appalling attitude that is victimizing and unhealthy. It is this idea that has created the self-destructive behavior of millions of victims. It would be "nice" to believe that the Biblical solution of an "eye for an eye" would relieve both society and the victim of any burden of reciprocity, thus alleviating a small measure of the forever damage done to the victims of rape. In our civilized society, we must instead offer recovery and restoration help.

There are millions of victims of a crime beyond the imagination. They are raped and ravaged persons who must be cared for with nurturing, a feeling of unwavering and undemanding love, respect, truth and hope. There has been an unfortunate lack of this in the past for victims of rape.

These most hurt and wounded victims of society have been ignored and neglected to an alarming degree. This

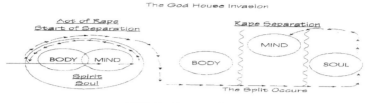

negligence has led to a lack of culpability in many avenues
of victim services being offered to rape victims. Victims
need to be reassured that there are trustworthy and
conscientious people who will minister to their holistic
needs.

Humpty-Dumpty Can't Ever Be Put Back Together Again

In examining the God House invasion and
understanding the importance of this event within the
victims, one must understand the impact of what has
happened in the mind, spirit and body. In this review
summation, a more detailed background explanation is
given in Figure 4.

Figure 4

As you can see in this God House invasion drawing,
the act of rape starts a separation that is a real occurrence
for the victim. This is depicted by the arrow piercing
through the drawing on the left side showing the spirit
already moving into the spiral of separation with the mind
and body and beginning the splitting process as seen on the
right side. As in the story of Humpty-Dumpty, the egg falls
off the wall and separates; this is comparable to what
happens in rape separation. The egg contains three distinct

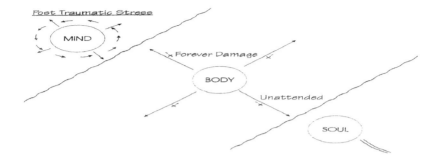

Figure 5

sections and once these three parts are separated, there is no way to put them back together. This is comparable to the separation found in the God House invasion. It can occur in all sexual abuse traumatic events whether the victim is young or old. This rape separation results in the Post-Traumatic Stress Syndrome which takes over. The trauma of rape is so severe that until now there has not been much detail, reporting or examination done to explain the splitting apart that occurs when the victim is attacked. This damage and the effects of this are permanent. For the purposes of having a viable explanation, the abuse damage is referred to as the Humpty- Dumpty Syndrome or a damage that cannot be put back together again.

In Figure 5, note the forever damage the victims will be dealing with during recovery and restoration. This Figure depicts the total separation that is experienced in the aftermath of rape. The mind spirals into Post Traumatic Stress Syndrome and is alienated from its proper position in the developed inner circle of life that is depicted in The Garden of Eden Creation Expectations from the aggressive act of abuse in the God House Invasion. The mind is thrown into a rotational effect that leaves the victim with many of the symptoms listed in the section Journey to

Freedom: What abuse does to the abused. The scientific idea of the earth, moon, and sun in rotational sync is used to explain this model.

Millions of victims live with the forever damage sustained during their assaults and many are never able to return to their full functional reality because of the lack of understanding on the part of treatment specialists. Victims face multiple health problems after rape. Many victims never get beyond just mending these physical problems and turn to drugs, alcohol and other self-destructive behaviors. They fail to become established in community health support groups to heal their minds leaving their souls neglected. The soul is allowed to shrivel up into nothingness because of the lack of understanding by clergy, community, and educational misunderstanding. This leaves the victims feeling disassociated from those around them, dysfunctional from sexual unhealthiness, self-hate, and low-self-esteem and alienated from family, children, and friends; unable to accept help. Many will suffer mental trauma that will leave them emotional cripples for the rest of their lives."

If trauma teams are trained to intervene in the first days after the rape, then the victim will be given the assurance and help needed to become functional. On the next page, Figure 6, shows the Functional Reality Rotation Model. This model shows there is hope for the functional recovery of the victim. Many may never gain the healing of this model, but there are many who fight through their pain and fear and gain at least this much hope of functional recovery: This is the Advanced-Post Rape Recovery Stage.

Figure 6

The victims' goal during this stage of recovery is to work through the symptoms of victimization and realize that she can become a survivor. This model is based on the physical law of the moon rotating around the Earth and the Earth's rotation around the Sun. In this Functional Reality Rotation Model, the mind can heal enough to keep the victim in reality even though it rotates around the body and

Functional Reality Rotation Model

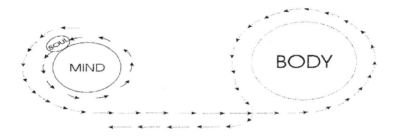

Advanced Post Rape Recovery Stages

the soul becomes attached to the mind, and then rotates around the body. This is where an advanced recovery and restoration program can lead the victim toward survivorship. Abuse victims can return to near normalization which can become acceptable for their mental, spiritual and physical health through hard work and taking responsibility for their personal recovery and restoration. This fundamental understanding is necessary for the person desiring to work and heal using the principal of functional reality to find recovery and restoration for a future. Many will recover working through this stage. This recovery and restoration model is intrinsic and vital in developing a model for the abused to follow as it gives workable ideas of how the mind is affected from PTSD and how it affects the body's reaction, making it possible for the idea of the full functional rotational recovery to be acceptable. The use of this model will help the victim to grasp, work through and gain strength until she is at the level of Figure 5, in dealing with the separated parts of themselves. The goal of this program is to offer support and encouragement to each victim to believe she can reach the Advanced Post-Rape Recovery Stage and live with the idea of Functional Reality Rotation to become happy and healthy.

This letter validates the winning of the VA lawsuit.

DEPARTMENT OF VETERANS AFFAIRS
Office of District Counsel
805 West Franklin Street
Boise ID 83702–5560

July 5, 1994   In Reply Refer To:

General Accounting Office
Claims Division
441 G Street, N.W.
Washington, D.C.   20548

Re: Voucher for payment under the Federal Tort
      Claims Act, Public Law 89-506
      Claimants: Catherine L. Snow - Amount Approved - $ ████
                                   - Amount Approved - ████
                                   - Amount Approved - ████
                                   - Amount Approved - ████

Gentlemen.

Transmitted herewith are the originals and three (3) copies of each
Standard Form 1145, Voucher for Payment Under the Federal Tort Claims Act,
in the amount ████ executed by the claimant, Catherine L. Snow;
in the amount of ████ executed by the claimant ████; in
the amount of ████ executed by Catherine L. Snow, Conservator of
the estate of ████ by Court Order in ████ and
████ executed by Catherine L. Snow, conservator of the estate of
████ by Court order in Cause ████

Also transmitted is herewith a copy of the Standard Forms 95 for each
of the above claimants setting forth claims against the government in the
amount of $1,000,000.00 each.

This claim arises as a result of he care and treatment by the Department
of Veterans Affairs Medical Center, Boise, Idaho, beginning in 1986. The
veteran's wife and children complained of abuse in the home by the veteran
but the matter was not reported to the child protective services.
Subsequently, the veteran was accused of and pleaded guilty to sexual
misconduct with the children. The failure to report was a direct and
proximate cause of the subsequent abuse suffered by the mother and the
children.

After consideration of all aspects of each of the claims, and, pursuant to
the authority delegated to me by Veterans Administration Regulation 6(E),
[38 Code of Federal Regulations 2.6(e)], I have determined that these
claims are proper for payment in the amounts of ████ to Catherine L.
Snow; $ ████; and
████ to ████, under the Federal Tort Claims Act as
amended by Public Law 89-506. It is requested that your office process the
enclosed vouchers for payment pursuant to the provisions of 28 U.S.C.,

10/3/03

Your Honor,

    It's hard to express what that man did to me. The reason I call him that man is because he doesn't deserve the honor of being called daddy. He has been touching me wrong for so long I don't even know what a good touch is supposed to be like from a father. He has put my family and me through living hell. Your honor, please put my nightmares of his hands on me to rest. He deserves to be put away for the maximum sentence for the rape of me and my sister.

Thanks,

The above letter was presented to the court by my oldest daughter.

RICHARD L. HARRIS

PROSECUTING ATTORNEY
CANYON COUNTY
STATE OF IDAHO

CHIEF CIVIL DEPUTY:
Charles L. Saari

CHIEF CRIMINAL DEPUTY:
Timothy W. Spencer

DEPUTIES:
Gearld L. Wolff
Gary W. Barr
Kenneth F. Stringfield
R. David Butler, II
John A. Christensen
Robert B. Richbourg
Jim J. Thomas

Canyon County Courtho
P.O. Box 668
Caldwell, Idaho 83606-0(
(208) 454-7391
Fax (208) 454-7474

Child Support Division
(208) 454-7343

Victim/Witness Division
(208) 454-7304

August 24, 1992

Kathyrn Snow
~~████████████~~
Middleton, ID 83605

RE: State of Idaho v. Noel Snow
     Case No. CR 91-08467

Dear Kathyrn:

As you are aware, the defendant in the above-referenced case entered a plea of guilty to the charge of Sexual Abuse in Canyon County District Court.

The Sentencing Hearing in this case has now been scheduled for Monday, October 5, 1992 at 2:00 p.m. You may attend this hearing if you wish. Please let this office know if you do plan to attend, and please call to verify that the hearing is still scheduled for that date and time the day prior to the scheduled date.

Please feel free to contact me should you have any questions.

Very truly yours,

RICHARD L. HARRIS
Prosecuting Attorney

BENITA M. MILLER
Victim Witness Coordinator

57882801R00189

Made in the USA
Charleston, SC
24 June 2016